Invincible Generals

GUSTAVUS ADOLPHUS
MARLBOROUGH
FREDERICK THE GREAT
GEORGE WASHINGTON
WELLINGTON

Philip J. Haythornthwaite

Indiana University Press

Bloomington and Indianapolis

Published in the United States 1992
by Indiana University Press

Copyright © 1991 by Firebird Books Ltd
Text copyright © 1991 by Philip J. Haythornthwaite

Manufactured in Great Britain

Library of Congress Cataloging-in-Publication Data
Haythornthwaite, Philip J.
    Invincible generals: Gustavus Adolphus, Marlborough, Frederick the
Great, George Washington, Wellington / by Philip J. Haythornthwaite.
      p.   cm.
    Includes bibliographical references and index.
    ISBN 0-253-32698-2
    1. Military art and science—History. 2. Military history.
Modern. 3. Military biography. 4. Generals—Biography. I. Title.
U39.H39 1991
355'.009—dc20   91-21497

1 2 3 4 5 95 94 93 92 91

Contents

George Washington – Father of his Nation 143

Wellington – The Iron Duke 189

Bibliography 235

Index 237

Introduction

The history of warfare has been dominated by the so-called 'great captains', those generals or commanders who not only bestrode their own age but who also left a lasting mark upon posterity; and who advanced military theory and the practice of the 'profession of arms'. Whilst in some eyes this might be considered a dubious distinction – given that a progression in military theory usually results in more effective methods of destruction – it cannot be denied that the great captains left an indelible mark upon the course of history.

Much debate can ensue from a consideration of which of the military commanders of the past might legitimately be numbered among this exclusive band; but in any list of these distinguished characters, the five who are the subject of this book unquestionably would figure. The five separate sections each cover the career and significance of one general. The period itself might be described as the era of 'sword and musket', the two centuries or thereabouts which bridged the gap between medieval or post-medieval/renaissance warfare, and the onset of what is often considered as the beginnings of 'modern' war.

The active lives of these five generals did not overlap, so an account of their careers and of the progress of the art of war in their time (and often a progress as a result of their actions) serves also to chart the basic course of strategy and tactics during this most significant period.

The styling of these five great men as 'invincible generals' may be considered debatable. After all, Gustavus Adolphus died on the field of battle; Marborough was undone by politics; Frederick suffered defeats, though ultimately emerged triumphant. Taking the case of Washington, whilst he was never completely invincible on the field of battle, it was his foresight and appreciation of strategic realities which were invaluable to the struggle for American independence. Even Wellington, who conquered another undisputable military genius at Waterloo, had his difficult moments and almost over-reached himself, especially in the attempt on Burgos. Nevertheless, like Alexander and Caesar before them, all five stand so far above their contemporaries that none can dispute their position as being among the most able soldiers and greatest historical figures of all time.

PJH

Gustavus Adolphus
LION OF THE NORTH

Portrait of Gustavus Adolphus, attributed to Albert Cuyp around 1630.

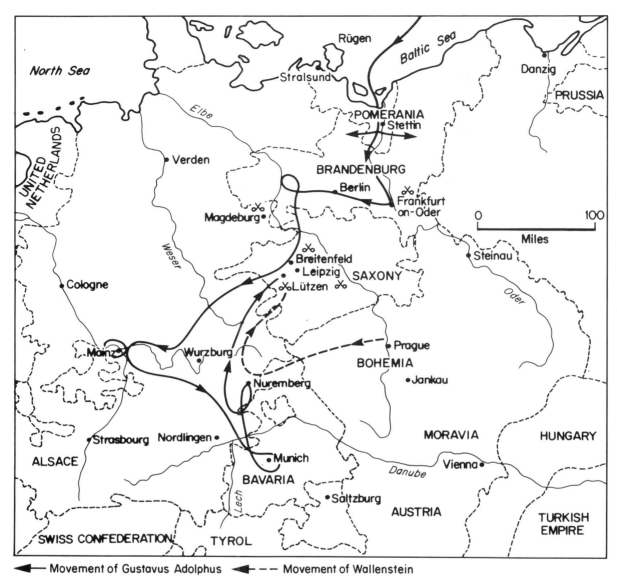

North Sea

Rügen

Baltic Sea

Danzig

Stralsund

PRUSSIA

Elbe

POMERANIA

Stettin

Verden

BRANDENBURG

Berlin

Frankfurt on-Oder

UNITED NETHERLANDS

Weser

✂ Magdeburg

0   100

Miles

Steinau

Breitenfeld

Cologne

✂ Leipzig

SAXONY

Oder

✂ Lützen ✂

Mainz

Wurzburg

Prague

BOHEMIA

Nuremberg

Jankau

Strasbourg

Nordlingen

MORAVIA

HUNGARY

Munich

Vienna

ALSACE

BAVARIA

Danube

Saltzburg

AUSTRIA

TURKISH EMPIRE

Lech

SWISS CONFEDERATION

TYROL

◄—— Movement of Gustavus Adolphus   ◄— — Movement of Wallenstein

Gustavus Adolphus' man-oeuvres in Germany during the Thirty Years War.

Part of an engraving, from a contemporary pamphlet, show-ing the German cities captured by the Swedish forces in the Thirty Years War.

The true greatness of his spirit was such that in all his actions he placed ostentation behind, and conscience before him. . . .

The Great and Famous Battle of Lützen

A good Christian can never be a bad soldier. . . .

Gustavus Adolphus quoted by J. Mackay in *An Old Scots Brigade*

Gustavus the King

On 19 December 1594, at Stockholm Castle, Duke Charles of Sweden was provided with an heir when his wife Christina, daughter of Duke Adolphus of Holstein–Gottorp, gave birth to a son. The advent of the child was of greater import than providing Sweden with a crown prince (for after a brief civil war, on 19 March 1600 Duke Charles was proclaimed as King Charles IX of Sweden). The infant was named Gustavus Adolphus after his grandfathers; his paternal grandfather was the great King Gustavus I of Sweden, founder of the Vasa dynasty. The new prince was to become one of the greatest generals of recorded history, a man who may fairly be said to have contributed more than any other to the advent of 'modern' warfare.

The background into which Gustavus Adolphus was born had much influence on the course of his actions. The Swedish monarchy was both vehemently Protestant and overtly military, the two factors which most governed Gustavus' life. Charles IX, head of the Protestant party in the country prior to his election as King, remained one of the foremost anti-Catholic princes in Europe. It was at his instigation that the Swedish parliament sanctioned the establishment of a regular army, each district being liable to provide a set number of soldiers for the benefit of the state. This was a remarkably modern policy in an age when armies were largely raised only in wartime and disbanded in time of peace.

From the beginning of his reign, Charles was involved in conflict with Poland and Russia in attempts to extend Swedish territory, and latterly in a fratricidal conflict with Denmark (the so-called War of Kalmar, named from the area of chief conflict). Thus, it was against a backcloth of continual war and the aspirations of Swedish expansionism that Gustavus was raised.

From the first, his education was directed towards making him a fitting successor to the throne, and he was groomed by his austere parents to be the prop of the Protestant religion in northern Europe. Extensively schooled in the classics, he became an extraordinary

Musketeer with separate powder-flask and bullet-bag. Gustavus' musketeers sometimes carried a 'twelve apostles' bandolier instead; and latterly carried pouches with 'prepared' cartridges to facilitate loading. Light helmets were sometimes worn by musketeers in place of the more usual felt hat; this version is a type known as a cabasset.

9

linguist. Bilingual in Swedish and German from the earliest age, by the time he was twelve he had mastered Latin, Italian and Dutch, and subsequently became fluent in Spanish, Russian and Polish. Charles IX ensured that his son's education was directed to the practical experience of a ruling prince. As early as the age of nine he began to perform public engagements; by thirteen he negotiated officially with foreign ministers; at fifteen he administered the Duchy of Vestmanland and from 1610 was virtually co-ruler with his father. When he succeeded to the throne in 1611 as King Gustavus II, at the age of seventeen, he was thus not only experienced and capable but recognised as the uncontested leader of his country. Despite a somewhat volatile temperament and an iron and almost inflexible will, his inherent feeling for the values of truth, the Protestant religion and upright conduct impressed even those who were his enemies. These characteristics influenced his policies and conduct in the almost continual warfare in which Sweden was involved from his accession.

Despite holding the crown, Gustavus' rule was in one sense an administration of consent. Unlike almost every other European state (except England), in which the ancient representative councils were to be subjugated to absolute monarchy, under Gustavus the Swedish *Riksdag* (parliament) grew into an integral portion of the constitution. The Riksdag ordinance of 1617 converted the haphazard mob of *riksdagsmen* ('drunken boors') into a dignified national assembly, meeting regularly and debating according to rule and order, organised in four estates (nobles, clergy, burgesses and peasants). At the start of each session, the King presented his proposals or bills, which were debated in congress. Whenever the estates' opinions conflicted, the King selected the opinion which to him seemed the best. The rights of the Riksdag were guaranteed, and though the King had the initiative to table legislation, they could decline to agree, and were also consulted on foreign policy. The eleven Riksdags held by Gustavus were concerned largely with measures to conduct or finance his various wars. Yet such was his prestige and the nation's admiration for him that their religious and patriotic zeal shrank from no sacrifice to further his campaigns or policies. To the devotion of his people, Gustavus owed as much as to his own abilities and successes as a general and empire-builder.

The Art of War

Gustavus Adolphus was not the greatest strategic or tactical genius. His military skills were subordinate to his greatest asset and contribution, that of an administrator and theorist scarcely equalled in military history. It is these qualities which advanced him to the position of the greatest soldier of his age. However, before considering the course of his career and his military innovations, it is necessary to consider the state of the art of war which existed in Europe in the early seventeenth century at the time of his accession.

Musketeers

Military tactics had been revolutionised by the growing importance of firearms. By the late 1590s the dominant weapon was the infantry musket, a ponderous, muzzle-loading weapon. It was of such immense weight that in order to 'aim' (usually no more than pointing it, at breast height, in the general direction of the foe) it required a support for the barrel. This took the form of a spiked pole stuck in the ground in front of the musketeer, with a U-shaped top into which the musket-barrel was placed, supporting its great weight.

The musket fired a spherical lead ball which could inflict a horrifying injury. However, the weapon took a very long time to load, with loose gunpowder inserted into the barrel. Musketeers generally wore a bandolier over the shoulder from which were suspended a number of wooden tubes, each tube containing a measured amount of powder sufficient for one shot. Known from the commonest number of tubes as the 'Twelve Apostles', such bandoliers were not only slow to operate, but had other deficiencies – most notably a fearful habit of catching fire and exploding, and in rattling so loudly that on occasion officers' commands could not be heard over the din.

Ignition of the gunpowder in the musket-barrel was achieved by plunging a lighted taper or 'match' into a depression or metal 'pan' containing a small amount of gunpowder on the side of the barrel. The match was held in the jaws of a spring-operated cock connected to the trigger, which when depressed ignited the powder with a 'flash in the pan', communicating a spark to the main charge via a touch-hole drilled in the side of the musket-barrel. The charge then exploded with a loud noise and a cloud of smoke, sending the bullet on its short and erratic course.

Pikemen

Though the musketeer was also armed with a short sword (the heavy musket also made an effective club) and was sometimes equipped with a light helmet, musketeers were largely defenceless during the time it took them to load; so protection had to be provided. This was given by large bodies of pikemen, infantrymen usually wearing not only a breast-plate and heavier helmet, but frequently arm-defences and 'tassets', or thigh-armour as well. They carried a pike, or spear, of enormous length, 18 feet being quite common. In a tightly-packed mass of infantry, the pikes presented an impenetrable hedge of spikes into which cavalry could not penetrate, and which only a similar body of infantry

Musket-drill (opposite and above) in an engraving by N.C. Goodnight (after Hexham's Principles of the Art Militarie 1637) Musket-drill was extremely complicated but necessary to ensure discipline in combat. This sequence shows the loading of the musket, including ramming-home the musket-ball and charge.

An officer of pikemen in conventional pike-armour depicted in an engraving by N.C. Goodnight. It was worn throughout Europe, but discarded by many of the more forward-thinking armies (including latterly the Swedes) as being a greater encumbrance to movement than its defensive capacity warranted. The breastplate and helmet were often retained, but the articulated thigh-guards (tassets) were often removed.

could engage. In such confrontations, 'at push of pike', two phalanxes would stab at each other until one gave way – or until the musketeers (ranged among or on the flanks of the pikemen) shot down a sufficient number of foemen for the enemy to be discouraged and retire.

The evolution of such dense masses of pikemen – originating with the columns of the Swiss and the *tercios* of Spain, the latter with as many as 1000 to 2000 pikemen crushed closely together – entirely negated the chief tactic of cavalry which had existed since the middle ages, i.e. the armoured charge which rode down the enemy. The cavalry lance, a relic of medieval warfare, was in rapid decline due to the great effort and practice required to master its use; even in the hands of a trained lancer, it could scarcely reach beyond the spiked hedge of 18-feet infantry pikes. Thus, firearms had become the cavalry's main weapons, aided by the development of a second system of ignition, the wheel-lock.

Wheel-lock and Cuirassier

This expensive and easily-damaged device overcame the necessity of carrying a glowing match, which was extremely difficult to manage on horseback. Instead, the gunpowder was ignited by sparks struck from iron pyrites held in the jaws of the cock, which, upon pressure on the trigger, was crashed against a metal plate. The resulting sparks ignited the powder in the pan and fired the weapon.

Short muskets were carried by some cavalry – loosely termed 'harquebusiers' after their firearm, the harquebus – but more common were long-barrelled pistols. In the management of these, however, the traditional rôle of the cavalry was lost, for charges were no longer made. Instead, the universal tactic of trained cavalry was the *caracole*. In this manoeuvre, successive ranks of horsemen advanced at a slow pace until within pistol-range of the enemy, whereupon they fired, and wheeled away to re-load while the succeeding ranks kept up the fusillade. Thus, the offensive impetus of the cavalry was lost entirely, charges with the sword only occurring when the enemy was in flight or when isolated parties of musketeers were encountered. Only in Poland was the offensive capability retained.

There were two basic varieties of cavalry, cuirassiers and harquebusiers. Cuirassiers retained almost full armour, much of it of sufficient strength to be shot-proof. Consequently, it was very heavy and

Wheel-lock holster pistol of the type favoured by cavalry; with a mechanism more temperamental than the matchlock, but easier to handle on horseback.

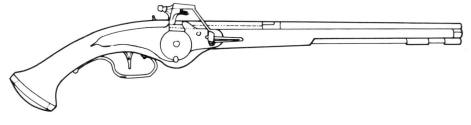

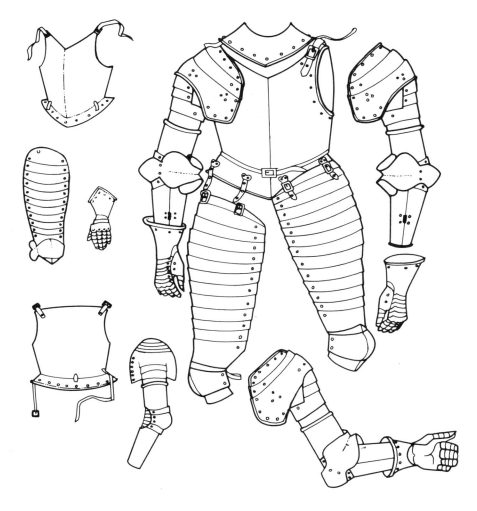

Armour of the period shows (above) pikeman's armour with a typical corselet comprising breastplate and backplate, tassets and helmet. The tassets here include a not uncommon feature in detachable lower plates, which would be removed to facilitate movement whilst still retaining an iron 'skirt' to protect below waist-level. The 'half armour' for a cuirassier (left) was so termed because of the lower leg being usually unarmoured. The suit included either a close helmet or an open-fronted 'pot'.

cumbersome, requiring the use of huge horses. The harquebusiers however were lightly armoured or protected only by a thick jerkin of buff-leather. A third variety, dragoons, were not true cavalry at all, but mounted musketeers who rode into battle but generally dismounted to fight.

Artillery

The army's third arm was the artillery. Although cannon were regarded as symbols of status and of use in besieging towns, they were generally regarded as noisy and not very efficient evils which had to be tolerated. The concept of an aggressive use of artillery was largely unknown, due to the ponderous weight and slow rate of fire. Only two projectiles were in common use: 'solid shot', metal or stone balls; and grapeshot or 'canister', bags or handfuls of musket-balls or scrap iron fired at close range, turning the cannon into a giant shotgun.

Cavalry 'cornet' (standard bearer), with detail of the socket on the stirrup into which the butt of the lance fitted.

Deadlock

The result of these developments was that decisive victories became difficult to achieve. The infantry was formed in blocks, largely impenetrable by the enemy. Simultaneously, the cavalry had lost its striking power, and the artillery was largely ineffective.

The decline of the concept of decisive victory was accelerated further by the composition of armies, many states being unable to raise sufficient numbers of men from their own inhabitants or citizens without damaging agriculture and commerce. Thus, mercenary armies attained the greatest importance, similar to the medieval *condottieri* of Italy and Switzerland, but ranging more widely, so that soldiering became the profession for thousands, who changed their allegiance according to the location of current wars.

The evils of the system were obvious: feeding and equipping were a continual drain upon the resources of a state, discipline was often non-existent and the cruelties committed upon the inhabitants of a region through which an army passed were appalling. By the time of the Thirty Years War, into which Gustavus Adolphus entered in 1630, massacre and atrocity were commonplace.

The combination of the prevalent tactics, the growing importance of fortified places, difficult and costly to capture, and the increasing difficulties of supplying ever-larger armies with ammunition and food (even though the latter was usually taken by force from the unfortunate local civilians), all impelled generals to avoid battle unless success was reasonably assured. Thus, many wars and campaigns were prolonged and stalemated.

Maurice of Nassau

However, attempts were made to break the deadlock, several generals attempting to institute new formations and manoeuvres, most directed towards obtaining the greatest benefit from the maximisation of infantry musketry. Most notable were the reforms of Maurice of Nassau, Prince of Orange (1567–1625) who led the Dutch fight for independence against Spain.

Though he won no truly decisive victories (still eschewing battle except in favourable circumstances), his reforms were far-reaching. Based on ancient Roman patterns (influenced in particular by Aelian), he increased the number but reduced the size of units in his army. Thus, his companies of pikemen stood only five deep, and were flanked by platoons of musketeers. Not only were these smaller units more manoeuverable than the vast and unmanageable masses of the Spanish *tercios*, they also enabled all soldiers to come into direct contact with the enemy. (In the huge *tercios* the men in the middle never even came within pike-range of the foe.) In his passion for geometrical order and system (Maurice was said to have waged war as if playing chess), he

14

refined the concept of fortress warfare and the technical branches — engineers and artillery — and went some way towards making the heavy gun of more consequence on the battlefield.

His methods were copied throughout Protestant Europe, but not until Gustavus was the reformation truly completed. Maurice's progression was largely one of training and administration; it required Gustavus to complete the work and put it into practice.

The Great Reformer

The military system of Maurice of Nassau and his own study of classical texts were only the starting-points for the reform of the Swedish army instituted by Gustavus Adolphus. The reforms were not achieved overnight, but formed a continuing process. Thus, the Swedish army was probably not truly perfected until the late 1620s, or until Gustavus entered the Thirty Years War proper in 1630.

When he succeeded to the throne, he found the Swedish forces under-strength, poorly organised and equipped, badly led and generally unprofessional, and it was a work of some labour to correct the defects. It was also extremely expensive: over half the annual national budget was spent on the army — though it should be remembered in this regard that states at this period had only a limited number of calls upon their finances.

Sweden was fortunate in being able to sustain a continual war-effort, having natural resources of copper, tin, iron-ore and forests to provide both wood and charcoal. Indeed, the war benefitted Swedish industry in the increasing export of armaments, encouraged by the Crown: between 1626 and 1646 the export of Swedish cast-iron guns rose from 22 tonnes per year to 1000. However, Sweden could not afford to employ vast numbers of mercenaries, so the manpower problem had to be solved from within.

In this, as in everything else, Gustavus found the most practical solution. Though reading widely in the classics (his favourite textbooks were Xenophon's *Cyropaedia* and *Anabasis*, and Grotius' *De Jure Belli et Pacis*), he was equally interested in the newest scientific and technological developments, and being both liked and respected by his people as a man of humane temperament and high conviction without bigotry, his reforms were accomplished without opposition. He was, perhaps, the first general to approach the study of war with the mental philosophy of the Renaissance.

The National Army
Like Maurice of Nassau, who had created a professional army of native-

Another cavalry cornet bearing the three crowns of Sweden. The fluted lance to which it was fastened had a bracket for attachment to a shoulder belt.

Cavalry trooper with iron elbow gauntlet worn as protection for the bridle hand and left forearm only; it was not worn on the right arm.

born Dutchmen drawn from a wide social spectrum, Gustavus determined to create a professional army that was basically Swedish in composition, leavened with only the best and most trustworthy of mercenaries. Of these, his especial favourites were the Scottish and, to a lesser extent, English professional soldiers.

To create the 'national' army he regulated the process of conscription which had evolved over the previous half-century to ensure that it was fairer, that it provided a regular supply of men and that the average calibre of the individual recruit was higher. Gustavus himself preferred the conscripts to come from the property-owning class, especially the small farmers who he thought would at least be adequately nourished and of robust constitution, and if selected upon a district or regional basis, they would form closely-knit regiments with a common bond of province and a background in the soil of the homeland. Maurice of Nassau's guiding principle for the formation of a professional army was that it should be paid adequately for its services, to make the common soldier proud of his calling, to prevent looting in wartime and desertion in time of peace; but unlike the rich Dutch provinces Gustavus could not afford the same level of cash payment.

His solution was brilliant. His conscripts had to serve twenty years, or until the age of fifty, when they were discharged; upon which occasion their recompense for service was given in land. In the case of officers, the system was simple, in the gift of a farm, usually on crown

Lower gun deck of the Wasa, *the warship launched in 1628 and representing Gustavus' attempt to build a fleet to control the Baltic. The vessel was holed and foundered on her maiden voyage on 10 August 1628. In 1961, she was rediscovered, raised and is now restored.*

lands, and with it the right to collect rent from the tenant-farmer. For the ordinary soldiers, the system was more complicated but even more effective. In addition to a yearly wage and clothing-allowance, the private soldier would be allotted a share (usually one-eighth) of a homestead, where he would actually be billetted when not on campaign. The farmer who owned the land was allowed to deduct the equivalent amount from his taxes or rent, and would pay it over to the soldier, who was equally bound to work on the farm in exchange for his board and lodging. Thus, the ordinary soldiers were given a personal stake in the country, bound to the land and assisting with its maintenance. The fact that much of the civilian population was thus involved with the army and its support created a truly national army of men who were an integral part of the community, not regarded as dangerous outcasts, as were the soldiers of most other states.

In order to support the war effort, Gustavus expanded Swedish commerce, developed industries and exploited the country's natural resources. The government operated on a regular annual budget with a reformed fiscal system. Drafts to supply men to the regular army were taken from the militia, the home-defence force in which all able-bodied men over the age of fifteen were liable to serve.

These fundamental reforms produced a Swedish army which was quite different in character and generally superior to those of any other European power. In these matters, as in so many others of national importance, Gustavus was indebted to the administrative skill of his invaluable chancellor, Axel Oxenstierna (1583–1654), who transformed Gustavus' ideas into reality. Responsible for the administration and supply of Gustavus' armies in the later campaigns, Oxenstierna proved to be Gustavus' right hand and the most loyal of servants and collaborators.

Typical officer's costume, with armour restricted to the gorget and the large waist sash often used to identify the nationality or army of the wearer. The gorget itself, worn with a buff-coat as neck protection later became the symbol of an officer's rank.

The method of recruitment resulted in a raising of morale among the ordinary soldiers, strengthened by the concern shown by Gustavus for the men he conscripted. In wartime, soldiers engaged on campaign were paid regularly (by a monthly allowance of hard cash whenever possible) to remove discontent and obviate the necessity of plundering to keep body and soul together, something prevalent in other armies. Gustavus ensured that his men were properly fed and clothed – they received one of the earliest regular issues of warm clothing – and properly equipped. He established supply depots in the rear of the army's sphere of operations, ensuring that the necessary provisions were at hand, and even set up a hospital administration. These actions were all proof of his concern for the well-being of his soldiers, an attitude of mind which was highly unusual for the time.

Tactics Reorganised
Gustavus' second great reform was tactical and represented a major

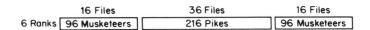

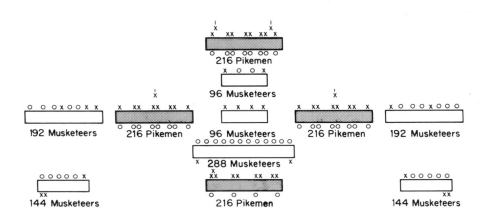

Swedish infantry formations: (a) the squadron; (b) a brigade of three squadrons, with regimental artillery and arrows indicating the direction of fire that was possible with this formation; (c) a brigade of four squadrons, showing the positions of officers [x] and NCOs [o]

progression from the work of Maurice of Nassau. The reform was directed towards Gustavus' philosophy of war in which the destruction of the enemy force was paramount, overriding all other considerations.

To achieve this, he had to restore the previously declining power of offensive action by increasing firepower and its effectiveness, and restoring shock action by both infantry and cavalry. Simultaneously, he had to ensure that though decisive in attack and capable of rapid mobility, the army still retained its capacity for stout defence.

The infantry was reorganised into tactical units or 'squadrons' each of 408 men – 216 pikemen and 192 musketeers – plus officers and non-commissioned officers, the number of which were increased greatly to give a capacity for close command previously undreamed of. These units were smaller and thus even more flexible than those of the Dutch, whose battalions contained 250 pikes and 240 muskets. Gustavus' pikemen were formed in a central block, six ranks deep, and the musketeers in bodies of 96 men, also six ranks deep, on each side.

The pattern of musket was improved, so that the weapon became lighter and more manageable, and more wheel-locks were introduced. 'Prepared cartridges' were devised, in which the musket-ball and its propellant charge were assembled into a paper tube, greatly speeding

18

the process of loading the musket and thus increasing the rate of fire. Attempts were also made, largely successfully, to standardise the calibre of firearms to ease the problems of re-supply. The pikes were shortened slightly in 1616, and the head of the shaft shod with iron to prevent the points from being lopped off, and the infantry armour was reduced, greatly facilitating movement.

The principal emphasis was on firepower, Gustavus adopting the Spanish practice of countermarch, by which the front-rank musketeers retired to the rear to reload, their places being taken by the succeeding ranks; but since the loading process had been speeded, Gustavus was able to have two ranks fire simultaneously. The countermarch was so designed that in its execution, the whole formation moved forward – in effect a rolling barrage. Later, the *salve* or salvo was perfected, in which three ranks of musketeers fired simultaneously, resulting in even greater hitting-power. With the salvo, musketeers were unprotected whilst they re-loaded, when the pikemen were needed as their shield, but from it being previously a defensive weapon, Gustavus transformed the pike into a means of offence, charges being executed by the pikemen whose reduction in armour allowed them to move quickly. This aggressive use of pikes was in itself innovative, in an age which elsewhere was beginning to question the value of the pike even in a defensive role.

The linear formations which had originated with Maurice of Nassau had resulted in the maximum number of weapons being brought to bear at once, but his insistence on rigidly-held geometrical formations had resulted in the loss of manoeuverability. Under Gustavus, increased freedom of movement was the result of his more flexible formations. Three or four squadrons formed a brigade, which could be arrayed in different formations according to circumstances. Each squadron was subdivided into platoons, normally six ranks deep – 36 files of pikes in the centre, with two wings of 96 musketeers each, each with a frontage of 16 men. Arrayed in the common T-shaped formation, with pikes and muskets mutually supporting and equally capable of offence, the brigade was described as resembling 'a little moveable fortress with its curtains and ravelins'. The combination of flexible formations and smaller, highly-disciplined units combined with the aggressive use of infantry proved immeasurably superior to the massive and immobile *tercios*. Disordered by musketry, the wavering enemy would find themselves assailed by a charge of pikemen, and such was the inherent weakness of the tightly-packed *tercio* that any rupture in their front could not be countered, manoeuvre being impossible due to the density of the formation.

Equally dramatic were Gustavus' reorganisations of the cavalry. Under ancient obligations, the Swedish nobles were responsible for filling a quota of heavily-armoured cavalry or cuirassiers. However, the system was so unpopular that in the year of Gustavus' accession (1611),

This engraving by N.C. Goodnight (after Jakob de Gheyn) shows a musketeer with the musket in firing-position, supported by the forked rest. The lighted match had only to be clamped into the jaws of the 'cock' for the musket to be ready to fire.

The lighter-armed cavalry were often termed 'harquebusiers' (from their firearm or harquebus), though in Swedish service the sword was regarded as the principal weapon. Although a cuirass (breast- and backplate) might be worn, the universal protective garment was the buff-coat, a waist- or thigh-length leather jerkin, with or without sleeves.

Cavalry trooper shown wearing a harquebusier equipment in an engraving by N.C. Goodnight (after Cruso's Militarie Instructions). This typical costume includes a waist-length buff-coat, with 'wings' protecting the shoulders, and a burgonet-style helmet (though a lighter helmet was more commonly worn).

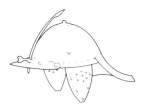

Cavalry helmets of the Zischagge type, with laminated neck guards and 'nasal', or nose protection bar, which slid through a slot in the peak.

only thirty cuirassiers were thus recruited. Even Gustavus never succeeded in compelling the nobility to serve, and as late as 1630 only two squadrons could be formed. Instead, Gustavus had to rely upon voluntary enlistment. Thus instead of the enormous mounts and costly armour of the cuirassiers, he obtained largely lighter-equipped cavalry on smaller, faster horses. Nevertheless, by the continual training which all branches of the Swedish army were compelled to perform, even in time of peace, Gustavus made it more than a match for any other cavalry in Europe.

The New Cavalry

Maurice of Nassau had made little attempt to reform cavalry tactics, but Gustavus' developments were crucial. Realising the moribund nature of the *caracole*, Gustavus prohibited the manoeuvre. In its place he developed the cavalry in line with his objective of achieving a decisive victory, by utilising the speed and impetus of a well-disciplined charge. In 1620, the establishment of each squadron was set at seventy-five, and in 1628 two such squadrons were formed into the first provincial cavalry regiment, the Västgöta. In the early years a regiment on campaign comprised 974 men and 1000 horses, organised in a small headquarters and eight squadrons, each squadron of three officers, two non-commissioned officers, a quartermaster, muster-clerk, provost, farrier, chaplain, barber (who doubled as a medical orderly under the supervision of the regimental surgeon), two trumpeters and 120 men. By the 1630s the formation had become even more flexible by the reduction of the regimental strength to 570, in eight squadrons each of seventy men.

In battle, a squadron was arrayed four ranks deep, later three, who fought in the style of the Poles whom Gustavus had witnessed in his early campaigns. Instead of merely harassing the enemy with often-ineffective pistol-fire, the Swedish cavalry's main tactic was to charge home with the sword, overthrowing any enemy in their path. Only the first one or two ranks fired their pistols, and then only immediately before engaging the enemy with the sword. The remaining one or two ranks held their fire for use in the ensuing mêlée, or when the enemy was broken and in flight. It is unclear whether charges were executed at a gallop or a fast trot; but what mattered was the devastating effect of well-disciplined and determined men charging home with cold steel, with cavalry regiments of small size and situated in the line of battle. Consequently, disorganisation in the enemy forces was exploited rapidly, often with a rapid dash into any gap in the enemy line which had been blasted by the Swedish artillery or musketry.

Even the heaviest Swedish cavalry were usually armoured only with breastplate and helmet, greatly increasing their mobility; the lighter cavalry often had no armour save a stout buff-leather jerkin. Among other innovations, Gustavus' dragoons were given shorter muskets to

enable them to fire from the saddle, and boxes of prepared cartridges instead of the inconvenient bandoliers.

Science of Artillery

But wide-ranging as were Gustavus' innovations in infantry and cavalry tactics, perhaps his greatest single contribution to the development of military science was in artillery. In this he was aided by the greatest gunner of the age, Lennart Torstensson (1603–51) who at the age of fifteen had become Gustavus' page. He accompanied Gustavus in the campaigns in Livonia in 1621–23, where he showed sufficient promise be sent to study under Maurice of Nassau himself in the Netherlands in 1624. Torstensson returned to Sweden in 1626, and at the age of twenty-seven was given command of the Swedish artillery, which had already benefitted markedly from Gustavus' reforms, producing the first modern field artillery in Europe.

Maurice of Nassau had first classified guns according to the weight of their projectile, and by 1630, Gustavus had reduced the previous sixteen types of guns in Swedish service to just three main varieties or 'natures' each designed for a specific rôle: the 24-pounder, the 12-pounder and the 3-pounder. This standardisation radically improved the problems of re-supply.

The design of the cannon was refined, the largest and least mobile being discarded in favour of lighter pieces. For example, the massive 48-pounder siege-gun, which required a team of up to 39 horses to move it at ponderous speed, was abandoned in favour of the 24-

Laying a gun by means of a sighting disc, a wooden crescent with a vertical slot, used to align the barrel with the target.

Gunner wearing short buff-coat and long stockings; and carrying a shovel used to improve siting of gun positions.

Bouget or 'budge barrel' used for carrying gunpowder. The staves were bound were bound with rope, so as not to strike sparks, and the fabric lining kept the powder dry.

pounder. Continuing efforts to improve the quality of gunpowder allowed the thickness and length of the barrel to be decreased without compromising range, hitting-power or safety, so that for the first time in history the field artillery was truly mobile and able to keep pace with the movements of the rest of the army.

By 1630, Gustavus' artillery-train of 80 guns required only 1000 horses and 100 waggons, whereas in 1625 the army's 36-gun train had needed over 1000 horses and 220 waggons to operate it in the field.

The vast natural mineral resources of Sweden made the creation of a large artillery force (and the continuing process of improvement by experimentation) a realistic possibility, so that by 1630 the ratio of guns to men in the Swedish forces was an amazingly high 9.4 per 1000 soldiers. The 12-pounder was the ordinary field-gun, and the lightest fieldpiece had been the 'leather gun', a thin copper tube bound with rope and covered with leather. By the time Torstensson assumed overall command of the artillery, the 'leather gun' had been largely withdrawn; though a major technological development, it sacrificed too much to lightness and mobility. It was replaced by the 'regimental gun', a light 3-pounder – known as a *pièce Suèdoise* which could be moved by a single horse or only two or three men. It could be transported anywhere and one was usually attached to each squadron in order to provide immediate fire-support for the infantry. It was designed to take the newly-developed artillery cartridge, in which the shot and propellant charge were wired together to facilitate loading. This so increased the rate of fire that the Swedish artillery could discharge eight rounds of grapeshot to six shots by a musketeer. Indeed, at the Battle of Breitenfeld, the Swedish gunners were so skilful that they fired three shots to every one of the enemy. Accuracy was insisted upon, which, together with constant practice, resulted in the Swedish artillery being immeasurably superior to that of their opponents. The science of artillery may properly be said to have been invented by Gustavus.

Gustavus Adolphus, the 'father of modern artillery', positioning the guns to cover the crossing of the River Lech, assisted by his artillery chief, the brilliant Lennart Torstensson.

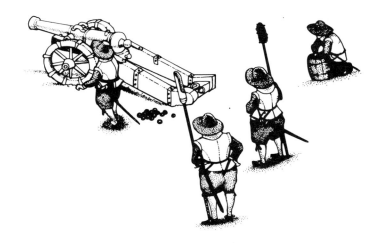

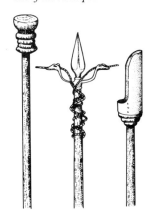

Gun crew in action: the gun captain prepares to ignite the charge whilst the others stand out of the recoil path.

Artillery sidearms (left to right): rammer, linstock with slow match in position; powder ladle.

Arms and the Man

The result of all Gustavus' innovations was to produce a Swedish army which was radically different from any other in Europe. It was a well-equipped, well-supplied force with high morale, constantly trained and highly disciplined, whose linear formations were vastly more mobile and flexible than those of their opponents. Although Gustavus was constantly seeking to improve and alter his tactical dispositions, in general he assembled his army in two shallow lines about 300 paces apart, infantry in the centre and cavalry on the flanks, with the wedge-shaped infantry formations having a striking-point of pikes flanked and supported at the rear by musketeers. Behind each line was a strong reserve, and between each cavalry regiment was usually a body of up to 200 musketeers. The heavier artillery was grouped in batteries, to bring the maximum firepower to bear, whilst the lighter regimental guns accompanied the infantry and cavalry. In fact, the artillery was suffi-ciently mobile that it could be directed to whichever point of the battlefield it was required. In addition, the comparatively small size of units (especially cavalry) and their high level of discipline and training allowed the battle-line to change its formation rapidly and advance at speed to exploit any retrograde movements or unsteadiness in the enemy ranks. The army operated as a cohesive whole, all 'arms' being interdependent and mutually supportive. Though initially small in numbers, its aggressive handling made the Swedish army the finest in Europe.

Soldiers of Fortune

Gustavus only employed mercenaries out of necessity, and never the cut-throat bands which ravaged central Europe, but professional

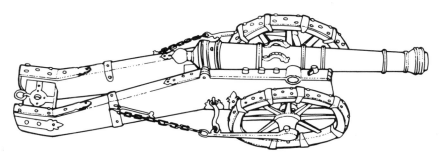

soldiers who accepted the stern discipline in return for treatment as good as that received by native Swedes. Indeed, probably the best infantry in the Swedish army was the Green Brigade (brigades were commonly named after the colour of their flags), which was almost exclusively Scottish in composition. It was led by such distinguished soldiers as Robert Monro and Alexander Leslie (both of whom became Swedish field-marshals) and Sir John Hepburn.

Some of the component regiments were formed specifically for Gustavus' army, but the career of Mackay's Regiment of the Green Brigade is typical of that of mercenary units at the period. With the permission of King Charles I of England the regiment was formed initially to fight with the Protestant army of Graf Ernst von Mansfeld (1580–1626), a somewhat unprincipled mercenary who overlooked his own Roman Catholic religion to fight against his co-religionists of the Imperial army in a series of campaigns. Mansfeld died before the Scots under Sir Donald Mackay (1st Lord Reay) could join him. Consequently, Mackay took his regiment into Danish service, before transferring in 1629 to Gustavus. So good were the Scottish troops that the Scots Brigade was formed in March 1631, command being given to Sir John Hepburn, and consisting of four of the best regiments in Swedish service: Hepburn's own, Mackay's Highlanders, Stargate's, and Lumsden's Musketeers. It is conceivable that the name 'Green Brigade' was derived equally from the tartan clothing worn at least by Mackay's, which apparently retained its Highland national dress and even its bagpipers.

At this time, Gustavus had some 13,000 Britons in his service, mostly Scots and including six generals, thirty colonels and fifty-one lieutenant-colonels. Other mercenaries included the Black, Blue and Yellow Brigades who were largely German in composition. In fact, only about half the Swedish army was truly 'Swedish'.

The Swedish–Polish war provides other examples of a typical use of mercenaries. From 1621 King Sigismund III of Poland had formed several British units, some raised from 'vagabonds and unpropertied Scots resident in Poland' and others recruited in England and led by the two Sir Arthur Astons, father and son. The elder Aston died in 1624 but the younger (who had begun his career in Russian service) fought with

his English against Gustavus until he was captured near Danzig in 1627. Despite being a Roman Catholic, he took service with Gustavus and followed him until Lützen. Like many of Gustavus' veterans, he later plied his talents in the English Civil War, where the barbarous habits he had assimilated in Europe made him the terror of enemy and friend: 'very much esteemed where he was not and very much detested where he was'. Clarendon, who thought him a man of much greater reputation in war than he deserved, portrayed him well in a good general description of the genus of mercenary throughout Europe at the time, except, perhaps, under Gustavus' discipline:

a man of rough nature, and so given up to an immoderate love of money that he cared not by what unrighteous ways he exacted it.

Aston later became the extremely unpopular Royalist Governor of

Gustavus Adolphus at the head of his élite unite of Scottish mercenaries, the 'Green Brigade'.

25

Oxford, until he lost a leg in a riding accident, showing off before some ladies; later he went to Ireland and was killed in the storm of Drogheda, where it was said his brains were beaten out with his own wooden leg!

First into Battle

Perhaps the most important factor in the excellence of the Swedish army was the presence of the King himself. Unlike the majority of generals of the period, and alone among reigning monarchs, he led by personal example. No task was too small or menial for Gustavus to perform, if by so doing he set an example to the army – even to the digging of trenches. Like Maurice of Nassau, Gustavus realised the importance of field fortifications. Indeed, it was said of him that his successes in Germany owed as much to the spade as to the sword, for he only gave battle when he believed it appropriate, and at other times was too strongly entrenched to be attacked by the enemy. Many mercenaries in particular thought it above their dignity to dig trenches and raise earthworks, so Gustavus was always the first to pick up a shovel to set the example. Equally, Gustavus was always the first in battle, directing from the front and even leading charges, as a contemporary wrote:

He did animate his soldiers rather by fighting, than exhorting; nor did he challenge to himself any advantage above the meanest of them . . . He well understood that faith and loyalty are not to be expected where we impose thraldom and servitude, and therefore at times he would be familiar, as well with the common soldier as the commander . . . he never persuaded any man to an enterprise, in which he would not himself make one. He taught them as well by hand, as tongue . . .[1]

Wherever possible, despite being short-sighted, he even preferred to make his own reconnaissances. At least one of these almost ended in disaster. As the King walked along a frozen marsh near the besieged town of Demmin, 'of intention, with a perspective-glass, to spie into the enemie's workes'. The ice gave way under his weight: 'his Majesty falls up to the middle in water'. Gustavus waved away the Scottish soldiers nearest him lest they were injured, for the besieged garrison had begun to fire at him. Despite 'above a thousand shot of musket at his Majesty [Gustavus] at last wrought himselfe loose' and retired to sit by a camp-fire. The Scottish captain Dumaine remonstrated with the King for risking his life and thus risking depriving the Protestant party of their champion, 'and which was worse, what would become of many brave cavaliers of fortune, who had no further hopes than to live and be maintained under his Majesty?'.[2] Gustavus excused himself, saying that he could never believe anything well done unless he did it himself – a revealing insight into his approach to the task of command.

Right, Truth and Religion

Religion was one of the motivating passions of Gustavus' life. A most devout man without being a bigot, he saw himself as the champion and

Musketeer with light harquebus and cabasset-style helmet.

defender of Protestantism. 'A good Christian', he declared, 'can never be a bad soldier; and the man who has finished his prayers has already got over the best part of his day's work'.[3]

This belief supported him, and equally was responsible for his insistence on the most strict discipline within the army.

Gustavus' *Articles of War* bound both Swede and mercenary to a rigid code of conduct, both in and out of battle. They were read to the army regularly, and forbade swearing, blasphemy, drunkenness and fornication. Punishments for minor offences were humane (flogging was forbidden), which improved morale and had a civilizing influence. In contrast pillage, rape and 'despising divine service' were punishable by death. A similar attitude was adopted by Gustavus towards the enemy towns he occupied. In Munich, for example, harsh treatment was expected where the clergy had preached of Gustavus as the Antichrist. What they actually received at the hands of the Swedish army astonished the citizens. Instead of the army levying contributions of money and goods (the common practice even with friendly armies), Gustavus exacted a sum from the rich and distributed it to the city's poor. The idea of a victorious army distributing alms to its defeated enemy was unheard of, even though not entirely altruistic in that did no harm to the Swedish cause in German eyes.

Despite his love of 'right, truth and religion', Gustavus' temperament was not the easiest to handle, though his fairness usually triumphed. As he admitted, 'I bear my subjects' errors with patience, but they too must put up with my quick speech'![4]

A story was told of his altercation with a British mercenary, Colonel Seaton, whom Gustavus struck in public. Seaton demanded his discharge, but Gustavus followed him until they had left Swedish territory. The King called upon Seaton to dismount:

That you have been injured I acknowledge; I am, therefore, now come to give you the satisfaction of a gentleman, for being now out of my own dominions, Gustavus and you are equal. We have both, I see, pistols and swords; alight, sir, immediately, and the affair shall be decided.

Astonished, Seaton fell to his knees, saying that it was satisfaction enough to be described as Gustavus' equal, and begged to be reinstated. Apocryphal or not, the story demonstrates how Gustavus' fair manner won the devotion of his followers.

Less happily resolved was his altercation with the famous Scottish commander Sir John Hepburn, who resigned after seven years in Gustavus' service. The cause of the quarrel is uncertain, but may have arisen over Gustavus' neglect of Hepburn's forces or Hepburn's religion (though fighting for the Protestants he was himself a Catholic). Whatever the case, Hepburn refused to accept an apology and somewhat theatrically drew his sword, then returned it to its sheath, vowing, 'Now sire, I shall never draw it more in your behalf'.

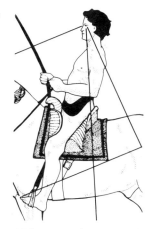

Mid-seventeenth century riding posture, with 'long' stirrups, as shown in L'Art Monter à Cheval published in Paris, 1642. It is shown here with the 'great saddle' used by cuirassiers shown below.

Imperialist cuirassier.

27

Hepburn was as good as his word, for though the Swedes fought an engagement before he quit the army, Hepburn refused to become involved personally, but instead spent the action advising and encouraging his countrymen.

Early Campaigns

The reform of the Swedish army was a continuing process, and was not fully completed until Gustavus became involved in the Thirty Years War. For the first nineteen years of his reign, however, there was scarcely a time when Sweden was not planning or fighting a war, the whole of which added to Gustavus' and the army's experience.

In the earliest campaigns, however, the Swedish army was generally unequal to the demands of modern war, being recruited largely from woodsmen and peasants, skilled in forest-fighting but ill-organised and ill-equipped.

Typical horseman's boot, with turned-down top and lace 'boot hose' inside.

One of the first acts of the young king was to terminate the 'War of Kalmar' against Denmark, Gustavus' father having died on his way home after the summer campaigning-season of 1611. After the fall of Kalmar to the Danes, the war degenerated into a series of border skirmishes. The mediation of King James I of England resulted in the Peace of Knäred (28 January 1613).

War with Russia

Charles IX had been involved in campaigns in Russia, a period known in that country's history as 'the Time of Troubles'. In his conflicts with Poland (ostensibly a contest for domination of the Baltic, though the fact that Poland was Roman Catholic was also significant), Charles had first allied with Czar Basil IV against their common enemy, the Poles. However, the deposition of Basil led to a change of policy and hostilities commenced between Sweden and Russia, Charles having an idea of making his second son, Philip, the Czar.

As the Russian war was political speculation rather than national danger, Gustavus was eager to end hostilities. In 1613, Moscow sent an expedition against the Swedish-occupied city of Novgorod, but the Russian force was intercepted by Swedish troops and defeated. Gustavus himself led an expedition into Muscovite territory in 1614. Pskov, the strongest frontier fortress, was besieged unsuccessfully for seven months before Gustavus withdrew to Swedish territory. With the rallying of Russia around the new Czar Michael Romanov, Gustavus became convinced of the impossibility of partitioning Muscovy and establishing a trans-Baltic empire, which had been the dream of some Swedish statesmen. Moscow expected a Polish invasion, and with

Another horseman's boot, with a garter below the breeches, and lace 'boot hose' to protect stockings chafing against the leather.

Gustavus planning a descent on Polish Livonia, it was clearly in the interest of both states to terminate the war. The Russians recognised the necessity of buying-off the Swedes by a concession of territory. Thus, the Peace of Stolbova (27 February 1617) which ended the war was very advantageous to Sweden, the Czar surrendering the provinces of Kexholm and Ingria, renouncing all claims to Livonia and Estonia, and paying an indemnity of 20,000 roubles. In return, Gustavus acknowledged Michael Romanov as Czar and restored Novgorod. Gustavus had thus succeeded in excluding Muscovy from the Baltic and he announced the fact quite graphically to the Stockholm diet (parliament):

'I hope to God that the Russians will feel it a bit difficult to skip over *that* little brook'.

War with Poland

The war against Poland was a very different matter. Essentially, it was a conflict for control of the Baltic coast, but was complicated by a number of additional features. Gustavus perceived a danger to Protestantism from Catholic Poland, though in truth the threat never really existed. In fact, the Polish diet prevented the later martial monarch Wladislaus IV from intervening in the Thirty Years War on the Catholic side. Nevertheless, Gustavus magnified the threat until it assumed major proportions, and this was the reason he formed an alliance with Denmark to defend Stralsund in 1628, for he believed that a divided Protestant Scandinavia would result in the destruction by the Catholic states of both Denmark and Sweden. There was some truth in his belief that the Scandinavian monarchies represented the pillars of Protestantism.

Gustavus was convinced of the legitimacy of his cause and of the threat from Poland. This was reinforced by the fact that the Polish Vasas denied the legitimacy of Gustavus' possession of the Swedish crown, and by the rivalry to control the Baltic. So Gustavus took advantage of Poland's simultaneous involvement in wars with Muscovy and Turkey and reconquered the eastern littoral of the Baltic. In 1617 he captured several Baltic ports in Livonia, and compelled the Polish *Hetman* Krzysztof Radziwill to conclude an armistice until 1620.

Gustavus resumed the offensive in 1621, invading Estonia with 12,000 Swedes reinforced by 4000 Estonians. Riga, the political and commercial centre of Livonia, was invested on 13 August, and the city was captured on 15 September. On 3 October Mitau was occupied, but so severe was the sickness which afflicted the Swedish army that a further 10,000 reinforcements had to be called. However, Radziwill was again forced to conclude an armistice, from 1622 to 1625.

In the summer campaigning season of 1625, Gustavus occupied all of Livonia and Kurland against minor resistance, and in January 1626 he attacked the Poles at Walhof, destroying a fifth of their army and scattering the remainder. This action, remarkable as the first full-scale

The 'long boot', a version favoured by cavalrymen; the high top protected the knee.

29

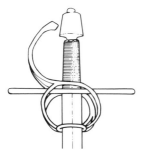

Hilt of a broadsword of the type carried by cuirassiers.

pitched battle fought by Gustavus, completed the conquest of Livonia and opened the way for a new theatre of operations.

Finding it increasingly difficult to support an army in the Dvina district, Gustavus resolved to transfer the offensive to Poland's Prussian provinces, with a view to securing control of the Vistula, as he had already secured the Dvina. The Swedish fleet, with 14,000 men aboard, arrived off the chain of sand-dunes which separated the Frische–Haff from the Baltic. Pillau, the only Baltic port then accessible to warships, was occupied, followed by all of northern Prussia, threatening Poland's access to the Baltic. In July, Gustavus conquered the bishopric of Erme-land, and the surrender of Marienberg and Elbing gave him possession of the easily-defensible Vistula delta, which was treated as a permanent conquest, with Axel Oxenstierna appointed as governor-general. Only Danzig rejected his demand of surrender, and it was blockaded by the Swedish army. The city's communications with the sea were cut by the erection of the first of Gustavus' famous entrenched camps, at Dirschau. The city was blockaded from the end of 1626, and though the Swedish army began to be harassed by Polish irregulars under *Hetman* Stanislaus Koniecpolski, the initial object of the campaign, to secure a base of operations, had been won.

In October, Gustavus returned to Sweden to organise reinforce-ments. While Gustavus was away, Koniecpolski launched a counter-offensive, attempting to reopen the Vistula and relieve Danzig. He captured the port of Puck, a fortress west of Danzig on the Vistula and intercepted some 4000 mercenaries recruited for Gustavus in Germany. Gustavus returned from Sweden in May 1627 bringing with him some 7000 men. The strength of his army was now some 14,000 against Koniecpolski's 9000, and the Poles were repulsed at the Battle of Tczew, where Gustavus was wounded. For the first time, Gustavus' cavalry was able to meet the Poles on equal terms, the reforms of the Swedish army having now taken effect, but Koniecpolski's superior strategical ability frustrated all Gustavus' attempts to destroy his army. At this time, Sigismund III organised a small fleet of privateers to harass the Swedish supply route across the Baltic. Such was Swedish naval power that Gustavus still retained control of the sea, a factor vital for the successes of the Swedish army, who thus maintained their line of com-munications with their homeland.

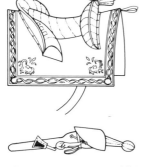

Cuirassier's 'great saddle' with holstered pistol. The in-ternal lining of the holster, shown folded down, could be drawn up over the butt to keep the pistol dry.

With his army increased to 32,000 men, after extensive preparations and having recovered from his injury, Gustavus took the offensive in 1628. Koniecpolski was forced to retire southwards; but as the Poles were content to fight a war of harassment, Gustavus was unable to bring about the decisive battle he sought. As the normal campaigning season drew to a close with the onset of winter, Gustavus withdrew to Prussia, breaking-up his camp on 10 September. The campaign had again confirmed Koniecpolski's skill: although his own forces were outnumbered and virtually unsupported by his own government, he had cost Gustavus some 5000 casualties.

Final Polish Campaign

In the campaign of 1629, Gustavus faced a stronger enemy. Already he was proposing to march into Germany to support the Protestant party in the Thirty Years War. In an attempt to prevent Swedish intervention, the Holy Roman Emperor (leader of the Catholic party) sent Sigismund III some 7000 men to aid Polish resistance. These troops were part of the mercenary army of the Bohemian adventurer Albrecht von Wallenstein (1583–1634), the archetypal self-centred freebooter, nominally in Imperial service but who was most concerned with his own interests.

With these reinforcements, Koniecpolski immediately went on the offensive in 1629, surprising Gustavus and a contingent of his army while on the march. At Sztum, on 29 June, the Swedes had the worst of what was generally an inconclusive cavalry action, in the course of which Gustavus was almost captured and severely wounded in the back. The two injuries he sustained in the Polish War prevented him from ever wearing armour.

Despite the reverse at Sztum, the Swedish hold on the Baltic coast remained unshaken. It was from this position of strength that Gustavus was able to negotiate the Treaty of Altmark (1629), which was highly advantageous to Sweden. Both sides wished to end the fighting, Poland from exhaustion and Gustavus to enable him to enter the war in Germany. The treaty brought peace between Poland and Sweden until 1634 and Sweden's position was confirmed. Poland surrendered all of Livonia north of the Dvina river, and Sweden was permitted to use all the Prussian ports excepting Danzig, Königsberg and Puck. The lower Vistula ports, including Marienburg and Sztum, were left temporarily in the hands of the Elector of Brandenburg. Success in the Polish war had won for Sweden a considerable Baltic 'empire', and had confirmed the reputation and abilities of her King.

Into the Thirty Years War

Gustavus' next campaign was his entry into a war which had already been waged for twelve years. It is not correct to regard the Thirty Years War as primarily a religious struggle. Although (initially at least) the war which ravaged central Europe was overtly a struggle between the Protestant Evangelical Union and the Holy Catholic League, political and dynastic motivations were of great significance. The war was not waged simply between nation-states or dynasties; the presence of mercenary armies, sometimes with only tenuous loyalty towards their employers,

Close helmet of the style worn by cuirassiers; the vizor is shown in open position.

31

was responsible for many of the appalling atrocities and massacres which characterised this most savage of European wars. The whole temper of the conflict was exacerbated by the belief of the righteousness of religious causes on the one hand, and total self-interest on the other.

Origins of the War

The conflict began in Bohemia in 1618, though its causes were rooted in the previous decade. Allegiances changed with circumstance, but the central conflict was between the Catholic League – at the head of which was the Holy Roman Emperor (Ferdinand II from 1619), with the power of the Hapsburg empire and alliances behind him – and the loose confederation of Protestant German princes who supported Frederick, Elector Palatine, appointed by the Bohemian Protestant party in 1619. Frederick was defeated at the hands of the army of the Catholic League commanded by the Catholic Prince Maximilian of Bavaria and the League's General Tilly at the Battle of the White Mountain, near Prague in 1620. The Protestants then rallied behind Frederick.

In 1624, France entered the war, but although a Catholic country, she supported the Protestant side, being already involved in a war with Hapsburg Spain. France withdrew two years later, though Cardinal Richelieu as controller of France's foreign policy continued to involve himself in the progress of hostilities. In 1625, King Christian IV of Denmark invaded Germany with the intention of rallying waning Protestant support. He was defeated in the following year at the Battle of Lutter, at which the Protestant (or at least anti–Hapsburg) fortunes were perhaps at their lowest ebb. The Danes were driven back in 1627, and defeated again by Wallenstein, the Imperial general; and in June 1629 Denmark withdrew from the war.

Wallenstein

Many Protestant princes, alarmed at the reverses in their fortunes and with the great Protestant mercenary general Mansfeld dead, made peace with the Empire, which now appeared on the verge of complete success.

Wallenstein was already vastly wealthy, owning virtually all of northeast Bohemia, and was a prince of the Empire from 1625. He had offered to raise and equip, at his own expense, a huge mercenary army of 24,000 men for the service of the Emperor. Ferdinand, with no other method of creating so large a force, had accepted the offer. Wallenstein was largely responsible for the defeat of the Danes and the success of the Imperial cause. By 1629, his army approached 70,000 in strength and its officers were commissioned not in the Emperor's name but in Wallenstein's own. Clearly, he was intent on carving from the chaotic debris of the war, a kingdom for himself in northern Germany, based on the Emperor's grant to him of the Duchies of Mecklenburg and Pomerania in 1628. Such was Wallenstein's position of strength that even the

Horseman's sword, with S-shaped quillons and shell guard; more sharply pointed than the usual 'stiff tuck', a typically robust and functional weapon shown below.

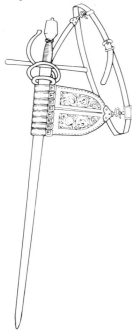

Waist belt and sword suspension of brocaded fabric and of finer quality than the plain leather belts normally used.

princes who most closely supported the Emperor were alarmed at the ambition and power of the ruthless mercenary general. They attempted to have him removed from command, but without success. From February to July 1628, Wallenstein laid siege to Stralsund in an attempt to gain control of the Baltic coast, a policy more in line with his own ambitions than those of his master; but he withdrew in the face of determined opposition and of Swedish threats.

Albrecht Eusebius Wenzel von Waldstein (1583–1634) – commonly called Wallenstein – Gustavus' most distinguished opponent.

Gustavus Intervenes

This was the situation in a Germany ravaged by war, famine and accompanying disease, into which Gustavus Adolphus intervened in 1630. His motives for entering the Thirty Years War were varied and he was encouraged by Richelieu, who was alarmed at the extent of Imperial success and had thus been instrumental in arranging the peace of Altmark to free Swedish resources.

Gustavus' correspondence with Oxenstierna shows that a major concern was his fear that the Emperor might gain control of the Baltic ports and build a fleet to threaten Sweden. Oxenstierna advocated a defensive war, using the fleet only; but Gustavus was convinced that security could only come from capturing enemy territory. Merely to blockade enemy ports with the Swedish fleet was impossible due to the insufficient number of ships; better to capture the harbours and fortify the best of them. As he wrote to Oxenstierna, 'If we await our enemy in Sweden, all might be lost by a defeat . . . we must carry the war abroad. Sweden must not be doomed to behold a hostile banner on her soil'.[5] Gustavus was aware of the risks of such an offensive, for his army was smaller than either of the two which might confront him – those of Tilly and Wallenstein. Once in Germany, he would not be without assistance or resources. He believed that the vast territory and garrisons which the Imperialists had to maintain would largely neutralise their numerical superiority, the strategic reasoning of an experienced soldier and statesman. Furthermore, an additional motive for his intervention in Germany was that of religion. Gustavus had the deepest sympathy for the German Protestants, and regarded himself as their divinely-appointed deliverer. Yet he was no simple crusader; his first duty was to Sweden, and by delivering the German Lutherans and Calvinists from a 'soul-crushing tyranny', Sweden would emerge as the leader of Protestant Europe, with all the advantages attached to such a position.

On 19 May 1630, Gustavus appeared before the Estates at Stockholm to take his leave, holding in his arms his sole heir, the four-year-old Princess Christina. (Gustavus had married Maria Eleonora, sister of the Elector of Brandenburg, in 1620.) Committing the child to the care of his people, he called upon the Estates to witness, 'in the sight of the Almighty' that he was embarking on campaign 'out of no lust for war, as many will certainly devise and imagine' but in self-defence and to deliver

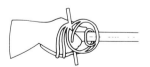

The commonest broadsword grip; the back of the blade was blunted for some distance to allow the thumb to rest along it.

33

his fellow-Protestants from oppression. On 7 June 1630, the fleet set sail with about 200 transports and 28 ships of war. On 24 June, Gustavus was the first of his army to disembark near Peenemünde and his first act on touching German soil was to kneel and give thanks to God for the safe passage. Answering some remark on this act of piety, he replied that 'A good Christian can never be a bad soldier; and the man who has finished his prayers has already got over the best part of his day's work'. When these words were circulated throughout Germany their effect cannot have been but beneficial among the Protestant states he had come to aid.

Gustavus' army was small, no more than about 13,000 strong, with an additional 6000 under his Scottish general Leslie in Stralsund. Alexander Leslie, later 1st Earl of Leven, was another of Gustavus' subordinates to use his Swedish training during the English Civil War. The gallant defender of Stralsund against Wallenstein, Leslie was knighted by Gustavus and later commanded the Scottish army in England, being joint leader of the Parliamentary forces at Marston Moor.

Despite the smallness of Gustavus' army, however, its quality was unmatched by any other in Europe, save perhaps the Dutch. Gustavus' reforms and his own genius had produced perhaps the first great 'modern' army, though the skills of its commander were perhaps the most vital factor. The immediate apprehension of the Imperial party, however, was not great; Gustavus was jestingly called a 'king of snow, held together by the frost of the north, who would soon melt under the influence of the southern sun'. In reality they were soon to realise that Gustavus' sobriquet 'The Lion of the North' was no joke.

Shortly after Gustavus landed in Germany, the Emperor Ferdinand was at last compelled to yield to pressure and dismiss Wallenstein, whose personal ambitions had reached an insupportable level. Wallenstein vowed revenge and began to negotiate with the Swedes for a joint attack on the Emperor and on the princes of Germany who had pressured for his dismissal. When the Emperor received news of these discussions, he hurriedly reappointed Wallenstein, on terms dictated by the ambitious general.

In the meantime, Gustavus' opponent would be the Emperor's other great commander, the loyal Johann Tserclaes, Graf von Tilly (1559–1632). Tilly, a Flemish-born mercenary, was employed by Maximilian of Bavaria to command the army of the Catholic League, and somewhat reluctantly assumed command of the Imperial army upon Wallenstein's temporary dismissal. A tough old soldier and an honest and moral man, he stood above most of his dubious contemporaries both by reason of his military skill and his loyalty to the cause which paid him. Yet his age of 71 in 1630 led some to doubt his capability for so large a command as Wallenstein's army as well as his own.

Gustavus' plan was to anchor his flanks with Stralsund in the west and Prussia in the east, and penetrate into Germany along the river lines. Stettin, the capital of Pomerania, was occupied and transformed into a major strongpoint, the key to the line of the river Oder; then Pomerania was cleared of Imperial troops. Gustavus retired to Stettin for the winter and to prepare for the campaign of 1631. The focus of the campaign was to be the city of Magdeburg, the strongest fortress in lower Saxony, which declared in Gustavus' favour. Wallenstein had planned its capture, but as he was no longer in command, the siege was undertaken by Tilly and his subordinate, Gottfried, Graf zu Pappenheim (1594–1632), best known as a cavalry commander. Born a German Lutheran, Pappenheim became a Catholic and engaged as a mercenary with the Catholic League, where he achieved a feared reputation as a difficult subordinate and a ruthless pillager. The Magdeburg garrison was strong and well-provisioned, and from the commencement of the siege in November 1630 the besiegers suffered more than the besieged, finding great difficulty in scraping provisions from the denuded countryside.

In the early part of 1631, two significant diplomatic events occurred. Firstly, in January, Gustavus concluded the Treaty of Bärwalde with France, which guaranteed financial support for the Swedish war effort, whilst Gustavus guaranteed freedom of worship for Roman Catholics in Germany and agreed to make no separate peace for five years. Secondly, in March the Protestant princes protested to the Emperor in the Leipzig Manifesto of the depredations of the Imperial and Catholic League armies and other discriminations against them. Doubtless the presence of Gustavus' army was a major encouragement to this protest, which the Emperor, not surprisingly, ignored. Nevertheless, the princes, led by John George of Saxony, were too timid to render military assistance to the Swedes at this stage, despite the fact that with reinforcements, Gustavus' army swelled to more than twice the strength of the original landing-force.

Frankfurt

In an attempt to divert Tilly's attention from Madgeburg, Gustavus marched on Frankfurt-am-Oder, where he arrived in early April 1631, after a brilliant surprise march. The Imperialist garrison in the town began to taunt the Swedes: 'What, you bacon-eaters! Have you eaten up all your leather guns for hunger?'. They derisorily hung a goose over the walls, alluding to their name for Gustavus as 'a wild goose lately come over the sea'.

These taunts soon rebounded on the garrison. After sermons and dinner on Palm Sunday, Gustavus launched an attack on the city. Led by the Scots, his forces stormed over the wall and either killed or captured the entire garrison. As many as 3000 Imperialists were slain, for the loss of some 800 Swedes (including about 300 Scots). Among the prisoners taken, and sent to Stettin as captives, was a Colonel Sparr. He was a Swede in Imperial service who was said to have been dragged

Wheel-lock pistol in holster, with powder flask and bullet bag attached and (left) the spanner used to cock the mechanism.

35

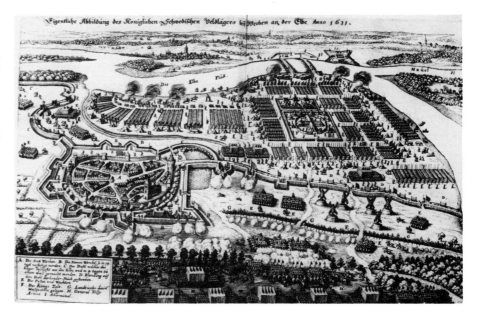

Engraving showing Tilly's troops bombarding the Swedish army at Werlben. Gustavus' camp is protected by the River Elbe, which is crossed by only two pontoon bridges. Elsewhere, the town's fortifications form a compact of an extended earthen rampart, which had been erected in just two weeks.

from his horse by his hair by none other than Gustavus himself. The capture of Frankfurt, however, did not relieve the pressure on Magdeburg.

Gustavus' conduct after the fall of Frankfurt – he ensured that none of the citizens were harmed, and ordered a day of thanksgiving – contrasted markedly with that of the Imperialists who stormed Magdeburg on 20 May 1631. The city was sacked by Pappenheim's troops, who ran amok once resistance had ended. Tilly was unable to stop the carnage, and only about 5000 of Magdeburg's 30,000 inhabitants survived. Tilly had intended to use the city as a base, but following the appalling scenes of rapine and massacre, fire broke out and raged unchecked until almost the entire city was consumed. It was the worst atrocity of a war characterised by violence and horror, and served no purpose except to throw Protestant Germany into panic and deprive Tilly of a base.

The Duke of Saxony still hesitated to ally with Gustavus, but the Swedish king compelled the conclusion of another alliance, with his brother-in-law the Duke of Brandenburg. The Duke was hardly a willing party, but incensed at lack of Protestant solidarity and co-operation, Gustavus declared that he would make the Duke a prisoner and capture Berlin unless an alliance were concluded. Even with the financial and material support of Brandenburg, Gustavus did not feel he had sufficient forces to meet Tilly in the open field, so formed an entrenched camp at Werben, at the confluence of the Havel and Elbe. Tilly made two attacks but was repulsed with heavy loss; and then marched into Saxony, laying it waste. At last, to save his state from the ravaging of the Imperial army, John George placed his army under the orders of Gustavus Adolphus. On 15 September, Tilly occupied Leipzig, his army numbering between 36,000 and 40,000 men. Opposed to them, Gustavus had some 26,000 Swedes and 16,000 Saxons, united at Düben, some 25 miles to the north.

Victory at Breitenfeld

Tilly took up a position at Breitenfeld, some four miles north of Leipzig, where he probably intended to wait for reinforcements. However, against his better judgement he yielded to Pappenheim's desire for a battle, perhaps under taunts that he was too old or timorous to meet Gustavus in a pitched battle, and probably influenced by a deliberately-falsified reconnaissance report from Pappenheim. The position Tilly took up at Breitenfeld was ideal for the use of the old-fashioned *tercios*: a flat plain with no major timber, the bulk of his artillery on raised ground in advance of his main line, with a small and marshy stream between the line and the direction of Gustavus' advance. The Imperial infantry was arrayed in a line of seventeen great *tercios*, tightly-packed squares of up to 1500 or 2000 men each, with cavalry on the flanks under Pappenheim on the left and General Fürstenburg on the right.

Line of Battle
Early on 17 September – 'as the Larke begunne to peepe' according to

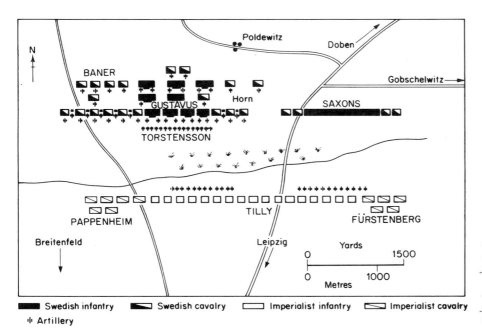

Battle of Breitenfeld, 17 September 1631. The Swedish infantry were arrayed in T-shaped units, with small squares of infantry at their front, between the cavalry regiments.

37

Colonel Monro of the Scots Brigade – Gustavus ordered the drums to beat and the army to get in motion. He had spent most of the night in conference with his main subordinates, and after prayers the army formed up and marched towards Tilly's camp-fires; the terrain was so clear of obstruction that the army marched in full array. Apparently, Tilly made little attempt to prevent the Swedish–Saxon army crossing the Loder stream, in advance of the Imperial line, though Pappenheim may have indulged in some desultory skirmishing. Gustavus assembled his forces in line, infantry in the middle in the mutually-supporting 'brigade' formations, including the Scots, with cavalry on the flanks. The right was commanded by General Johan Banér (1596–1641), the best of Gustavus' generals, and the left by General Horn. On the extreme left of the line were the Saxons.

Following usual practice, parties of musketeers were interspersed between Gustavus' cavalry regiments, and the regimental guns were distributed along the entire line; Gustavus had about 54 guns to Tilly's 26. In an age before recognisable national uniforms had evolved, armies distinguished themselves by the use of 'field signs', a temporary way of recognising friend from foe. On this occasion, the Imperialists wore white ribbons or white paper in their hats, and Gustavus' army wore green foliage. Their 'field-word', or password, was *Godt mit uns*; the Imperialists used *Sancta Maria*. According to Monro, Gustavus had 'instructed the Officers how to behave themselves in discharging their duties' and 'of the forme he was to fight unto'. Thus, everyone in the Swedish army knew exactly what was required of them.

Heat of Battle

When the Swedes had advanced within range, a great cannonading began, the Imperialist artillery being answered by the Swedish, whose numbers and excellence of training out-shot Tilly's gunners. After some two-and-a-half hours, Pappenheim could stand the galling fire no longer and, without orders, launched his 5000 horsemen at the Swedish right wing. Tilly was furious: 'They have robbed me of my honour and glory!'; but the parties of musketeers between the Swedish cavalry poured salvo after salvo into the ranks of the cuirassiers, attempting to perform the old *caracole*. Seven times Pappenheim charged, and seven times the musketeers threw him back; and on the last occasion Banér counter-attacked with his reserve and drove Pappenheim from the field.

On the opposite flank, the result was different. Thinking that Pappenheim's charge was the signal for a general advance, Fürstenburg on the Imperial right charged the Saxons on the Swedish left. The Saxons broke and fled with John George leading the rout. With the Saxons in full retreat – save those who paused to plunder the Swedish baggage – Tilly realised that he had the initiative. He ordered his army to advance obliquely to the right and then wheel to the left, falling upon Gustavus' disordered left; simultaneously Fürstenburg was ordered to attack the Swedish rear.

Against any other army, Tilly would probably have swept his opponents from the field; but the excellence of the Swedish training and the small, compact size of their units enabled them to move twice as fast as anyone else. Though the Swedish left was completely exposed, and now greatly outnumbered after the flight of the Saxons, Gustavus ordered general Horn to wheel his wing to the left to meet the incoming Imperial advance. Simultaneously, he brought the brigades of Hepburn and Vitzthum from the second line in the centre to reinforce the first. The Scots moved into the front line accompanied by their light regimental artillery. They poured roundshot and musketry into the Imperial ranks and charged 'unto them with push of pike, putting one of their battailes [*tercios*] in disorder, fell on the execution, so that they were put to the route'.[6] The Scots charged on, overrunning the Imperial artillery, but gunsmoke and the dust raised by the charge was so great that everything was blotted from view. Monro caused his drummers to sound the *Scots March*, the distinctive beat of the Scottish brigades, to rally his men and wait for the smoke and dust to clear.

The Great Captain

Whilst this action was in progress, Gustavus took the opportunity to strike the decisive blow. Riding to his right, he ordered Banér to send the West Gothland Horse down the Swedish front and charged Tilly's left flank. Placing himself at the head of four regiments, Gustavus made for the slope where the bulk of Tilly's artillery stood. He overran them and turned them upon their own army, while Tortensson brought forward the Swedish artillery reserve to pound the immobile *tercios*. The Imperialists stood bravely, and the fight was desperate; but assailed by infantry, artillery and cavalry, the whole mass broke and fled, pursued by the Swedish cavalry.

Tilly's army was destroyed; 7000 were dead, 6000 wounded and captured, and all the artillery and baggage lost. The Swedish pursuit lasted until 21 September, chasing the Imperial fugitives; 3000 more were captured on 19 September. Gustavus' loss, including the Saxons, did not exceed 3000 men, the greater part of whom fell to the opening artillery barrage. Of Tilly's army, only four regiments of experienced Walloon infantry, Belgian veterans, resisted to the end, making a final stand amid some timber at the rear of the Imperial position. Eventually, about 600 got away in good order, the wounded Tilly with them.

Breitenfeld was a battle of supreme importance. Politically, it prevented for ever the Imperial steamroller which threatened to turn all Germany into a Catholic province of the Empire; and it established Gustavus as the redeemer of the Protestant cause in the eyes of north Germany. Militarily, it was equally of paramount importance, and might be regarded as the first great land battle of the modern era, in which firepower and, above all, mobility emerged triumphant over numbers and the military systems of the previous age. Breitenfeld alone establishes Gustavus Adolphus as one of history's 'great captains', for it was the product not only of his tactical skill, which was considerable, but of the organisation and military theories which he had devised.

Consolidating the Victory

Gustavus has been criticised for not exploiting his victory by marching immediately upon Vienna to dictate peace terms to the Emperor, as advised by Oxenstierna. Had he done so, it has been asserted, the Thirty Years War would have been a Fifteen Years War instead. Probably, however, Gustavus took the correct course, for possession of Vienna was not of paramount importance to the immense Imperial territory. Furthermore, the route towards Vienna was fraught with danger, as Gustavus' supply-lines would be stretched and his base was not secure. The road would have passed through devastated Bohemia, winter was coming and hostile Bavaria would have been on his flank; and his allies of Brandenburg and Saxony in his rear were not above suspicion. By moving to the Rhine, the course of action upon which Gustavus decided, he was based in the Protestant Palatinate and able to supply his army from fertile territory – 'the Priests' Lane' as the Catholic areas of Würzburg, Cologne, Mainz, Worms, Bamberg and Spires were known – whose resources would thus be denied the Imperialists. By occupying the Palatinate, Gustavus saw that he could sever the Imperial link between their possessions of Italy and the Netherlands. Lastly, he intended to ensure that Tilly was not allowed to manoeuvre

Pamphlet of 1631 in which Gustavus' army is depicted as the Swedish lion chasing Jesuits and Catholic clergy from the prosperous area known as Pfannegrasse ('Priests' Lane') along the rivers Main and Rhine.

unhindered in his rear. Thus, he advanced to the Rhine, while the Saxons moved into Bohemia.

Gustavus occupied Würzburg on 16 October, pushed on to Frankfurt-am-Main and then to Mainz, which surrendered after a two-day siege on 22 December, and where he remained throughout the winter of 1631–32. Within three months of his victory at Breitenfeld, Gustavus had subdued the Rhineland and forced neutrality upon its Catholic princes. He was firmly established on both banks of the middle Rhine, rather to the alarm of Richelieu, who feared Gustavus' favouring of a Protestant federation under his leadership, which must threaten France as much as the Empire:

Means must be devised to check this imperious Visigoth, since his successes will be fatal to France as to the Empire.

(Cardinal Richelieu)

Lützen and Death

In order to bring about peace, the 'imperious Visigoth' decided in spring 1632 to take the field again, the signal for him to move being Tilly's sudden advance from behind the Danube.

Tilly had formed a new army since Breitenfeld, not as veteran as before, but again based on the forces of the Catholic League; for the Imperial army once more had Wallenstein at its head. Having realised his error in dismissing Wallenstein, the Emperor had recalled him in desperation, but at a terrible price: Wallenstein insisted upon being given unconditional control of the army and all confiscated territory,

41

and for the Emperor to issue no orders without Wallenstein's consent. Utterly devoid of morals and loyalty, Wallenstein had won for himself supreme power within the Empire.

Death of Tilly

Gustavus pursued Tilly into Bavaria, where he drew up his camp behind the River Lech, having stripped the country of every boat and all means of bridging the fast-flowing river. Gustavus crossed the Danube at Donauwörth and came up to the Lech, behind which Tilly thought himself secure. But Gustavus threw a thin bridge of boats across the river, his crossing covered by artillery fire, deceiving Tilly's army with clouds of powder-smoke and the burning of damp straw, so that the preparations of the Swedish army were concealed. Under cover of Torstensson's artillery barrage, Gustavus stormed across the river on 16 April and scattered Tilly's army, Tilly himself being severely wounded by a shot in the knee.

Gustavus sent a renowned surgeon (at Tilly's request) to treat his injured adversary, but the wound proved fatal and Tilly died at Ingolstadt a fortnight later. The death of this honourable man, who had outlived the age and tactics in which he had been trained, was lamented by all, except in Wallenstein's army, which expressed 'more joy than sorrow'. Gustavus himself is said to have remarked 'Honourable old Tilly! whose acts were so heroic in his lifetime, that after his death they are his everlasting monuments [which would make] his memory eternal'.[7]

The forces of the catholic League were now commanded by Maximilian of Bavaria, who extricated what he could (less baggage and most of his artillery, lost at the Lech) and moved to join Wallenstein, with whom he united at Schwabach. Gustavus occupied Augsburg, Munich, and all of southern Bavaria.

Wallenstein first chased the Saxons out of Prague, and then manoeuvred them out of Bohemia. Then, using the diplomatic powers he had wrung from the Emperor, Wallenstein attempted to separate John George of Saxony from Gustavus' camp by offering peace. To prevent wavering in the Protestant party, Gustavus marched towards Nuremburg en route for Saxony. However, finding that Wallenstein and Maximilian had united, and after a clash at Neumark, Gustavus abandoned his attempt to reach Saxony. Both armies confronted each other at Nuremburg, a city which gave Gustavus a strong base.

Wallenstein followed and entrenched an enormous camp, twelve miles in circumference, on the western bank of the River Regnitz, aiming to pin Gustavus to Nuremburg and then cut off the Swedish retreat northwards. The Imperial forces numbered some 60,000, against whom Gustavus originally had 20,000, increased to 45,000 by the arrival of reinforcements.

42

For two weeks the armies faced each other, generally immobile. Then, with supplies beginning to run low, Gustavus attempted to assault Wallenstein's camp at Alte Veste (31 August–4 September). The terrain around the camp was broken and thus unsuitable for the full deployment of the Swedish artillery and cavalry. After renewed attempts involving heavy fighting, Gustavus decided to abandon the action, having lost one of his most valued lieutenants, Torstensson, captured by the Imperialists as he fought 'within a paternoster' of the King.

Gustavus decided to march towards Vienna to draw Wallenstein away from Saxony, but the scheming Imperialist refused to be drawn, sending Maximilian to protect Bavaria and calling up Pappenheim with the intention of concentrating his forces against Saxony. Gustavus marched to support his ally, returning to Nuremburg, shortly to be joined by Prince Bernhard of Saxe-Weimar. Gustavus urged John George of Saxony to complete the concentration of the Protestant forces.

Costume worn by Gustavus Adolphus, including a buff-coat with laced front opening, plain doublet and breeches.

Wallenstein presumed that Gustavus was to go into winter quarters until the spring, so himself prepared his own camp around Lützen, sending Pappenheim away to prevent overcrowding. Though Wallenstein had thus far outmanoeuvred the Swedes, the division of his army in such circumstances was dangerous, and prompted Gustavus to attack, despite his own numerical inferiority.

At one o'clock in the morning of 15 November 1632, Gustavus set out for Pegau to unite with the Saxons. After a four-hour halt in which the Saxons had not appeared, Gustavus marched on Lützen in the hope that he would surprise Wallenstein while his army was still divided, but the road was so wretched that it delayed his march. At Rippach, Gustavus ran into a body of Croats and routed them after a sharp fight, and encamped that night in the open fields.

He held a council of war during the night; Gustavus' general Kniphausen was for manoeuvre, Bernhard of Saxe-Weimar for attack. But Gustavus was not to be swayed by advice. His mind was made up:

he said that 'the die was now cast and that he could not bear to have Wallenstein under his beard and not make a swoop upon him' because 'I long to unearth him, and see how he can acquit himself in a campaign country'[8]. He would attack on the morrow.

Wallenstein himself was anxious to avoid a battle at that moment, so spent the night 'in digging and intrenching, in embattling his army, and planting his artillery'. Learning of Gustavus' proximity, at two o'clock in the morning of 16 November he sent an urgent despatch after Pappenheim to say that the Swedes were advancing: 'Sir, let everything else be, and hurry with all your forces and artillery back to me. You must be here by tomorrow morning . . .'[9]

The frantic letter still exists, soaked in Pappenheim's blood. It does not tell the whole story of Wallenstein's discomfiture, for he was afflicted by a severe attack of gout which necessitated his commanding the army from a sedan chair.

Gustavus Adolphus' buff-coat as worn at the Battle of Lützen.

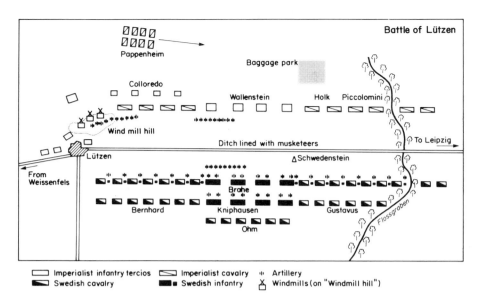

Pappenheim

Baggage park

Colloredo

Wallenstein   Holk   Piccolomini

Wind mill hill

Ditch lined with musketeers

To Leipzig

Lützen   △Schwedenstein

From
Weissenfels

Brahe

Bernhard   Kniphausen   Gustavus

Flossgraben

Ohm

☐ Imperialist infantry tercios	◁ Imperialist cavalry	◦Ⅰ Artillery
◀ Swedish cavalry	■◦ Swedish infantry	✕ Windmills (on "Windmill hill")

Battle of Lützen, 16 November 1632, showing the Flossgraben stream, lined with trees on both banks and the sunken Lützen – Leipzig road, described as the "ditch lined with musketeers".

Wallenstein marshalled his army a little north of the Lützen–Leipzig road, the right wing anchored on a low hill on which were some windmills, near to Lützen itself, which was slightly to the right of Wallenstein's army. Intending to fight a defensive battle, Wallenstein drew up most of his infantry in four enormous *tercios* under his own command, pikes in the centre and muskets at the angles, in the middle of his line; a fifth *tercio* was on the right and to the rear. On either side of the central *tercios* was arrayed the cavalry, commanded by Piccolomini on the left and Colloredo on the right. On his own side of the causewayed Leipzig road, he turned the ditches into trenches, which he lined with musketeers. His 60-odd cannon he arrayed in two batteries, one on his immediate front and one on his right centre, around the windmills. His exact strength is uncertain, but ranged between 20,000 and 25,000 men.

Gustavus moved forward 'by the peep of day', about eight o'clock in the morning of 16 November 1632. His object was to cut off Wallenstein from Leipzig, not only to sever him from his base but to open the road for John George and his Saxons, whom Gustavus expected hourly. Gustavus arrayed his infantry in two lines, each of four brigades, with a cavalry reserve at the rear. On each wing were assembled two lines of cavalry, with parties of musketeers between the regiments, as at Breitenfeld. His central battery of 26 heavy guns he positioned in advance of the infantry; the 40 'regimental guns' he allocated to the flanks, to accompany the mixture of cavalry and musketeers. Gustavus himself commanded the right of the army, Bernhard the left. The total was about 18,000.

A religious service was held in the Swedish ranks and Luther's hymn *A Mighty Fortress is Our God* was sung. A heavy mist descended, which caused the opening of the battle to be postponed until about ten o'clock in the morning.

Tragedy in the Mist

As the mist began to drift away, the artillery on both sides began to fire; but as Gustavus made his offensive movement, the mist descended again,'that we could not see one another' as one participant wrote. This mist has caused accounts of the battle to be confused and conflicting. Nevertheless, it is certain that Gustavus himself led forward his right wing, charging over the entrenched roadway and scattering the musketeers, then progressing on to rout a body of Croatian light cavalry and push back Piccolomini's heavy cavalry; seven Imperial guns were also captured, but were later recovered. Gustavus himself was wounded in charging the ditches by a shot through the arm, but pressed on with the attack. Lützen was set alight, and the smoke blew into the faces of Bernhard's wing of the Swedish army, making the visibility even worse; but Bernhard led his troops forward, and temporarily enjoyed some success before retiring again.

Gustavus' attack had been mounted in the brief period of brightness; but with the return of the mist, it is not clear exactly what occurred. It appears that Gustavus heard that his centre was retiring, so placed himself at the head of a regiment of cavalry and rode to its relief. He became separated from his men in the fog, so was accompanied only by

Gustavus Adolphus' original plan, in his own hand, for positioning of his forces at Lützen differs slightly from that which he finally adopted.

45

his cousin, the Duke of Lauenburg, his page Leubelfing, and his personal servant, Anders Jönsson. Suddenly, the small party rode into a body of Imperial cuirassiers. Gustavus was shot in the back, and again through the head, the latter perhaps when he had already fallen from his horse. Lauenburg fled, Jönsson was killed and Leubelfing wounded. The Swedish army only discovered that their king was dead when his horse, spattered with blood, trotted back to the Swedish lines.

Undoubtedly Gustavus had repeatedly risked his life needlessly in battle, but by so doing had been the cause of inspiration to his men; and now his fall served as exactly the same spur, at the moment it was needed, for about this time Pappenheim arrived with his cavalry, increasing Wallenstein's army by a further 8000 men. Now, with their fortunes apparently at their lowest ebb, as Pappenheim attacked the right wing and recovered all the lost ground to the road, the news of Gustavus' death filled the Swedish army with fanatical fury.

Pappenheim was struck by a cannonball and was removed from the battlefield in a cart; learning of the death of his great opponent shortly before he himself died. Leaderless, his cavalry retired as the Swedes, now commanded by Bernhard of Saxe-Weimar, counter-attacked and finally carried windmill hill and the battery beside it.

Wallenstein's army was not routed, but the Imperial commander decided to retire and extricate what he could from the mist-shrouded carnage. There was no pursuit; the Swedes were too exhausted to follow. Confused and severe as the cavalry fighting had been, it was the resilient Swedish infantry which probably won the day; as a British member of the army wrote: 'had not our foote stoode like a Wall, there had not a man of us come of[f] alyve'.[10]

It is difficult to assess casualties for the Battle of Lützen; Wallenstein probably suffered 12,000, and the Swedes 10,000. Tactically, the battle was indecisive; strategically, it was of the greatest importance in checking Imperialist intentions. But of greater consequence was the loss to the Protestant cause of their leader. Gustavus' body was recovered from the mud in which it lay, his spurs being removed as mementos by his Scottish A.D.C., Colonel Hugh Somerville.

Legacy of Command

The Thirty Years War dragged on until 1648, exhausting central Europe. Wallenstein lived only until 1634, when following renewed treachery aimed at further personal gain, he was assassinated upon the instigation of the Emperor.

Swedish fortunes declined after the death of Gustavus, a crushing defeat being suffered at Nördlingen in 1634 when Bernhard of Saxe-

Weimar was routed by an Imperial-Spanish army commanded by King Ferdinand of Hungary (the Emperor's son) and the Cardinal-Infante Ferdinand of Spain. Politically, this compelled the Catholic Cardinal Richelieu to assume direction of the Protestant cause. Gustavus was succeeded by his little daughter Christina, but due to her age the actual direction of the war devolved upon the capable Oxenstierna. His abilities, combined with those of Banér, enabled Sweden to get what she did from the Peace of Westphalia in 1648, which ended the Thirty Years' War, comparatively meagre though these territorial gains were. Nevertheless, for the next two generations Sweden was regarded as the leading state of Protestant Europe, a rôle which ultimately she had insufficient resources to sustain.

Jan Asselyn's painting of Gustavus Adolphus at the Battle of Lützen, 16 November 1632.

Like Alexander, Gustavus Adolphus died before his work was accomplished, though his impact upon Europe and European warfare was profound. His victories not only enfeebled the Emperor to a degree that no subsequent successes could restore his power fully, but also ensured the survival of the independent Protestant states of northern Europe.

47

Said to be the most realistic portrait of Gustavus Adolphus, this etching has often been (wrongly) attributed to Lorenz Straucher.

Militarily, his influence was vast; arguably the first great modern commander, his offensive techniques and infantry formations were still being copied some seventy years after his death, by so great a general as the Duke of Marlborough. If Gustavus' tactical innovations were themselves copied in part from the Dutch and Poles, and his codes of discipline were no more strict than those imposed upon Huguenot armies, the use of each innovation in producing a cohesive whole was the product of his own genius. The fact that the Swedish army did not disintegrate after his death is testimony to the training he imposed and the example he set, which left sufficient capable subordinates to carry on after Lützen.

A contemporary wrote:

All his great achievements were ever attended by devotion within, and circumspection without. He first praised God, and then provided for man, at once having an eye on his enemies' next designs, and his soldiers' present necessities. The greatest of his glories, purchased with blood and sweat, could neither change the estate of his mind, or copy of his countenance. The true greatness of his spirit was such, that in all his actions he placed ostentation behind, and conscience before him, and sought not the reward of a good deed from fame, but from the deed itself . . .[11]

A fitting epitaph is provided by his subordinate Monro:

If Apelles with his skill in painting, and Cicero with his tongue in speaking, were both alive, and pressed to adde anything to the perfection of our master, captaine and king, truely the ones best colours, and the others best words, were not able to adde one shadow to the brightnesse of his royall mind and spirit; so that while the world stands, our king, captaine, and master cannot be enough praised.[12]

References

1   *The Great and Famous Battle of Lützen* (1633), in *Harleian Miscellany* 1809; see also J.F.C. Fuller *Decisive Battles of the Western World* London, 1957, II pp. 53–54.

2   Monro; see J. Mackay *An Old Scots Brigade* London & Edinburgh 1885; pp. 122–23.

3   See Mackay *op. cit.* p. 92.

4   See T.A. Dodge *Gustavus Adolphus* I p. 400.

5   Sir E. Cust *Lives of the Warriors of the Thirty Years War* 1865, I. pp. 142–43; see also Fuller *op. cit.*, II p. 56.

6   R. Monro, *Monro, his expedition* (1637); see also Fuller *op. cit.*, II p. 63.

7   Quoted in Mackay *op. cit.*, p. 174.

8   Cust *op. cit.*, p. 211.

9   Quoted in C.R.L. Fletcher *Gustavus Adolphus* London, 1892, p. 277.

10   Camden Miscellany 'Fleetwood's Letter'; see Fuller *op. cit.*, II p. 71.

11   *The Great and Famous Battle of Lützen*; see also Fuller *op. cit.*, II pp. 53–54.

12   Quoted in Mackay *op. cit.*, pp. 186–87.

Chronology of Events

Conflicting dates may be found in certain references due to the dual calendar of the earlier Julian and later Gregorian systems

1594 19 DECEMBER birth of Gustavus Adolphus, son of Duke Charles of Sweden.

1598 25 SEPTEMBER Battle of St ng bro which decided the Swedish dynastic struggle in favour of Duke Charles and the Protestant party.

1600 19 MARCH Duke Charles proclaimed King Charles IX of Sweden.

1604 6 MARCH Duke Charles formally began to use the title 'king' after renunciation of rights by rival claimant, Duke John.

1611 30 OCTOBER Charles IX died at Nyköping; succeeded as King by his son Gustavus Adolphus II.

1613 28 JANUARY Peace of Knäred which ended the 'War of Kalmar'.

1617 27 FEBRUARY Peace of Stolbova which ended the war with Russia.

1618 22 MAY Defenestration of Prague, beginning Thirty Years War (actual hostilities commenced July, though Sweden not yet involved).

1619 29 AUGUST Election of Ferdinand II as Emperor.

1620 8 NOVEMBER Defeat of the Bohemians at Battle of the White Mountain by Imperial and Catholic League; widening of Thirty Years War as a Protestant crusade.

1621 15 SEPTEMBER Swedish capture of Riga; beginning of acquisition of Baltic empire.

1629 7 JUNE Peace of Lübeck; Danish withdrawal from Thirty Years War, leaving Protestant cause without strong leadership, a vacuum to be filled by Sweden.

1629 29 JUNE Defeat of Gustavus Adolphus at Sztum, leading to Treaty of Altmark (5 October), giving Sweden freedom to intervene in Thirty Years War.

1630 19 MAY Gustavus Adolphus took leave of the Swedish Parliament prior to embarking on campaign, committing his heir, Princess Christina, into their care.

1630 24 JUNE Swedes landed in Pomerania.

1631 13 JANUARY Treaty of Bärwalde between Sweden and France.

1631 13 APRIL Gustavus Adolphus captured Frankfurt.

1631 20 MAY Tilly captured Magdeburg.

1631 17 SEPTEMBER Tilly defeated by Gustavus Adolphus at Breitenfeld.

1631 22 DECEMBER Gustavus Adolphus occupied Frankfurt-on-Main.

1632 4–16 APRIL Actions along River Lech, ending in Swedish crossing and defeat of Tilly, who was mortally wounded.

1632 31 AUGUST–4 SEPTEMBER Gustavus Adolphus vainly tried to defeat Wallenstein at Alte Veste.

1632 16 NOVEMBER Wallenstein defeated by Gustavus Adolphus at Lützen, but Gustavus killed.

Marlborough

THE GREAT COMMANDER

Portrait of John Churchill as the First Duke of Marlborough (G. Kneller).

Embroidered cloth holster-cap design of Marlborough's time.

France, Flanders and the Lower Rhineland at the time of Marlborough.

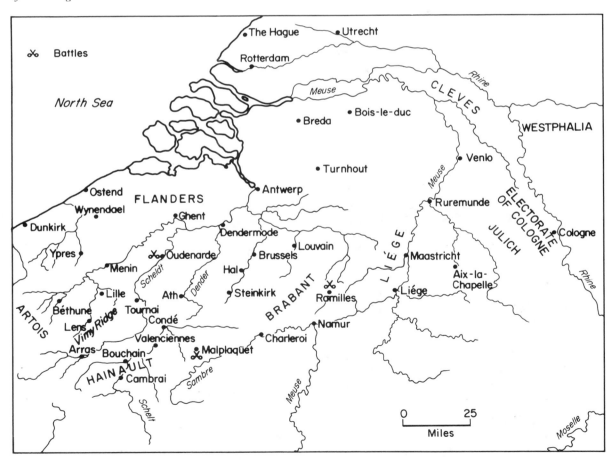

North Sea

⚔ Battles

The Hague
Utrecht
Rotterdam
Meuse
CLEVES
Rhine
WESTPHALIA
Breda
Bois-le-duc
Venlo
Turnhout
Ostend
FLANDERS
Antwerp
Ruremunde
Wynendael
Ghent
Meuse
ELECTORATE OF COLOGNE
Cologne
Dunkirk
Dendermode
JULICH
Rhine
Ypres
Oudenarde
Louvain
Brussels
LIÉGE
Maastricht
Menin
Scheldt
Hal
Aix-la-Chapelle
Lille
Dender
Ath
Steinkirk
BRABANT
Ramilles
Liége
Béthune
Tournai
Condé
Namur
Lens
Vimy Ridge
Valenciennes
Charleroi
Meuse
Arras
Bouchain
Malplaquet
HAINAULT
Sambre
Cambrai
Schelt
Moselle

0   25
Miles

The Greatest General

In his monumental history, the Hon. Sir John Fortescue quotes a letter concerning the great victory at Blenheim and notes that 'the message and the handwriting [were] both those of a man who is quite tired out':

I have not time to say more, but beg you will give my duty to the queen, and let her know her army has had a glorious victory, Monsr. Tallard and two other generals are in my coach and I am following the rest. The bearer, my aide-de-camp, Colonel Parke, will give her an account of what has pass'd. I shall doe it in a day or two by another more at large.

Marlborough[1]

Never in history has a victory of momentous proportion been reported officially in such terms; in a note on the back of a tavern bill, sent not to the sovereign of the victorious general, but to the general's wife.

That the letter was written by a 54-year-old general who had never before enjoyed a major independent command, or fought a battle in which he was general-in-chief, is even more remarkable. Of equal significance is the fact that he was arguably the greatest general of all time, of whom it was truly said that he never fought a battle which he did not win, or besiege a fortress which he did not capture.

Young Churchill

John Churchill was born at Asche House, Devonshire, on or about 5 June 1650. His background was neither overtly military nor aristocratic, but that known as 'country gentry'. His immediate forebears had been in the legal profession. However, during the English Civil War, his father, Winston Churchill, had fought for the King at Lansdown and Roundway Down as a Captain of Horse (cavalry). Thus, it is conceivable that young John first aspired to a military career as a result of his father's services. Unfortunately, they were services which cost the family dear in the interregnum when ex-Cavaliers were fined and otherwise discriminated against. John's mother, née Elizabeth Drake, came from the family which had produced the Elizabethan hero Sir Francis Drake.

The restoration of the monarchy brought a restoration of the family fortunes, including a knighthood for Winston, and an entry into the circles of Charles II's court.

Little information survives concerning John Churchill's earliest years, but the family connections with the royal court proved crucial. John's elder sister Arabella (1649–1730) became maid-of-honour to the Duchess of York, and mistress to the Duke (later King James II), to whom she bore several children, most notably James Fitz-James. It is one of those ironic twists of history that James became later Duke of Berwick, and a Marshal of France of great renown – and ultimately an opponent of his uncle, John Churchill!

A Misspent Youth?

John is believed to have shown an early interest in military affairs by his study of Vegetius' *De Re Militari*, but began his 'public' career as a courtier, being appointed page to the Duke of York at the age of 16, a position secured for him by Arabella. From the first, Churchill possessed the attributes of a good courtier: handsome (even in late middle age he was universally admired for his good looks, perfect complexion and trim figure), well-mannered and with great charm. From the Duke of York he received his first military commission, in the Foot Guards in 1667. At the age of 18 he experienced his first active service, with the garrison at Tangier, where he probably engaged in skirmishes with the Moors. Nor was his service exclusively military: in 1670 it is believed he served aboard ship in operations against the pirates of Algiers.

After an absence of three years, Churchill returned to court, where the handsome 21-year-old established a reputation for conquests of a different kind: among the ladies of a royal establishment noted for its laxity of morals. Most of the criticisms of Churchill's later behaviour can be traced to this period of peculiar characteristics, born in an atmosphere of revolution and raised amid corruption. The Duke of Wellington said that he had never understood the attitudes of the people of this era, or been prepared to excuse their vices, until he saw the effects of the French Revolution upon the minds and consciences of the French marshals and statesmen. Thus, the most reprehensible of Churchill's actions may be explained by the corruption of the society in which he spent his early career.

Among Churchill's liaisons was one with Barbara Villiers, Duchess of Cleveland (his second-cousin) and mistress of Charles II. For a number of years, Churchill conducted an affair with this famous beauty, producing an illegitimate daughter and including one awkward moment when the king caught them together. Charles II was remarkably easy-going in such matters and merely observed that Churchill did it to get his bread, believing his motivation was pursuance of advancement. It may have been: in 1674 Barbara Villiers gave him £4,500 which Churchill invested in an annuity which reputedly produced an annual income of £500 for life. (Perhaps arising from his family's early misfortunes, Churchill was known throughout his life for his acquisitiveness and thrift to the point of miserliness.)

Not all his life in this period was spent in the luxury of the court; during the Third Dutch War he served aboard the Duke of York's flagship *The Prince* at the battle of Solebay (June 1672), and in the same month was promoted captain in the Duke of York's Admiralty Regiment, the promotion-fee probably being found by Barbara Villiers. Of more import was the campaign in Flanders where Churchill gained experience of fighting in a French army, which may have had great effect on his later career.

In 1672, Charles II appointed his illegitimate son James Scott, Duke of Monmouth, as commander of the English contingent allied to Louis XIV of France in his war against the Dutch William of Orange. Part of the English force sent to assist the French was a detachment of the Admiralty Regiment, commanded by Churchill. After spending the winter at court, Churchill went to Flanders and singularly distinguished himself at the siege of Maastricht in June–July 1673. He was part of a small detachment, led by Monmouth, who captured the demi-lune ('half-moon battery'), an advanced fortification, on 24 June. When, on the following day, the Dutch attempted to recapture the position, he was part of a very small band which beat back the attempt. Among Churchill's companions in the latter action was a French soldier, Claude-Hector de Villars (whom Churchill was to meet again in different circumstances) and Monmouth himself, whose life was saved by Churchill and who reported to the King: 'To the bravery of this gallant officer I owe my life'. This action brought Churchill not only public recognition and a personal commendation from the French king, but established his reputation for personal bravery and the esteem of the common soldier, which throughout his career he never lost.

Military Apprentice and Husband

Although the erratic foreign policy of the Stuarts brought peace to England in 1674, a number of English regiments continued to serve in French pay, and Churchill was appointed to a colonelcy by Louis XIV. This was probably the most important part of Churchill's military education, serving in the army of the master tactician Henri de la Tour d'Auvergne, vicomte de Turenne (1611–75). He was the greatest general of his age and was admired intensely by Churchill, whose eventual system of war proved him to be Turenne's military heir.

Churchill fought in the battles of Sinzheim (16 June 1674) and Entzheim (4 October) in the campaign in the Palatinate. The latter

The cuirass (breast-plate and back-plate), the last relic of medieval armour, was worn by most cavalry in the earlier years of the eighteenth century. The projecting-lugs on the front of the breast-plate (top) were the means of securing the shoulder-straps (attached to the back-plate) to hold the two pieces of armour together.

included an advance by night planned by Turenne, a manoeuvre typical of Churchill's operations in later years. Churchill learned much from this apprenticeship, and in return Turenne recognised the spark of genius in Churchill, whom he described as 'my handsome Englishman'.

The period from late 1674 to 1677 is cloudy; Churchill may have been present in Turenne's celebrated winter campaign of 1674–75 and at Sasbach (June 1675) where Turenne was killed, but the only certainty is that he was in Paris in August 1675, and that he was appointed Lieutenant-colonel of the Duke of York's Regiment in January that year (the expense defrayed by Barbara Villiers) and promoted colonel in late 1677.

The most important event in this period – arguably the most important of Churchill's life – was his marriage in spring 1678 to Sarah Jennings, daughter of the sometime Member of Parliament of St. Albans, and the childhood friend and confidante of the Duke of York's daughter, Princess Anne. By his marriage to Sarah Jennings, Churchill gained vast influence and vital connections with the highest circles of the court. Yet this was an incidental extra: Sarah Jennings was the love of his life, for whom he abandoned his previous lifestyle and to whom he remained totally committed for the remainder of his life; his 'dearest soul' as he described her in 1704.

Sarah Jennings was handsome, highly intelligent and extremely virtuous, but self-willed and with a fierce temper which caused tremendous rows within her own family, even with her devoted husband. Even at the height of his fame and power, Sarah remained the dominating influence in his life, and eventually her quarrelsome nature resulted in the decline of her husband's fortunes. Nevertheless, without her and despite his huge talents, John Churchill would never have risen so highly in the first place. Patronage and political influence were of paramount importance in the attainment of high office in the late seventeenth and early eighteenth centuries, and most powerful influence was wielded by Sarah Churchill as a result of her close friendship with the Princess Anne. By overcoming the difficulties of their courtship (Sarah's moods and the opposition of both families on the grounds that neither was wealthy), John Churchill not only acquired a faithful and devoted partner, but a key to success and fortune.

The possibility of a war against France caused Churchill and his friend, the rising political star Sidney Godolphin, to be sent to the Hague to negotiate a treaty with William of Orange. This, Churchill's first diplomatic mission, greatly impressed William. In addition to his own qualities, the fact that William was married to Princess Anne's sister Mary was doubtless a further aid. As a diplomatic mission, however, the trip was abortive and Churchill was ordered to Flanders with the temporary rank of 'Brigadier-General of Foot'. The Peace of Nimwegen forestalled any action, and Churchill's active military career went into abeyance.

Domestic turmoil entered the scene at this juncture, with the attempt to have the Duke of York excluded from the succession on

account of his Roman Catholic faith. The fortunes of the Churchills were closely enmeshed with those of his patron, and Churchill accompanied the Duke in his temporary exile in Brussels in 1679. After his return, the Duke was wrecked in the North Sea upon the Lincolnshire coast when the frigate *Gloucester* foundered, both the Duke and Churchill narrowly escaping with their lives.

Churchill's fortunes continued to improve through the good offices of the Duke. He was created Baron Aysmouth in December 1682 and a year later was appointed colonel of the Royal Dragoons. After the marriage of Princess Anne to George of Denmark (to whom Churchill was chosen as escort to Britain), Sarah was appointed Lady of the Bedchamber, making her tie with the Princess even stronger.

Hinchliff's engravings (after G. Kneller) of Sarah Churchill and John Churchill, Duke of Marlborough.

Sedgemoor and Betrayal

The death of Charles II, in 1685, was the cause of a complete change in Churchill's career, though initially the accession of the Duke of York as King James II resulted in a further advance of the Churchill fortunes.

Churchill is reputed to have remarked: 'If the king should attempt to change our religion and constitution [i.e. to restore Roman Catholicism], I will instantly quit his service'.[2] However, he served James well in 1685, better perhaps than that unfortunate monarch deserved. Appointed a Lord of the Bedchamber and further ennobled as Baron Churchill of Sandridge (in Herefordshire), Churchill remained a loyal servant in the dreadful events of 1685.

The Pitchfork Rebellion

Churchill's erstwhile comrade-in-arms, the Duke of Monmouth, landed on the south western coast of England at Lyme Regis in an attempt to raise the forces of Protestantism and dissatisfaction, and to wrest the crown from his uncle's head. The expedition was both ill-timed and ill-led; the country had not yet grown tired of the new king and support was very limited. News of the landing at Lyme Regis was conveyed to the king by that town's Parliamentary representative, Sir

Winston Churchill; and Sir Winston's son John was immediately appointed as Brigadier-General and ordered to take command of the royal troops mustering to resist the invasion.

Initially, Churchill's forces were insufficient to do more than shadow the rebels, which he did with speed and skill (putting to good effect his tuition under Turenne), paying great attention to the smallest details of administration, supply and transport, a characteristic attribute throughout his career. As the royal forces prepared (including the Foot Guards, commanded by the Duke of Grafton, another of Charles II's illegitimates and thus Monmouth's half-brother!), Churchill received a severe shock when James II appointed Turenne's nephew, Louis Duras (the Huguenot Earl of Feversham), to overall command. Though Churchill felt greatly aggrieved, the King's decision is understandable, given Churchill's family connections in the west country, his friendship with Monmouth and his lack of experience in independent command; and despite their religious differences, Feversham did remain loyal to James throughout.

To his credit, Churchill co-operated fully with Feversham. The rebel army, largely comprising ill-armed peasants, became disheartened and began to melt away. In an attempt to win a quick victory, Monmouth executed a march at night to attack the royal camp at Sedgemoor, four miles from Bridgwater in the county of Somerset. It was a hazardous undertaking with experienced troops and doomed to failure with his poor peasantry. The royal camp was alarmed by a vigilant sentry and Churchill, as 'General officer of the day', organised resistance. The battle had already commenced by the time Feversham had roused himself and by daylight, the rebels had been scattered by the disciplined musketry of the royal army and a cavalry charge led by Churchill. The *London Gazette* reported how Churchill had 'performed his part with all the courage and gallantry imaginable'. It was a just reflection on his part in the preservation of James II's throne, and the first exhibition of his cool head and clear thinking when entrusted, however temporarily, with an independent command. The collapse of the rebellion was followed by a ruthless purge of Monmouth's supporters, including the infamous 'Bloody Assize' of Judge Jeffreys. However, Churchill had no part in this, being sent to London as bearer of the victory despatch.

The Pragmatist

The maltreatment of suspected rebel sympathisers rankled with Churchill, as did his subordination to Feversham, and fuelled the fire of his growing disillusionment with the King. James II's increasingly cavalier behaviour and his perceived wish to reinstate Roman Catholicism finally caused his downfall. Secretly, William of Orange was invited to assume the throne. Churchill was not one of the signatories of the invitation, but was knowledgeable of the plot. In August 1688 he declared to William: 'I am resolved to die in that religion that it has pleased God to give you both the will and power to protect'.[3] Doubtless Churchill's strong Protestant faith was a major contributory factor towards his break with James, but perhaps a greater motive was self-interest, the desire to be on the winning side irrespective.

When William of Orange landed at Torbay in November 1688, Churchill was appointed Lieutenant-General of the King's forces, again subordinate to Feversham, though that general begged the King to order Churchill's arrest. James was not prepared to accept the possibility of betrayal. After a council of war on 23 November (in which Churchill vainly urged an immediate attack on William), Churchill departed from the royal army and joined William, having seen, perhaps, that the chance of James' success was now slim. He had the decency to write to the King that his actions 'proceed from nothing but the inviolable dictates of my conscience, and a necessary concern for my religion'.[4] Underlying these noble sentiments is the suspicion that it was chiefly self-interest which led Churchill to desert the benefactor to whom he owed virtually everything.

How L'art Militaire Francais pour L'infantrie *(Colombon, 1680) showed the infantryman's method of musket loading This was the disciplined type of musketry used by John Churchill's forces against Monmouth.*

The assistance of Churchill's defection to William of Orange – by then King William III – was immense. It influenced much of the army to desert with him; and even Sarah Churchill played a part, helping Princess Anne to escape from London. James II bowed to the inevitable and went into exile, the 'Glorious Revolution' having been achieved with virtually no bloodshed. Churchill's apologists have made much of his patriotism and concern for religion, which certainly influenced his actions; but the determination to finish on the winning side was the mark of a typical seventeenth century politician, ensuring his own welfare before that of his master. That his actions were ultimately beneficial to his country is only evident with hindsight.

King William's General

Churchill probably expected great favours from William III following his actions in 1688. However, his hopes were largely unrealised. In April 1689, he was created Earl of Marlborough, a title once linked to his mother's family. Although he was given the task of reorganising the English army, the prize appointments – such as that of Master-General of the Ordnance – were not given him; he remained not a rich man.

For all his talents, his urbane and courteous manner, and all the influence he had (via Sarah) over Princess Anne – who it became increasingly obvious would succeed to the throne – William III could not be persuaded to trust Churchill completely. William never attempted to court the popularity of the English, regarding everything from a Dutch viewpoint; he placed more trust in his Dutch generals and regiments than in the English. However, his reforms of the English army, to which Marlborough contributed significantly, led to the King stating that by 1696 the English infantry was the best he had ever commanded. Yet more than his Dutch bias, he regarded the Marlborough family with suspicion, on the grounds that Marlborough had turned his coat once and might do so again. (William was not, as it transpired, unnecessarily suspicious.) Thus, Marlborough was not entrusted with an independent command but was instructed to lead the English contingent in Flanders in the war against France, under the command of the 69-year-old Prince of Waldeck. William III was preoccupied with Jacobite unrest in Britain, and the dispatch of Marlborough to Flanders removed from the scene a commander who, though enormously popular with the ordinary soldiers, was politically suspect.

Success in Flanders and Ireland

Despite a reputation for bravery, the English army in Flanders was in a poor state. It was lacking in order, included disaffected adherents of James II, and was administratively chaotic. Marlborough began immediately to improve discipline and morale. On 25 August 1689, the army was engaged by overwhelming French forces at Walcourt, but held on until Waldeck reinforced them and Marlborough counter-attacked, leading a cavalry charge in person. Walcourt was the only important action of the campaign, and served mainly to enhance Marlborough's reputation. Old Waldeck reported to William that in this short campaign Marlborough had not only behaved with great gallantry, but despite his age (he was only 39) he had shown greater military skill than most generals achieved in a lifetime. Yet, when William crossed to Ireland to crush James II's attempt to regain his throne (which William achieved with his victory at the Boyne in July 1690), Marlborough was given no field command. Instead, he was appointed as military adviser to the Queen's council, which ran the affairs of state during William's Irish campaign.

Due to the Marlboroughs' influence over the Princess Anne, Queen Mary disliked and distrusted them. Thus, she rejected Marlborough's scheme for an attack upon Cork and Kinsale to sever the Jacobite forces in Ireland from reinforcement from France. William, however, unexpectedly approved the plan and placed Marlborough in command, who proceeded to astonish everyone with the speed and efficiency with which he gathered the expedition. Rather pointedly, the reinforcements he was given were Dutch, Huguenot and Danish troops, conceivably so as to avoid the spectre of Jacobite disaffection.

In this, his first truly independent command, Marlborough captured both Cork and Kinsale in short order, both garrisons surrendering

King William III on horseback.

before an assault was made, having satisfied their honour by holding out until the besiegers' progress made their positions untenable.

Though these were military successes, Marlborough also scored a notable diplomatic success in his dealing with the commander of the reinforcement, the Duke of Württemberg, who insisted on sharing command. Using his tact and the skills learned as a courtier, Marlborough charmed the Duke, accepting joint command on an alternate daily basis, and chose 'Württemberg' as the password for the next day. Württemberg chose 'Marlborough' for the following day and in effect left complete control in Marlborough's hands.

Despite these successes, no more command came Marlborough's way. His reception on his return to England was cordial, but for the campaigning season of 1691 he was merely attached to the King's headquarters. Even here, he impressed the military experts with his capabilities. Indeed, by this time, his skill was probably almost perfected: experienced in the minutiae of close combat, with an obvious strategic sense (demonstrated by his plan for landing in Ireland), capable of conducting a siege, appreciative of the need for sound administration and organisation, possessed of first-hand knowledge of how the French army fought and how the Dutch combatted them, and capable of using his courtly skills in his dealings with difficult foreign allies. He appeared to be the complete military commander, possessing skill, intelligence and humanity; yet it was almost a decade before he again took an active command in the field.

Eclipse and Recovery

Following the 1691 campaign, Marlborough's fortunes went sharply into decline. Openly critical of some of William III's appointments, and feeling slighted at the lack of royal favours he had received, Marlborough exacerbated the position by championing Princess Anne in her family quarrel with the King and Queen. On top of this, his demand to be given overall control of the English troops in Flanders forced the King's hand.

Treason

In January 1692, Marlborough was removed from all his offices and colonelcies, and in May was arrested and imprisoned in the Tower of London. During the five-week incarceration, his younger son, Charles Churchill, died.

Although nominally indicted with bribery and extortion, it was treason of which he was suspected. Since the 'Glorious Revolution', Marlborough had kept clandestine links with James II's court in exile, a not uncommon practice by which a number of highly-placed officials endeavoured to keep their options open, should James ever succeed in recovering his throne. Marlborough's correspondence with James was known to King William. Indeed, it has been suggested that it was condoned and used to transmit false information to the Jacobites. Nevertheless, the connection with the deposed king and Queen Mary's hatred had completely undermined William III's trust. Released from the Tower under a writ of *habeas corpus*, Marlborough remained unemployed but not completely uninvolved in the war with France. In June 1694, the English expedition against Brest was roundly defeated, the plans having been disclosed by English Jacobites. Among those who appraised the French of the landing was almost certainly Marlborough. His apologists suggest that he was only disclosing what he already knew to be in French possession, but though unproven the suspicion of treason remains to stain Marlborough's character.

The Comeback

Queen Mary's death from smallpox in January 1695 led the way to a reconciliation with the King, though the process was not untroubled; in 1696 Marlborough was again charged with treason, but the King declined to indict him. The Marlboroughs were allowed to return to court in 1695, and in 1697 Marlborough was appointed guardian to Princess Anne's eldest son, the Duke of Gloucester, heir-apparent to the throne as it was now obvious that Anne would succeed the widowed King. Indeed, it is likely that William again began to favour Marlborough partly as a result of the friendship between Sarah and the princess. The death of the Duke of Gloucester, also from smallpox, in

1700 caused Marlborough and the King to draw closer. William realised that as Anne had now no direct heir, the constitutional problem of the succession – settled upon the Protestant rulers of Hanover – would require the acquiescence of the Tory party (to which Marlborough had shown some leanings) at the expense of the King's more diehard Whig ministers. Once more, favours were bestowed upon Marlborough and his relations; but what completed his rehabilitation was the imminent prospect of war with Louis XIV of France over the question of the succession to the throne of Spain.

Whilst hoping that France would not initiate hostilities, William realised that the need for allies was urgent, and that the only conceivable military commander was Marlborough. Thus, the Earl was appointed commander of all English troops in Holland and, as a singular mark of trust, the 'Ambassador-Extraordinary and Plenipotentiary' with diplomatic power to negotiate treaties without reference even to the King, if necessary. A hostile France threatened the very existence of Holland and the Protestant succession of England, Louis XIV recognising James II's son as lawful English king. The cornerstone of the resistance to France was the 'Grand Alliance' of England, Holland and Austria; but its determination was not tested in William's lifetime. In February 1702, the King broke a collar-bone when his horse stumbled on a mole-hill (the 'little gentleman in black velvet' toasted by the Jacobites!). He died on 19 March, aged only 52.

Changing Patterns of War

By 1700, warfare had altered quite markedly, a transformation in the previous half-century as a reaction to the horrors of the Thirty Years War (1618–48). In its latter stages, this terrible conflict had approached 'total war' nearer than ever before, affecting both soldiers and civilians alike. Combat, starvation and pestilence had reduced by one-third the population of central Germany, and made life almost unbearable for the wretched survivors. The military excesses had brought about widespread revulsion and the realisation that another such war would be even more devastating. Such opinion had combined with the onset of the 'Age of Reason' to bring about a changed perception of how war must be waged. Though combat remained as brutal as ever, the worst excesses against civilians were prevented, at least in the west, any outrages being condemned universally as offending against humanity. Campaigns were generally conducted in the period from late spring to early autumn, rarely extending into the bad weather during which armies would retire to 'winter quarters'. Practical considerations were largely responsible for this limitation of warfare, the warring states not

The most robust and practical of the early firearm-mechanisms, the flintlock (or 'firelock') musket appeared at the middle of the seventeenth century, had virtually replaced the matchlock entirely by the 1690s, and remained in use until the advent of the percussion cap in the mid-nineteenth century.

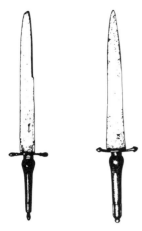

The first bayonets were of the so-called 'plug' variety, being jammed into position down the musket-barrel, so that it was impossible to fire the weapon when the bayonet was 'fixed'.

A crucial development from the 'plug' bayonet was the 'socket' variety, in which the hilt of the bayonet fitted over the musket-barrel and was held in place by a lug on the barrel. This allowed the musket to be fired even when the bayonet was in position.

wishing to expend vast sums in keeping their armies mobilised all year – quite apart from the physical difficulty of manoeuvre in bad weather. Furthermore, the increasing importance of fortresses was equally significant, such fortifications being vital as storage-depots and magazines.

Attack – but Nothing to Chance

Arguably the most influential character of the period was the French Marshal Sebastian le Prestre de Vauban (1633–1707), the greatest military engineer in history. By devising vast new systems of fortification, and turning siege-warfare into a precise science, he created a totally new conception of war. By creating or re-modelling over three thousand fortified places, he ensured that only by time-consuming and meticulous 'investment' (besieging) could fortifications be captured; and thus with such constraints and strong refuges for any defeated army, campaigns became indecisive, revolving around the siege of fortifications and similar short-term objectives.

Almost alone of European generals (the other exception being King Charles XII of Sweden), Marlborough pursued the goal of the swift offensive leading to a decisive battle, in preference to the mechanical manoeuvre and stalemated campaigns favoured by almost all the others. Marlborough's maxim was always 'attack', but equally, to avoid rash consequences: 'leave nothing to chance'. It was this latter ability which established his greatness, for in the administration of his army nothing was too trivial to be outside the scope of his attention. In this, he was almost unique. Whilst enjoying the supreme command and needing all his diplomatic skills to ensure the collaboration of his allies, at the lowest level he superintended the army's administration to the smallest minutiae of soldiers' footwear and rations. The whole was representative of his deep concern for the welfare of his troops and thus the maintenance of their morale; which was reciprocated in the virtual idolatry he was accorded from the ordinary soldiers under his command. The fact that they called him by the affectionate nickname 'Corporal John' is testimony to the unique position he occupied in the hearts of the men he led.

The Flintlock

The major technical innovations concerned the weaponry of the infantry. The cumbersome matchlock musket was at last replaced by a lighter and more efficient musket, using flintlock ignition. This system dated from the mid-seventeenth century, but though considerable numbers of these had been used as early as the English Civil War (1642–51), not until the end of the century had such 'firelocks' almost completely supplanted the matchlock.

The flintlock operated on the same basic principle as the matchlock; the musket was muzzle-loading, firing a plain lead ball, with ignition via a touch-hole in the barrel through which a spark passed from a pan

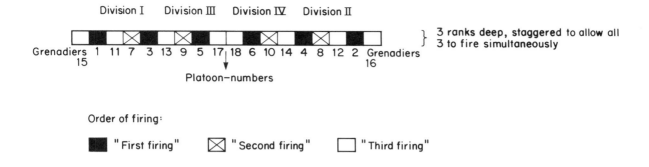

Division I   Division III   Division IV   Division II

3 ranks deep, staggered to allow all
3 to fire simultaneously

Grenadiers 1 11 7 3 13 9 5 17|18 6 10 14 4 8 12 2 Grenadiers
15   16

Platoon-numbers

Order of firing:

■ "First firing"   ⊠ "Second firing"   □ "Third firing"

on the side of the musket, in which a charge of priming-powder was burned. However, the powder in the pan was no longer ignited by the end of a smouldering taper or match, but by sparks struck from a wedge of flint held in the jaws of the 'cock'. The flint crashed against a piece of steel when the trigger was depressed.

The reduction of weight of the musket at last obviated the need for supporting the barrel in a rest, dramatically increasing mobility. Also, the flintlock system occasioned fewer misfires and greatly increased the rate of fire, a trained infantryman being able to discharge at least two shots per minute under combat conditions, though the musket remained wildly inaccurate.

Bayonets, Volleys and Grenades

A second major development was the elimination of the pike. Musketeers still required a means of defence, and found it in the invention of the bayonet, which turned a musket into a short pike. Initially the weapon was a 'plug bayonet', which fitted into the musket-barrel (making it impossible to fire when the bayonet was in position); but latterly the bayonet was attached by rings or sockets, so that the musket could be fired even when the bayonet was fixed.

The disappearance of the pike occasioned a radical change in infantry tactics, as all men now had a firearm. The linear formations developed by Gustavus Adolphus, to bring the maximum number of muskets to bear at once, was refined. The increased rate of fire allowed infantry to be arrayed in as few as three ranks, which were able to produce a continual barrage of musketry when required.

Most continental nations, including the French, fired by volley in ranks, producing a continuous fire along the whole frontage of a regiment. Conversely, British practice was for fire by platoon sub-divisions, all three ranks firing at once, so that a 'rolling volley' was produced. This began at one end of the line and extending by degrees to the other end, by which time the first end would have re-loaded and be able to fire again. This form of continuous fire was better adapted to take advantage of the gaps in the prodigious amount of smoke produced by

English 'platoon firing': a battalion in line, divided into 16 platoons with the line about 9 feet deep (3 ranks) by 270 yards long (260 ranks). By platoon firing, a continual 'rolling volley' could be maintained along the front of the line. Thus, by the time the 'third firing' had actually fired, the 'first firing' was re-loaded and able to recommence the sequence.

65

muzzle-loading muskets, so that the men would be able to see the target at which they were firing. In order for all three ranks to fire simultaneously, the front rank knelt, the second stood half-a-pace to one side and the third a full pace to the other side.

Another development of the late seventeenth century was the hand grenade, an iron sphere filled with combustible material, ignited by a wick in the top and lit from a length of slow-match. Once alight, it would be lobbed at the enemy. Grenades were especially useful in the storm of fortifications, the infantry equipped with them – styled 'grenadiers' – leading the assault and thus, from their exceptionally hazardous duty, coming to be regarded as the élite of their battalion. Even after the decline of the grenade as a weapon in the early eighteenth century, the term 'grenadier' was retained to distinguish the battalion's élite company.

Manoeuvres, Firepower and Siege Warfare

The disappearance of the pike had a major effect on the ability to manoeuvre. The earlier formations of Gustavus Adolphus, though an immense improvement on previous practice, were still of limited flexibility. Marlborough insisted that his troops be able to move more freely across the battlefield, introducing drills whereby sub-units could be manoeuvred in any direction.

The increased rate of fire and the quantity of firearms had a more terrible effect, however. Although hand-to-hand combat declined markedly, the casualty-rate rose. For all its limited range (musketry was usually commenced between 100 and 150 yards from the enemy), the musket was a fearful weapon *en masse*, as statistics demonstrate.

66

At Steenkirk, an infantry fight in 1692 then regarded as one of unparallelled savagery, the combined casualty-figure for both sides was around 4½ per cent of those engaged. At Blenheim in 1704, with the improvement in weapons-technology and increase of firearms, the Allies lost 24 per cent and the Franco-Bavarians 40 per cent. Though such statistics may be influenced by unusual conditions, the general trend was obvious and provided another reason which discouraged commanders from engaging in full-scale battles unless they were certain of the outcome. This resulted in the increasing sterility of warfare and the growing importance of fortifications and the lengthy sieges required to reduce them.

As careful geometry was involved in the construction of fortresses, so their besieging attained the level of a science. Trenches parallel to the defences were pushed progressively nearer the walls, and the besiegers' artillery bombarded a selected part of the defences until a breach was deemed 'practicable'. Though bitter fighting might occur for possession of the outlying defences (outworks), once the main defences had been breached, the defenders' honour was deemed satisfied, and rather than expose the inhabitants of the fortress to the horrors of an assault – equally costly to the attackers – the defenders usually surrendered 'on terms' which might allow the garrison to march away unhindered. Equally, a fortification might be blockaded and the garrison starved into submission, often a very lengthy undertaking.

A principal requirement for a siege was heavy artillery, but few improvements were made in this branch of military science. Immense 36- and 48-pounder guns and huge mortars which lobbed 'bombs' (explosive shells) were gathered in siege-trains which were cumbersome in the extreme, slow-moving and requiring vast numbers of draught horses, ammunition and supplies.

The field artillery was more mobile, but still a drag on an army's movements; the largest field-guns normally employed were those firing a 24-pound shot, but the standard was probably the 9-pounder, just about sufficiently mobile to keep pace with the formations to which it was attached. The smaller guns, down to miniscule 1½-pounder 'regimental' guns, were of limited effect. In battle, field-guns were normally grouped in batteries of six or eight pieces, and unlike the majority of generals, Marlborough always paid the greatest attention to the siting of his artillery.

Mobility and Support

To support an army, immense numbers of waggons and draught

A cannon-barrel of typical form. The projecting lugs ('trunnions') rested in depressions upon the gun-carriage, allowing the barrel to elevate or depress; the projections on top of the barrel (or 'dolphins') were lifting-handles. The ball at the opposite end to the muzzle was termed the 'cascabel'.

67

Musket-drill: ramming the charge of powder and ball down the barrel of the musket. This was followed (right) by tipping 'priming-powder' from a small flask into the open 'pan' of the musket-lock, immediately before firing.

animals were required, obstructive of the army's facility to manoeuvre. Systems of supply were not sophisticated. Although depots would be established in an army's rear, from which supplies could be transported (such depots serving to provision an army during its half-year's winter quarters), supply-trains and the need for regular halts in order to allow bread to be baked greatly slowed the process of a campaign.

In these affairs Marlborough exceeded all others, his concern for regular supply evolving the best system yet seen. No detail was too small for his personal attention; for example, he encouraged the adoption of a light, sprung, two-wheeled cart drawn by only two horses as the army's principal transport-vehicle, increasing mobility.

Aided by his friendship with Godolphin, the Lord Treasurer, Marlborough usually had sufficient funds for the purchase of necessaries from the areas on which his troops were billetted, so that 'free quarter' (the forcible requisition of provisions from the local population) was rarely necessary, ensuring greater harmony between soldiers and civilians who might otherwise have been hostile.

Soldiery

Although the profession of arms had been regarded in some quarters as a noble calling, by the late seventeenth century it was largely discredited due in part to the excesses of the Thirty Years War and the perceived tyranny of military administrations, such as that of the Commonwealth after the English Civil War.

68

Musket-drill showing (left) *'present' (as in 'present fire', i.e. take aim) and* (right) *'give fire'.*

Apart from the higher echelon of officers – still largely the province of the nobility – armies were usually recruited from the lowest or most desperate elements of society, the almost universal absence of conscription making wider social strata unavailable as a source of recruits. One of Marlborough's greatest works was his humane treatment of such men. According to his earliest biographer it had a great effect on his forces:

[he] secured the affection of his soldiers by his good nature, care for their provisions and vigilance not to expose them to unnecessary dangers . . . the poor soldiers who were (too many of them) the refuse and dregs of the nation, became tractable, civil, orderly, and clean, and had an air and spirit above the vulgar.[5]

In addition to the 'national' troops of each army, most states extensively employed mercenaries. Britain, for example, used Huguenots (French Protestants) and hired Hanoverians and Hessians; the French had Irish Catholics and Jacobites, Swiss and Bavarians; the Dutch hired Danes and Prussians. In 1709 as many as 81,000 of a total of 150,000 British forces were 'allied' troops. Whilst such paid professionals rarely had any deep attachment to a cause, they could be inspired by a charismatic leader; of which Marlborough was the most successful in this regard.

Battle Tactics
Though decisive battles were comparatively rare, when they occurred they were often fought under reasonably precise rules. Both sides were usually given time to assemble (a lengthy process), which allowed an opponent time to escape if he considered the position unadvantageous;

69

A typical 'Marlburian' order of battle – very different from the standard French deployment, which had infantry in the middle and cavalry on the flanks.

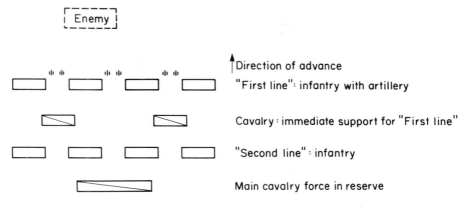

┌─────────┐
| Enemy |
└ ─ ─ ─ ┘

↑ Direction of advance

"First line": infantry with artillery

Cavalry: immediate support for "First line"

"Second line": infantry

Main cavalry force in reserve

Marlborough was uniquely skilled in getting close to his enemy before his intentions were revealed, by the use of night marches, for example. It was usual for an army to be arrayed in two lines, infantry in the centre and cavalry on the flanks, with artillery between units and a reserve (often cavalry) at the rear.

Battles were largely attritional, with both sides blasting at their opponent until one decided to retire, though attempts were often made to exert pressure on one or another of the enemy's flanks in the hope of driving back part of his line.

The French and their allies had not fully mastered the new art of firepower, and clung to infantry formations four or five deep, greatly inferior to the Anglo-Dutch three-rank line and rolling volley by platoons, inspired by Marlborough.

Even greater difference was evident in the handling of the cavalry of the two sides. The French were still largely reliant on the *caracole*, by which successive ranks of horsemen rode towards their enemy and fired their pistols and carbines, and only when the enemy was disordered by this fusillade did they charge with the sabre. These tactics were rejected totally by Marlborough, who insisted (like Gustavus Adolphus) that the cavalry's main advantage was the shock effect of the charge, actually conducted at a fast trot so as not to disorder the formations. To reinforce his insistence on the charge with the sabre, Marlborough allowed his cavalry only three rounds of pistol-ammunition per campaign.

An additional factor which made Marlborough's cavalry especially effective was his use of infantry as support, concerted action by two or more 'arms' being a most vital factor in his system of warfare.

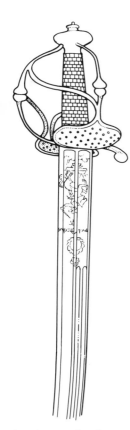

An Austrian broadsword of the late seventeenth or early eighteenth century: the semi-basket hilt protecting the hand is a style typical of the period.

War of the Spanish Succession

The accession of Queen Anne to the English throne almost immediately

70

elevated Marlborough to the most powerful position in the land. Within days he was confirmed as commander-in-chief of the English forces at home and in Flanders, appointed a Knight of the Garter (a long-sought award) and Master-General of the Ordnance, giving him total military power. Within two years he was receiving over £60,000 per annum (plus a percentage of army bread contracts); and Sarah, to whom the Queen referred by the nom-de-plume of 'Mrs. Freeman', remained Anne's closest confidante and received appointments worth over £5000 per annum.

The most immediate need was not for Marlborough's military skills, but for his diplomacy, in aiding the Queen to assemble an acceptable Ministry and confirming the Grand Alliance. The creation of a Tory Ministry (Anne being deeply suspicious of the Whigs) with Sidney Godolphin as Lord Treasurer provided Marlborough with the backing he required for his campaigns, for Godolphin was a friend of 40 years and connected to Marlborough by marriage. Together with Robert Harley, Speaker of the House of Commons, they formed the triumvirate within the Ministry which virtually ran the country for almost the next decade.

A Coming War

For nine years, Marlborough was largely in actual (if not official) control of British fortunes in the war of the Spanish Succession; his rôle as commander-in-chief of the British forces extended far beyond the management of the army, to the determination of alliances and foreign policy, a role almost unparallelled in British history. That he was able to make a success of this immense task is a tribute not only to his military, diplomatic and administrative genius, but also to his capacity for hard work and an unwillingness to leave anything unsupervised.

Yet even Marlborough could not surmount the problems arising from the collaboration of states united only by their opposition to France; all his attempts at a co-ordinated strategy to assail France on all fronts, by land and sea, were frustrated. Only where he commanded in person was there unrelieved success.

King Charles II of Spain was childless, which left the main contenders for the throne as Louis XIV's grandson Philip of Anjou, and the Emperor Leopold's son Charles. Hostilities between the Holy Roman Empire and France began in 1701, and in September of that year the Grand Alliance against France was formulated, between the Empire, Britain, Holland, many German states (including Brandenburg or Prussia) and (later) Portugal. In the French camp were Mantua, Cologne, Savoy (which soon changed sides) and (later) Bavaria. Although the war was fought in several theatres, including Italy, the Iberian peninsula and the Mediterranean, the most important battles were fought in the area of Flanders to the Danube, where Marlborough was to exercise his talents for the next eight years.

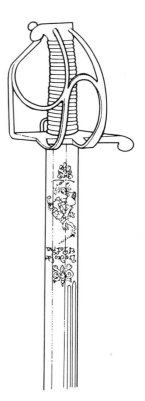

Bavarian cavalry broadsword of the late seventeenth or early eighteenth century. On the finer-quality weapons, it was usual for patriotic inscriptions and figures of cavalrymen to be etched onto the blade.

71

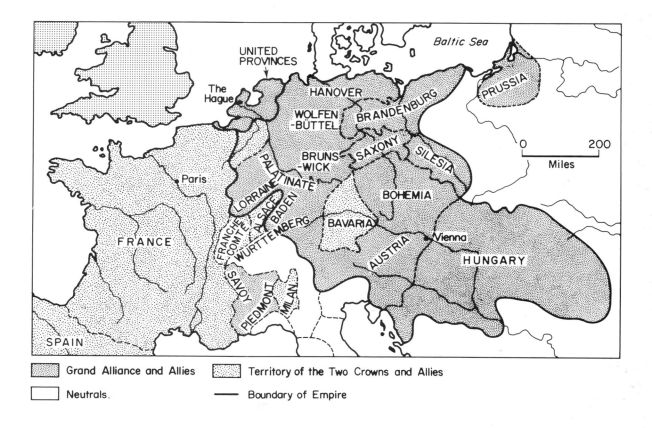

European territories of the Grand Alliance.

Frustration of Command

When war was declared against France on 15 May 1702, Marlborough was sent to Holland as captain-general of the combined Dutch and English forces. From the very outset he encountered the problem which was to beset him throughout his career in command of a polyglot army: the lack of overall control he was allowed to exercise over the allied troops. Only over the English troops had he unrestricted command; the other nationalities exemplified the problem of an alliance in which the aspirations of the component nations were different. Principally, the Dutch government wished to preserve their own territorial integrity as the first priority, rather than make offensive operations in support of the alliance's overt aims; and in addition to Dutch lack of co-operation in Marlborough's wider plans, he had also to contend with the jealousy of commanders nominally his inferiors. To anyone without Marlborough's skills in diplomacy, and what must have been a winning manner, the problem might have been insoluble. As it was, it required all his skill and tact to mould the multi-national contingents and their commanders into a cohesive whole, though he was never able fully to develop his plans without hindrance.

Such hindrance was evident from his first assumption of command, when in June/July Marlborough with some 50,000 men (12,000 British) invaded the Spanish Netherlands (roughly what is now Belgium) from Holland, in an attempt to bring to battle the French army of Marshal Louis, duc de Boufflers (1644–1711). Marlborough out-manoeuvred the French and in early August had them in a perilous position, open to attack on their line of withdrawal.

However, though commander of the allied army, Marlborough's authority over his Dutch regiments was dependent upon the acquiescence of the five Field Deputies appointed by the Dutch States-General to 'assist' him; in effect, they were political commissars. These fainthearts, unwilling to risk Dutch lives even though a major victory was the prize, represented to Marlborough that an attack was unnecessary as the French were already retiring. Although Marlborough could have over-ruled them and secured his victory, the diplomat in him realised that to cause a potential political crisis so early in the alliance was not worth the risk.

In the next few days, three more opportunities were lost for the same reason, so that when the French had finally reached safety Marlborough sent to them a trumpeter under a flag of truce, bearing an apology for not engaging them, a somewhat ironic and old-fashioned courtesy! Nevertheless, by consistently out-manoeuvering the French Marlborough had the upper hand, and confirmed his dominance by his operations on the lower Rhine and Meuse rivers late in the year, capturing the Meuse fortresses of Venlo, Ruremonde and Liège. (As there was no chance of a major battle and as their trade-routes were involved, the Dutch co-operated!)

At the end of 1702, Marlborough returned to London, whilst the army went into winter quarters. However, he was almost captured *en route* when his party was intercepted by the French. Marlborough had no current *laissez-passer* documentation (passports, habitually granted by a nation to eminent enemy personages). He bluffed his way through by using an old document of his brother's and (it appears) the promise of a Dutch commission for the French subaltern in command! Such were the common courtesies of early eighteenth-century warfare.

Marlborough's first major command had thus been a great success, virtually the only one for the Grand Alliance, and in gratitude Queen Anne elevated him to the rank of Duke.

Professional Headway, Personal Tragedy

The campaign of 1703 produced no decisive battles in the theatre which concerned Marlborough, but elsewhere was greatly successful for France, putting Vienna itself under threat by a series of victories over the Imperial troops. Marlborough's intended operations were to re-open communications with Austria via the Rhine, and then penetrate the French cordon of forts in the Spanish Netherlands and seize Antwerp.

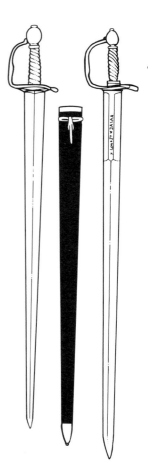

French cavalry swords of about 1700: the straight-bladed weapon was still almost universal, the curved blade of light cavalry style generally being a later development.

73

A secrete was an iron frame-work which was fitted inside, or over the top of, a felt hat, providing much of the protective value of an iron helmet but without the tiring effects of the weight; they were used from the mid-seventeenth century.

Again bickering with the Dutch confounded the operations, but the capture of Bonn in May opened the Rhine valley; and as early as late summer Marlborough was planning for the following year's campaign.

He returned to England in November, not wholly dissatisfied with the year, though French successes against the Dutch had forced the abandonment of the Antwerp enterprise. His frustrations with the Dutch generals and politicians, which had brought veiled threats of resignation as early as June, probably contributed to the attacks of migraine which afflicted him at critical moments throughout his career.

On a personal level, he had been devastated by the death from smallpox in February of his only surviving son, the 17-year-old Marquess of Blandford; it delayed his embarkation for the campaign and almost led to his retirement.

Despite his troubles, his successes in 1702–03 had been considerable. The existence of Holland was no longer under threat; ten fortresses had been regained, and though no major battle had been fought Marlborough's reputation was now of international repute (his presence as commander-in-chief probably had considerable influence on Savoy's change of side in 1703 and on Portugal's joining the Grand Alliance). That this was achieved in an atmosphere of jealousy and obstruction by the Dutch is testimony of his military and diplomatic skill. The most impressive tribute was that given by the Dutch general-in-chief Godart van Ginkel, Earl of Athlone (1630–1703) who admitted that the 1702 successes were entirely due to Marlborough, despite Ginkel having opposed him on principle at every step, as the Dutchman admitted.

Blenheim – Astonishing Triumph

In late 1703, the alarming situation in southern Germany, following the French successes, caused the Emperor to recall from Italy his best and most experienced general, Prince Eugene of Savoy-Carignon (1663–1736). Born in Paris to an ex-favourite of Louis XIV, Eugene had been refused entry to the French army (his mother having been banished under suspicion of black magic and of having poisoned her husband), so had joined the Imperial army instead. After distinguishing himself against the Turks in the relief of Vienna (1683), by the age of 30 he had risen to the rank of field-marshal, an unprecedented achievement for a foreigner of little influence or resources.

Partners

Marlborough experienced constant trouble from his foreign allies and subordinates, but in Eugene of Savoy – himself a commander of the highest ability – he found the ideal partner. So harmonious and

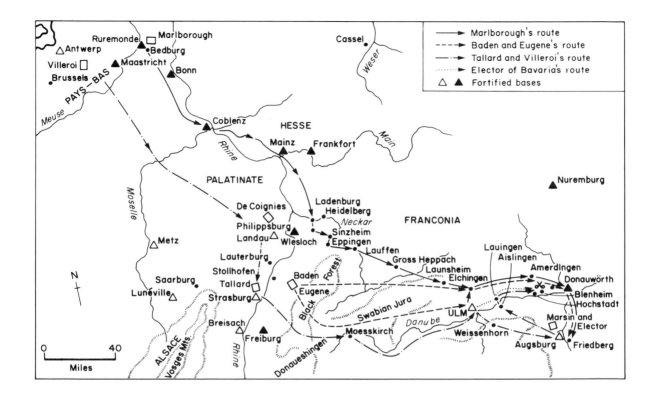

unselfish was their co-operation that popular medals were struck depicting them as Castor and Pollux, and one reason for their friendship was Eugene's attitude to war. Never content with the common formalised, sterile theories, Eugene preferred audacity and enterprise; he used terrain brilliantly, made much of the offensive and reconnaissance capacities of the cavalry, and inspired his men by the force of his personality. In other words, in such regard he resembled Marlborough himself.

Following their successes of 1703, the French planned that in 1704 Marshal Count Camille de Tallard should reinforce Marshal Count Ferdinand de Marsin and the Elector of Bavaria and thrust towards Vienna, whilst Marshal François de Neufville, duc de Villeroi (1644–1730) contained Marlborough on the Netherlands frontier. As captain-general of the Anglo-Dutch forces, Marlborough sanctioned an expedition to Lisbon, to move against Spain, and another to attack Toulon in support of Huguenot rebels in southern France; but these were only diversions, the main preoccupation being the saving of Vienna. Marlborough and Eugene intended to concentrate their forces in the Danube valley, drive the French from Germany, and knock Bavaria out of the war. It is not clear which of the allied generals was primarily responsible for the plan; both Marlborough and Eugene were capable of it, but it was Marlborough's actions which brought it about.

Marlborough's march to the Danube during the Blenheim campaign of 1704.

Prince Eugene of Savoy in the engraving by Bonon (after Toresanus).

75

To the Danube

At the outset, the situation was not hopeful. Already there was dissent in English politics, the Whigs favouring the appointment of the Hanoverian heir to the throne, Elector George, as supreme commander. Marlborough was prepared to accept demotion in the common cause, but thankfully Queen Anne would not countenance such a move. Eventually, a new Ministry had to be constructed by Godolphin and Marlborough, allowing the Duke to concentrate upon his military task; which was awesome, for Vienna was threatened by overwhelming Franco-Bavarian forces, and its capture would occasion the collapse of the Grand Alliance. Marlborough realised the need to march to its relief; but the Dutch, as usual, were concerned only for their own territorial integrity and were unwilling to risk their troops far outside their own boundaries. As the situation deteriorated for the Imperial troops, Marlborough embarked on a 250-mile march across Germany, a manoeuvre quite unprecedented. Knowing that it was hopeless to expect the Dutch to co-operate, he left their troops in the Netherlands and marched with his own British and Germans drawn from a number of allied states, whose rulers Marlborough had to influence with all his diplomatic skills to guarantee their collaboration. Eventually, on guaranteeing that he would return to Holland if any threat appeared to their territory, Marlborough extracted from the Dutch a reinforcement of Danish troops in Dutch pay.

The march to the Danube was fraught with danger. Nevertheless, informed of French movements by his network of spies, and decoying the French into thinking his destination was an incursion into Alsace, Marlborough progressed unhindered. His administration and meticulous planning ensured that his troops arrived at their destination in fighting condition. He had established advance depots (for example, every man received a new pair of shoes at Heidelburg), and for each day's march, advance-parties laid out the next afternoon's camping-ground, so that the troops had nothing to do but pitch their tents and light their camp-fires. By contrast, the French force which shadowed the march lost almost a third of their strength in keeping pace with Marlborough. Leaving his slow-moving baggage in the Netherlands, Marlborough took over 40,000 men more than 250 miles in the amazingly short time of just over five weeks, losing only 1200 sick *en route*. It was a work of administrative genius.

Medal commemorating the Victory of Blenheim. The reverse shows the defeat of the French army and the obverse has portraits of Marlborough and Eugene of Savoy – who are compared in the inscription to Castor and Pollux!

Battle is Absolutely Necessary

Having successfully moved into the same theatre as Eugene's outnumbered Imperial army, Marlborough had considerable difficulty in persuading the French to offer battle, though a minor success was gained in July when Marlborough captured the fortified Schellenberg Hill overlooking Donauwörth. Tallard, uniting with the army of Marsin and the

The 1st Foot Guards at Blenheim depicted by C. du Bosc (after Laguerre).

Elector, expected the campaign to be one of manoeuvre, in the usual style, perhaps without a major action. Indeed, he was especially sure of his position when he drew up his forces to the north of the Danube, just south of the river Nebel, with his right flank anchored on the village of Blenheim and his centre on the village of Oberglau, both of which

77

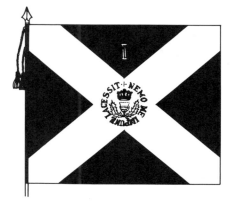

Infantry colour of the 1st or Royal Regiment (later, the Royal Scots) of the Marlborough's period: white saltire on a blue ground bearing a green thistle with purple flower, golden crown and motto Nemo Me Impune Lacessit. The silver 'I' at the top indicted the company of the regiment's First Captain, as each company commander retained his own.

Also captured at Blenheim was a French cavalry standard (right) featuring Louis XIV's very common device, the 'sun in splendour' and motto Nec Pluribus Impar.

were fortified. When on 13 August 1704, the Allied army appeared out of the early morning mist (having been on the march in the dark since 2 a.m.) it was a total surprise.

Marlborough's army occupied the left of the Allied position, and Eugene's the right; they had 52,000 men and 66 guns against Tallard's 56,000 Franco-Bavarians and 90 guns. Marlborough was all too aware that attacking a superior enemy in an entrenched position was hazardous in the extreme.

I know the difficulties but a battle is absolutely necessary, and I rely on the discipline of my troops.

Contrary to convention, Marlborough concentrated his cavalry in the centre of his line, instead of on the wings. After inspecting his line and checking the position of his artillery, he commenced the battle at 12.30 p.m. by thrusting against the fortified village of Blenheim on the French right, the attack being made by Lord Cutts and the British infantry.

From his love of heavy fire Cutts was nicknamed 'The Salamander', but on this occasion he received fire heavier than he could overcome, for twice the British infantry surged up to the palisades of the village, and twice were beaten back with heavy loss. Brigadier Row who led them stuck his sword into the palisading, but was mortally wounded and the attack driven back. Marlborough ordered that no further lives be thrown away, the British instead keeping the French occupied with long-range musketry; but although the attack had failed to capture the village, it paralysed the French right and had drawn into Blenheim much of their reserve.

One of the trophies captured by the British at Blenheim was this colour of a Bavarian infantry regiment, which incorporated the national blue and white chequers and gold orb.

Meanwhile, the remainder of Marlborough's army had struggled across the Nebel and, in the face of heavy fire, had established themselves on the French bank. Eugene had no such success, for Marsin and the Elector on the French left bitterly disputed the crossing; but he at least held his own. At 3 p.m. Marlborough was ready for his decisive blow, concentrating his bombardment against the weakened French

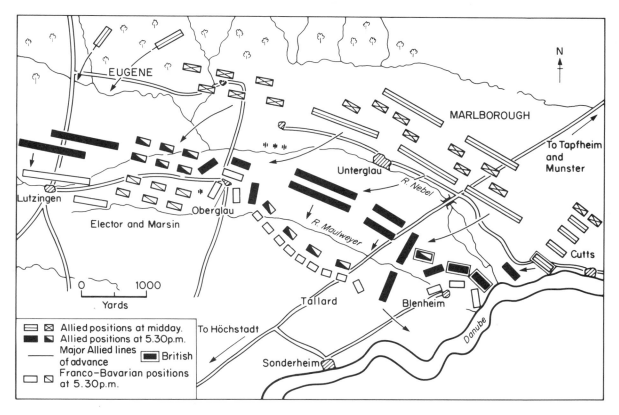

Within the map:

N

EUGENE

MARLBOROUGH

To Tapfheim
and
Munster

Lutzingen

Unterglau

R. Nebel

Elector and Marsin

Oberglau

R. Maulweyer

Cutts

0   1000

Yards

Tallard

Blenheim

Danube

Allied positions at midday.
Allied positions at 5.30p.m.
Major Allied lines
of advance   British
Franco–Bavarian positions
at 5.30p.m.

To Höchstadt

Sonderheim

Battle of Blenheim, 13 August 1704.

Marlborough at Blenheim, as depicted in a typical period engraving.

Charge of the Allied cavalry at Blenheim, depicted in a print of Dupray's painting.

centre. As soon as the French began to waver, Marlborough launched his cavalry into the charge. As the French line split under the pressure, Marlborough sent his whole force of cavalry into the gap. The French army was split asunder and their whole centre began to flee towards the Danube, pursued by the Allied cavalry. Hundreds were killed, hundreds were drowned in the river and thousands surrendered. Of Tallard's forces on the French right, only the troops in Blenheim remained on the field; and seeing their centre annihilated, Marsin and the Elector managed to extricate much of their left wing, hotly pressed by Eugene. The French in Blenheim were surrounded and powerless. Exclaiming 'What will the King say? Whatever will the King say?', they surrendered unconditionally.

Laurels of Victory

Blenheim was a stunning success, coming as it did after one of the greatest strategic marches in history. Tallard was captured and his army destroyed; Allied losses amounted to some 12,000 (the highest proportion from the small British contingent), but those of the French were almost 39,000. For the first time in forty years a major French army had been routed, destroying their reputation of invincibility; Vienna was saved, and Marlborough's reputation was assured. It was the highest point of his fortune: his bold night advance which established the Allied army in front of Tallard, his personal control of the battle at crucial stages, and his advanced preparations which had welded his army into a cohesive whole and had ensured that it was in fighting trim even after such extensive manoeuvres, had all been vital. He was fortunate to have Eugene as so capable an ally, and troops of such good heart; but the laurel indisputedly belonged to Marlborough.

Ramillies – Crushing Success

Before returning home for the winter, Marlborough had to conduct diplomatic duties in Germany, where he was hailed as the saviour of Europe. Upon returning home, he was honoured by the gift of a manor at Woodstock and the promise of a palace to be built there (named, appropriately, Blenheim). Amid the success, however, there were already signs of dissent, with the need for Godolphin and Marlborough to shift their stance slightly towards the Whig party which was making ground in the House of Commons; and the Queen was beginning to cool in her relations with the difficult Sarah.

Stalemate

After the triumph of Blenheim, the 1705 campaigning-season was a disappointment, and Marlborough's problems began to increase. Stalemate continued in the Netherlands, all Marlborough's offensive intentions once again being blocked by the excessive caution of the Dutch; and the campaign against Villeroi and the Elector of Bavaria ended without a decisive result. Increasingly frustrated with the Dutch government, who took little notice of his entreaties for offensive action, Marlborough's only success in 1705 was diplomatic, a tour of allied courts and headquarters to cement the alliance, which had been strained by internal political pressures. Yet even amid the stresses of campaign, such was Marlborough's concern for ostensibly the most trivial matters that he found time to write to Godolphin regarding 'a young woman of quality' who was in 'a very virtuous love' with the comte de Lyon, then at Litchfield, and enquiring whether the count might be permitted to go to France to marry the girl, 'As I do from my heart wish that nobody were unhappy'.[6] Marlborough's human side, so often overlooked, included a warm heart.

For the 1706 season, Marlborough's capacity for strategic planning was demonstrated by his suggestion of marching to Italy to defeat the French there; but as all the allied nations were opposed, his 1706 campaign again took place in Flanders. In his preparations he was as usual beset with the personal supervision of even small matters, most especially a shortage of cavalry horses which the Dutch declined to supply.

Battle by Chance

In France, Louis XIV was considering peace, but to increase his scope for negotiation decided to take the offensive; and in the Spanish Netherlands, Villeroi advanced with the desire of avenging Blenheim and emboldened by his confidence of being able to out-general Marlborough. Believing that Marlborough's objective would be the capture of the fortress of Namur, Villeroi moved towards the Dutch border; for both sides actively to seek action was indeed a singular occurrence. The armies ran into each other almost by chance, on 23 May at the village of Ramillies, where Marlborough was intending to camp. Running into the French advance-guard about 1 a.m., Marlborough drew his army into line-of-battle, as did Villeroi, who used the village of Ramillies as the centre of his line. Both sides fielded around 60,000 troops, but Marlborough was stronger in artillery (which, as usual, he sited with extreme care), and enjoyed a major advantage in the slightly convex frontage he adopted. This tactic made it easier to transfer troops from one wing to the other; the longer, concave French line could only manoeuvre along its length with difficulty.

In a typical manoeuvre, Marlborough made probing attacks on both flanks from about 1 a.m., that on the right (principally British) apparently only a feint intended to draw French support from the centre and occupy their reserve. Whether the British attacks *were* a feint is not clear – the marshy terrain was unsuitable for cavalry action and Marlborough always tried to co-ordinate the operations of all 'arms' – but it had the desired effect. Villeroi payed heed to his instructions from the King to pay special attention to the attack of the British contingent, and the red-coated battalions could hardly be mistaken.

A Risk for Victory

Meanwhile, French advances in the centre had threatened Marlborough's line, to stabilise which Marlborough himself led two cavalry charges, in one of which he almost came to grief, being thrown from his horse and ridden over. Covered by two Swiss battalions in Dutch service, Marlborough's aide Captain Molesworth dismounted to give the general his own horse, but the fight was so hot that when Marlborough transferred to his own spare horse, his equerry Major Bringfield[7] was killed by a roundshot as he aided Marlborough to mount. Though it was perilous to risk his life in this manner, Marlborough probably realised that his personal presence was needed to rally his centre.

The blunting of the French attack in the centre allowed time for allied troops to be transferred from the flanks, the battalions leaving

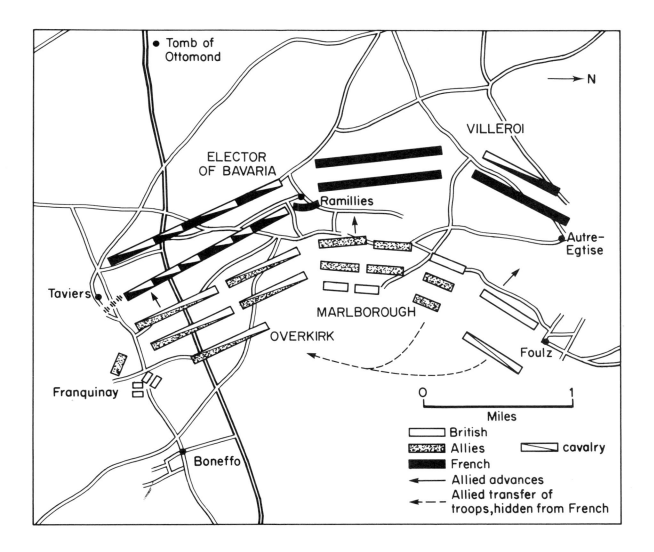

Inside the map:

- Tomb of Ottomond
- N →
- VILLEROI
- ELECTOR OF BAVARIA
- Ramillies
- Autre-Egtise
- Taviers
- MARLBOROUGH
- OVERKIRK
- Franquinay
- Foulz
- Boneffo

0 ———————— 1
Miles

British
Allies   cavalry
French
← Allied advances
←--- Allied transfer of troops, hidden from French

Battle of Ramillies, 23 May 1706.

their colour-parties in their original positions to decoy the French into believing that they were still there. Thus, Villeroi was unaware that Marlborough was massing in the centre for the decisive blow, which was made about 6 p.m. Too late Villeroi realised that he had been outwitted, and too late tried to form a new line of defence in his rear; the Allied forces swept on, driving the French away in chaos.

Total Allied casualties were about 3700, against which at least 13,000 French had fallen, and perhaps up to half Villeroi's army was lost in subsequent surrenders and desertions. It was a crushing victory, demonstrating again Marlborough's ability to use the advantages of terrain and the concerted action of all elements of his army. The pursuit was conducted vigorously, giving the French no chance to re-form, whilst Marlborough, after 20 hours in the saddle, folded himself in his

Marlborough being presented with the captured French colours at Ramillies (after Dupray).

cloak and slept on the open ground. His defeated opponent Villeroi had no such rest, lamenting that the happiest day he could foresee would be that of his death; but his old friend Louis XIV was more philosophical, remarking that 'At our age, one is no longer lucky'!

Triumph Confounded

As a consequence of Ramillies, the French in Flanders were flung into chaos as Marlborough swept through the Spanish Netherlands, capturing Antwerp in June, Dunkirk in July, Menin in August, Dendermonde in September and Ath in October, taking around 14,000 additional prisoners in the process. By the end of 1706, Louis XIV was making tentative approaches towards peace, and French fortunes seemed on the wane.

In the event, once the Allies had rejected Louis' terms as not sufficiently generous, it was Allied fortunes which suffered in 1707, once again to a considerable degree the result of disagreements within the Alliance and the difficulty of achieving an overall plan of action. Marlborough proposed a holding operation in Flanders, with the main Allied effort being made in Italy, where in the previous year Eugene had conducted a brilliant campaign, with further offensives in Spain and

84

a landing at Toulon, preparatory to a march into the heart of France to compel Louis to accept terms of surrender at any price. Allied discord was not the only reason for failure, however; the Duke of Berwick won a major victory over the Allies' General Galway at Almanza (Spain) in April; the Toulon expedition failed; and on the Rhine Marlborough's old comrade-in-arms, Marshal duc de Villars (1653–1734) – perhaps the most competent of Louis' generals – won a victory over the Imperial army at Stollhofen in May and followed by raiding south-central Germany as far as Bavaria.

In Flanders, with Marlborough bereft of the opportunity of a major offensive and divisiveness among the Allies, stalemate continued. The new Emperor Joseph I (Leopold I having died in 1705) offered Marlborough the Governor-Generalship of the Spanish Netherlands. Despite the £60,000 p.a. it would have brought him, Marlborough with some regret declined the position in order to pacify the Dutch. At home, relations between the Queen and Sarah were becoming more strained, and political in-fighting was gradually isolating Marlborough and his friends. In all, the position did not appear propitious.

Oudenarde – Bitter Encounter

In 1708 as many as 100,000 French troops prepared to renew the war in Flanders, nominally commanded by the young Duke of Burgundy (the king's grandson), but actually under the direction of Louis, duc de Vendôme (1654–1712), transferred in late 1706 from the Italian front.

The Plan
In April, an Allied conference at the Hague determined the year's strategy. Eugene would march to join Marlborough in the Netherlands when a newly-formed Allied army could replace him on the Rhine, but Eugene was not to move until fully relieved. In Spain and Italy, the Allies were to defend, Marlborough intending that Flanders should be the decisive sphere, where a victory was imperative, if not for purely military purposes then to revive the flagging resolution of the Alliance. The comparative weakness of his own army would, he hoped, tempt the French into battle, whereupon once they were committed he could unite with Eugene and overwhelm them. Marlborough's diplomatic skill, continually in demand, was needed to pacify the Elector of Hanover, who was jealous of Eugene, and the friction caused when the Electoral Prince (son and heir of the Elector, and later George II of England) took service with Eugene simply to annoy his father![8]

As Marlborough's plans had frequently been spoiled by internal dissent, so now were those of the French. The young and inexperienced

Duke of Burgundy and the able Vendôme viewed each other with mutual antipathy, so that their planning was fraught with argument and conflicting strategic intent. As a prince of the royal blood, Burgundy usually had his way, a considerable advantage to the Allies. Nevertheless, when it came, the French offensive took Marlborough by surprise and for once he was caught unprepared. In early July the French fell upon Ghent and Menin, and thus recovered much of the Spanish Netherlands, a severe blow to Marlborough's prestige. At the time he was suffering from ill-health, fever and migraine; to the Duchess he described himself as 'a good deal out of order' and to Godolphin that 'my blood is so extremely heated',[9] which perhaps helps to explain his discomfiture.

The Allied garrison of Oudenarde was under threat, but though it could have been captured, Burgundy over-ruled Vendôme and settled for a blockade of the town. Though the French should have struck before Eugene had time to arrive, their internal dissent gave the Allies the respite they needed. Though the Imperial forces were still some days away, Eugene himself rode ahead to join Marlborough and, seeing that both armies were approximately equal in size (around 80,000) urged battle. Marlborough seized the initiative and made a most audacious advance. He covered up to 50 miles in 60 hours, a speed quite unprecedented for the time, which staggered Vendôme.

Burgundy favoured withdrawal, but Vendôme, convinced that Marlborough might cut them off from France, persuaded him to fight. The battle, fought near Oudenarde on 11 July, was not to be a classic eighteenth-century encounter in which both sides arrayed their forces before commencing, but an 'encounter battle' with troops joining as they arrived. Marlborough's men were tired by their march and had only light artillery (the heavier, slower guns having been left behind), but their spirit and confidence in their chief was immense.

The Allied army having safely crossed the Scheldt river (upon which Oudenarde stands), thanks to the confusion in the French command which prevented them from opposing the crossing, the first action occurred on the Allied right where a French probing advance was overwhelmed. As more Allied troops came over the Scheldt, Marlborough was able to press forward into terrain of cultivated fields, unfavourable for the deployment of the French cavalry, giving the Allied infantry a major advantage. Throughout, the fight was bitter and confused, but the divided French command proved crucial; Burgundy misunderstood Vendôme's plan and, at a critical moment, declined to support Vendôme's attack. Nevertheless, it made good ground against the Allies on the French right, where Vendôme had achieved local superiority in numbers, and leaving Eugene in command of the Allied right, Marlborough rode over to take personal command. Marlborough again demonstrated his cool head in confused circumstances, switching units from the centre to secure the right wing (leaving their colour-

Medal struck to commemorate the Battle of Oudenarde.

86

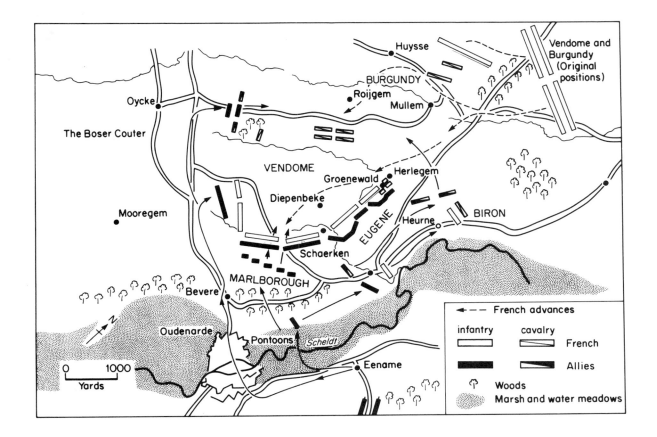

parties to delude the French, as at Ramillies), whilst preparing a major counter-attack on the left. When it came, led by Dutch and Danes in the early evening, it swept the French army from the field, though the onset of night and heavy rain allowed many French to escape; Marlborough called off the pursuit to prevent his own troops firing upon each other in the darkness.

Total Allied losses were about 3000; the French lost perhaps 6000, with 7000 prisoners and several thousand more scattered or deserted. At one blow the initiative in Flanders had been wrested from the French, and triumph again was Marlborough's own. Despite his ill-health, his eye for terrain, ability to husband his resources, exploit the weakness of the enemy and skill in being able to improvise and remain calm in a crisis again proved that he had no equal.

Consolidating the Initiative
With the initiative given by Oudenarde, Marlborough planned an audacious march to the Channel, and then an advance along the coast, by-passing the huge frontier defences to invade France, supported and provisioned by the Anglo-Dutch fleet. But only he could envisage the

87

Medal commemorating the surrender of Lille.

possibility of such an army/navy 'combined operation'. The Dutch and even Eugene thought it too great a risk, so Marlborough acquiesced for diplomatic reasons, and instead besieged the supposedly-impregnable fortress of Lille. Eugene conducted the siege whilst Marlborough's army provided the covering force to prevent its relief, turning back an attempt by Vendôme.

Lille fell in December after a gallant but costly defence, and despite the lateness of the season Marlborough was in no mood to retire to winter quarters. Deciding to force the French from western Flanders, he besieged and captured Ghent and Bruges in January 1709. The French withdrew to their own borders and both sides prepared for a renewal of the war in the spring.

Malplaquet – Last Victory

Despite his victories, Marlborough's position was becoming ever more threatened as a result of the withdrawal of royal favour. Queen Anne, by now, regarded him as a hard-line Whig, unjustly as the Duke always despised party factionalism; only the necessity to ensure the prosecution of the war had caused any affiliation with the Whigs. To consolidate his position, Marlborough asked to be appointed Captain-General for life, but was refused. Ageing and no longer in robust health, he yearned for peace.

Nevertheless, the Duke embarked on the 1709 campaign with determination. The year's plan was to breach the French frontier defences or tempt the French army into leaving their lines in a position favourable for the combined Allied armies of Marlborough and Eugene. The French, now commanded by Villars, were instructed to avoid battle, but though the early operations were inconclusive (the Allies capturing Tournai in July), the threat to the French fortress of Mons in September prompted Villars to offer battle. The French commander concentrated about 90,000 men in the vicinity of Malplaquet, where he entrenched, knowing that this threat would divert the Allies. Leaving about 20,000 to continue the siege of Mons, Marlborough and Eugene advanced with 90,000 more men to accept the French challenge.

Savage Shock

On 11 September 1709, the armies met at Malplaquet. The Allies adopted what might be termed a classic 'Marlburian' plan. Advancing with Eugene on the right and Marlborough on the left, both made holding attacks on their respective flanks, while the main concentration held the centre and then punched through the French line once Villars' reserves had been committed on the flanks.

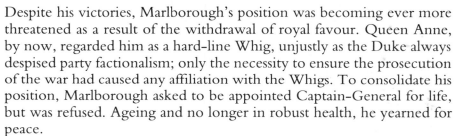

Battle of Malplaquet, 11 September 1709.

88

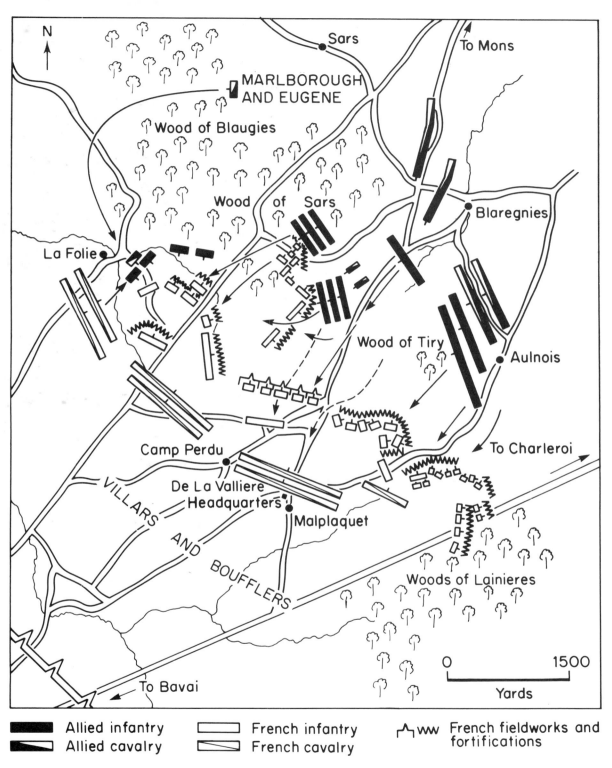

N

Sars

To Mons

MARLBOROUGH
AND EUGENE

Wood of Blaugies

Blaregnies

Wood of Sars

La Folie

Wood of Tiry

Aulnois

To Charleroi

Camp Perdu

De La Valliere
Headquarters

VILLARS

Malplaquet

AND

BOUFFLERS

Woods of Lainieres

To Bavai

0   1500

Yards

Allied infantry   French infantry   French fieldworks and
                                                  fortifications
Allied cavalry   French cavalry

- - - -   The Allied cavalry attack   Allied advances
          through the centre

However, this was the first time in which they had confronted a general as competent as Villars, whose position was strongly fortified, especially in the centre where he expected the main Allied effort would be made. Clearly, Villars had become aware of how to counter a typical Marlborough plan. The battle which began on the morning of 11 September was to shock all involved with its savagery.

From the start, things did not go well for the Allies despite super-human efforts from their flank-attacking forces, especially the Dutch and the Highland regiments in Dutch service, Tullibardine's and Hepburn's. The Dutch 'Blue Guards' (William III's favourite troops) were all but annihilated. Despite the losses, however, the attacks were made with such resolution that Villars had to commit part of his reserves. As Marlborough advanced his centre to occupy the French central position, to launch his main assault through the newly-won ground in the customary way, Villars was struck in the knee by a musket-ball. Like Eugene, who had earlier been grazed behind the ear, Villars refused to leave his post, but fainted with pain and was carried away. Command of the French army passed to the duc de Boufflers, the courageous defender of Lille who had, despite his superior rank, placed himself under Villars' orders.

Worthy Resistance

Boufflers handled the remainder of the battle with great skill and exceptional bravery, following Villars' plan and counter-attacking in the centre. Leading the *Maison du Roi*, the French Household Cavalry, Boufflers forced back the Allied cavalry in the centre six times, only to be halted on each occasion by the musketry of the British infantry, proving once again how vital was Marlborough's skill at arranging mutual support for his infantry and cavalry.

Despite the heroism of the French, weight of numbers finally began to count, and the French flanks began to retire under renewed pressure. Boufflers with some reluctance ordered the centre to retire with them, and capably organised an orderly withdrawal. He was not seriously harassed; the Allies were too exhausted to pursue, for it had been a Pyrrhic victory. Marlborough stated that never had he seen the French fight better, and as a French officer claimed of Marlborough and Eugene, 'till then they had not met with resistance worthy of them'.

All of the above accounts for the horrific scale of Allied casualties, perhaps as high as 25,000. Blunders in the Allied command, especially the Prince of Orange's Dutch attacks on the flank which were needlessly costly, were also responsible, though none of the blunders were Marlborough's. French losses may have been as low as 13,000.

Malplaquet was Marlborough's least successful victory, and is a tribute as much to the determination of Marlborough and Eugene for persevering after early setbacks, when others might have called off the

fight, as to any great tactical genius. For all the carnage, it achieved only limited success, allowing for the capture of Mons in October.

Rear of the Allied line at Malplaquet (after Dupray).

Final Eclipse

Following Marlborough's great successes, the campaigns of 1710–11 were inconclusive, with no great battle to tip the balance one way or the other. The French constructed a new and stronger frontier-protection, sometimes termed the *Non Plus Ultra* or *Ne Plus Ultra* lines ('nothing further is possible'),[10] though in June 1710 the Allies captured Douai, and Béthune in August.

In April 1710, the Queen received Sarah for the last time, the Duchess' tetchy and imperious disposition having finally caused her to be supplanted in the Queen's affections by her new favourite, Mrs. Masham. It was a precursor to the end of Marlborough's career. His staunch friend Sidney Godolphin was cast aside after eight years of constant hard work, and in October the Tories gained a landslide in the election. Only pleading by Eugene and Godolphin himself prevented Marlborough from resigning at this point:

I suppose that I must every summer venture my life in battle, and be found fault with in the winter for not bringing home peace, though I wish for it with all my heart and soul'.[11]

In 1711, the eclipse was completed. Though the Queen said that she still intended to employ Marlborough's military talents, he was told not to seek any vote of thanks from Parliament, and the Queen demanded the return of Sarah's golden key of office. Not even Marlborough's humiliation – he begged the Queen on his knees to retain Sarah – could change her mind, so far had royal favour fallen from the Duke.

Bouchain and Bread

Yet the 1711 campaign (conducted without Eugene, who was protecting Frankfurt during the coronation of the new Emperor, Charles VI) included one last example of Marlborough's genius, in the complete out-manoeuvering of Villars to pierce the much-vaunted *Non Plus Ultra* lines, and the siege and capture of the fortress of Bouchain. This was a culmination of Marlborough's talent, but again no major battle ensued, Villars declining to fight as, possibly, did the Duke himself, perhaps fearing the political repercussions or sheer human misery of another carnage like Malplaquet.

The breaking of the lines and the capture of Bouchain may have been a triumph, but Marlborough's reward was scant. In late 1711 he was accused of 'financial irregularities' over the bread-contracts for the army and the payment of foreign auxiliaries. His political enemies had at last found the opportunity they had sought, for no matter how honest were Marlborough's explanations for his acquisition of the sum in question, the Queen was persuaded of his guilt and ordered his instant dismissal. (The amount involved was £63,319 3s. 7d. as perquisite from the bread contract, which Marlborough claimed was a traditional allowance to fund the secret service, and £282,366 as a 2½ per cent levy on the money paid to foreign troops.)[12] The letter the Queen wrote to her general, one-time friend and greatest servant was apparently so insulting that the Duke, rarely a hot-tempered man, pitched it straight into the fire.

The Last Years

Cast out by the land in whose service he had spent his life, Marlborough went abroad for a brief self-imposed exile, where he was fêted by his foreign allies. His enemies, French and domestic, were jubilant, and the war in Flanders ended with a revival of French fortunes and the recapture of some lost territory, now that Marlborough was no longer there to exercise his skill. The Treaty of Utrecht in 1713 brought peace to all except the Empire, which fought on for another year, and in 1714

George of Hanover succeeded to the British throne upon Queen Anne's death.

Marlborough's services were once more called upon, but though George treated him kindly he was never employed in anything but an administrative capacity. His final years were marked by failing health and personal sadness: his favourite daughter, Anne, died from tuberculosis in 1716, and Sarah's ill-temper (directed largely at their surviving daughters) marred their domestic harmony.

His old age is perhaps epitomised by the story of his standing before his portrait by Kneller, painted in his prime, and remarking sadly, 'That was once a man'. Suffering from a series of strokes, one of which permanently impaired his speech, he formally laid down his office of Captain-General and retired from public life in 1721. He died on 16 June 1722.

The Talents of 'Corporal John'

There is good reason to regard Marlborough as Britain's greatest general, and rank him among the 'great captains' of all time. He possessed every military talent – personally brave, an administrative genius, a strategist and tactician of the first rank, with imagination and flair in abundance. More than military skill, he exercised the greatest talent as a statesman, to win the support of foreign rulers, and though a lifelong intriguer, had little interest in the more devious paths of party politics. Brilliant though his campaigns were, they are only a shadow of what might have been achieved but for the constant obstruction of his allies. Throughout his career, he had to fight a threefold battle, military, diplomatic and political, and only in the last was he finally undone.

Perhaps his greatest effect was his demolition of the theory of passive campaigning. Yet although he restored the concept of offensive warfare, he was no hothead; as Wellington stated, he was 'remarkable for his clear, cool, steady understanding', and as Marlborough once remarked to Godolphin, it was patience which alone could overcome all things. In his offensive operations, every possible use was made of terrain and natural conditions such as the cover of darkness. Although his favoured tactical method was relatively simple – flank-attacks to divert enemy resources and then the drive through the centre – only at Malplaquet was any effective counter devised. Marlborough's insistence on platoon-firing, the shock action of the cavalry, correct siting of artillery and especially the co-ordination of all three ensured that the strategic plans would culminate in a successful battle. Although he had capable subordinate commanders, and the most cordial of relationships with his friend and colleague Eugene, it was his own skill which was paramount.

The Soldier's General

Above all, perhaps, it was the care he took of his men which gave them the unshakable faith in his leadership and raised their morale to overcome any difficulties, especially impressive when it is considered that the army was composed of so many nationalities. Marlborough's genius for administration ensured that they would be well-equipped, paid and fed. Yet their devotion to him – and their consequent outrage and disbelief upon news of his dismissal – was founded on more than mere material concern, as their affectionate nickname 'Corporal John' would seem to testify. As one of his officers, Robert Parker, remarked, it was impossible to appreciate the joy with which a glimpse of Marlborough was greeted unless one was actually part of the army, every man of which realised that no lives would be risked unless he was confident of success; and never was an action fought that did not result in victory.

Marlborough raised the British Army to a reputation higher than it had enjoyed at any time since the Hundred Years War; well might his men lament (to the tune of *Over the Hills and Far Away*):

> *Grenadiers, now change your song*
> *And talk no more of battles won.*
> *No victory shall grace us now,*
> *Since we have lost our Marlborough*[13]

If not in politics, on the field of battle Marlborough truly was the invincible general.

References

1 Fortescue, Hon. Sir J. *History of the British Army* Vol. I, London, 1899 p. 442 notes that 'the message and the handwriting both those of a man who is quite tired out'.

2 In conversation with Lord Galway; see, for example, Coxe, W., *Memoirs of the Duke of Marlborough* Vol. I, London, 1847 pp. 16–17.

3 See Coxe *op. cit.*, I p. 21; he had been in contact with William as early as May 1687.

4 Coxe *op. cit.*, I p. 22 notes that in this context it is common to find 'the most upright characters maligned, and the purest principles misrepresented'!

5 Lediard, T., *Life of John, Duke of Marlborough* London, 1736, Vol. I p. xx; comments in such vein were typical of the mid-eighteenth century!

6 The full text of this lengthy and generous letter is quoted in Coxe *op. cit.*, Vol. I p. 321.

7 The name is also given as 'Bingfield': e.g. see Coxe *op. cit.*, Vol. I p. 413.

8 Such at least is the construction made by Fortescue *op. cit.*, Vol. I p. 493!

9 The amount of correspondence which he undertook even when ill is evident from Coxe *op. cit.*, Vol. II pp. 266–67.

10 For the origin of this phrase, see (for example) Chandler, D.G., *Marlborough as Military Commander* London, 1973 p. 288.

11 See Fortescue, *op. cit.*, Vol. I p. 239, where there is particular (and justifiable) criticism of the 'party' machinations which brought about Marlborough's downfall.

12 Coxe *op. cit.*, Vol. 3 p. 278 provides this calculation in pounds sterling; it was actually paid in Dutch guilders.

13 Though probably contemporary with Marlborough's downfall, this was apparently first recounted in Donkin, R. *Military Collections and Remarks* (1777); see Winstock, L. *Songs and Music of the Redcoats* London, 1970 pp. 37–38.

Chronology of Events

Conflicting dates may be found in certain references due to the dual calendar of the earlier Julian and later Gregorian systems; at this period, dates were often given with the suffix O.S. or N.S. ('Old Style' or 'New Style'). Old Style was commonly used in Britain at this period, the difference in the seventeenth century being ten days, and eleven days from 1700. Thus, by British reckoning, the Battle of Blenheim was fought on 2 August 1704; but by Continental reckoning on 13 August. For convenience all dates here are rendered in New Style, which was used at times by Marlborough himself. A common convention in correspondence was to give a dual date on letters, e.g. 2/13th August; or for the date of Malplaquet '31st August/11th September'.

1650   c.5 JUNE Birth of John Churchill, son of Winston Churchill.

1672   23 JUNE Churchill promoted Captain in the Duke of York's Admiralty Regiment (commission dated 13 June 'old style').

1673   24 JUNE Churchill distinguished at the siege of Maastricht.

1674   16 JUNE Churchill present at Battle of Sinzeheim.

1674   4 OCTOBER Churchill present at Battle of Entzheim.

1677   SPRING (date unknown) Churchill married Sarah Jennings.

1682   15 MAY Shipwreck of the *Gloucester* in which Churchill narrowly escaped.

1685   6 JULY Churchill distinguished at the Battle of Sedgemoor.

1688   23 NOVEMBER Churchill deserted James II and joined William III.

1689   25 AUGUST Churchill, now Earl of Marlborough, distinguished at Battle of Walcourt.

1692   20 JANUARY Marlborough formally relieved of his posts and offices, nominally on charges of bribery and extortion.

1700   1 NOVEMBER Death of King Charles II of Spain, leading to the beginning of the War of the Spanish Succession.

1702   19 MARCH Death of King William III and succession of Queen Anne.

1702   15 MAY England declares war on France; Marlborough commander-in-chief of Anglo-Dutch forces.

1704   20 MAY Marlborough begins his march to the Danube.

1704   2 JULY Marlborough captures the Schellenberg Hill near Donauwörth.

1704   12 AUGUST Marlborough unites with Eugene's Imperial army.

1704   13 AUGUST Marlborough and Eugene defeat Tallard, Marsin and the Elector of Bavaria at Blenheim.

1706   23 MAY Marlborough defeats Villeroi at Ramillies.

1706   6 JUNE Marlborough captures Antwerp; 6 JULY Dunkirk; 22 AUGUST Menin; 5 SEPTEMBER Dendermonde; 4 OCTOBER Ath.

1708   11 JULY Marlborough and Eugene defeat Vendôme and Burgundy at Oudenarde.

1708   11 DECEMBER Marlborough and Eugene capture Lille.

1709   11 SEPTEMBER Marlborough and Eugene defeat Villars and Boufflers at Malplaquet.

1711   31 DECEMBER Marlborough recalled in disgrace and ceases active military career.

1713   11 APRIL Treaty of Utrecht ends the War of the Spanish Succession for all except the Empire, which fought on until the Treaties of Rastatt and Baden, 1714.

1714   1 AUGUST Death of Queen Anne and succession of George I.

1722   16 JUNE Death of Marlborough.

Frederick the Great
FOUNDER OF THE PRUSSIAN ELITE

Frederick the Great in the J.G. Glume portrait, which now hangs in Schloss Charlottenburg in Berlin. An orange sash partly covers the embroidered silver star of the senior Prussian award of the Order of the Black Eagle.

Standard of the Bayreuth Dragoons (Dragoon Regiment No. 5), one of the most famous regiments of Frederick's army. The black standard had silver centre, bearing a black eagle, which was gold trimmed (including crowned "FR" on the breast). With gold decorations and fringe, it bore the motto Pro Gloria Et Patria.

Boundaries of Prussia and the scene of Frederick the Great's campaigns.

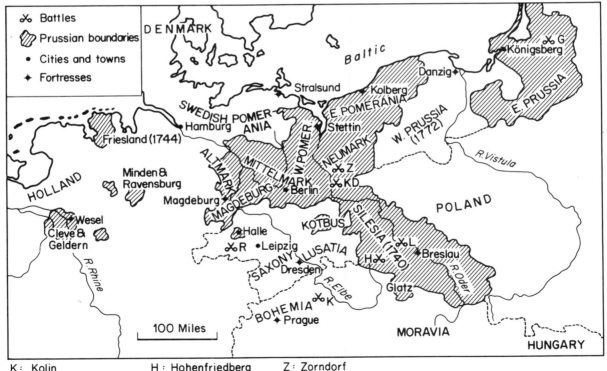

K: Kolin
KD: Kundersdorf
G: Gross-Jägersdorf

H: Hohenfriedberg
L: Leuthen
R: Rossbach

Z: Zorndorf

With troops like these, the world itself might be subdued . . . let them be well supplied with provisions and you might attempt anything with them.

Frederick the Great on the Prussian Army

The Great Captain

Frederick the Great's place in history stems in part from his almost unique position as a 'great captain', and also as the ruler of an important state with power totally and unchallengeably concentrated in his hands. In the immediate aftermath of the Seven Years War, the triumph of Prussia against quite incredible odds, and its resilience despite circumstances which would have crushed most states, Frederick assumed the rôle of hero not only amongst his own people but to the world at large. Even his opponents could not fail to be impressed by his military skill, courage in the face of adversity and, to not necessarily a lesser degree, by his appearance as the *beau idéal* of an 'enlightened' monarch, even though he had been the cause of such slaughter and misery.

Frederick might well be regarded as the founder of Prussian militarism, continuing the work of his father (who probably deserves the title more). Nevertheless, it was Frederick's campaigns which assured the prominence of the Prussian state, consolidating its position as a great power. The survival of Prussia during the Seven Years War provided posterity with a rôle-model for Prussian discipline, courage and fortitude which lasted until the present century. It inspired future generations of German warriors, and especially the reawakened German nationalism from 1813. An upsurge of interest in Frederickian history, lore and legend from the middle of the nineteenth century was fuelled by a number of influential biographies and histories and the publication of Frederick's own work. Much of it might be romanticism which overlooked the mangled limbs and reeking battlefields of reality, but the effect was profound. Even as late as 1945, the miraculous salvation of Prussia was quoted as evidence that history might repeat itself; though no matter what his failings, it is manifestly unjust to associate Frederick with the ravings from the *Führerbunker*. Without Frederick, however, the Prussian militarist tradition would probably have been still-born; and modern history might have been unrecognisably different.

Brandenburg

In the closing days of October 1806, following his crushing defeat of the Prussian army at Jena and Auerstädt, the Emperor Napoleon paused in his pursuit of the shattered remnants to visit Potsdam. For ten minutes the French Emperor stood in silent homage over the tomb of Frederick, before resuming his advance to capture Berlin. His admiration notwithstanding, he took away with him the sword, sash and decorations of the King of Prussia in an act of posthumous revenge.

Until the middle of the seventeenth century, Brandenburg had been a small north-German electorate of modest pretensions, ruled by the family of Hohenzollern which originated from south-west Germany. Officially accorded the hereditary electorship in 1415, the family acquired additional territory by basically peaceful means: East Prussia in 1618 and Cleves, Mark and Ravensburg in 1666. The territory thus controlled by the Hohenzollerns was unadvantageously sited; Brandenburg in the middle, East Prussia on the Baltic coast separated from Brandenburg by Polish West Prussia, and the other enclaves in western Germany. The resources of these areas were limited and the inhabitants of the eastern territories were regarded by the rest of Germany as little better than barbarians. The lands had been devastated during the Thirty Years War, the armies of both sides ranging virtually unchecked, with the Hohenzollerns ultimately being compelled to ally with Sweden. The Elector George William (1597–1640) was an ineffectual ruler, and though he made peace with the Imperialists after the death of Gustavus Adolphus, no attempt was made to eject the Swedish forces. Not until the succession of his son, Frederick William, did the fortunes of the oppressed and backward state improve.

Army and Crown

Frederick William realised that further ravaging could only be prevented by making Brandenburg a leading military power, an awesome task given the state's lack of resources and the fact that it was occupied by a foreign army whose upkeep it was forced to undertake. Having persuaded the Swedes to leave by the payment of an indemnity, Frederick William set the state upon a firmer foundation, reorganising its finances and breaking the power of the noble assembly so that the Elector's will was absolute. His small army gained a formidable reputation which was confirmed by a decisive victory over the Swedes at Fehrbellin (18 June 1675). Thus, when he died in May 1688, Frederick William had fully deserved his sobriquet of 'the Great Elector'.

His successor, the Elector Frederick III, lived in some opulence and died on 25 February 1713 with considerable debts, but consolidated his father's achievements by reforming the army on modern lines, instigated largely by his general Prince Leopold I of Anhalt-Dessau, alias 'the Old Dessauer' (1676–1747). Frederick III had supported William of Orange in 1688, fought against the Turks and, more significantly, against the French in the War of the Spanish Succession under Marlborough. Yet his most tangible achievement was the acquisition of a crown in 1701, largely in return for military support of the Emperor against Louis XIV of France. Consequently, on 18 January 1701 he ceased to be Elector Frederick III of Brandenburg and became King Frederick I of Prussia, the name of the kingdom being taken from his most eastern province; officially the title was 'King *in* Prussia', to emphasize the fact that West Prussia, separating Brandenburg and East Prussia, still remained in Polish control. The acquisition of kingship had profound effects, giving his various subjects a common identity and allowing the birth of a degree of nationalism, of which the benefit was felt by his successors. Frederick I continued to expand his territory by peaceful means. The acquisition of the crown of Poland by the Elector of Saxony in 1697, requiring his conversion to Roman Catholicism, left Prussia as the unrivalled champion of Protestant Germany.

Emergence of Prussia

Frederick I was succeeded by his son, Frederick William I, whose own infant son, later Frederick the Great, thus became Crown Prince and heir to the dynasty. Frederick William I was totally opposite in character to his father, obsessed with military matters from youth and an austere man who despised all learning beyond that necessary to read military orders. Born in 1688, he spent much of his early life at the court of his grandfather, Elector Ernest Augustus of Hanover, and his taste for military affairs was deepened by acquaintance with Marlborough, Eugene and 'the Old Dessauer'. Immediately upon his accession in 1713, he transformed his father's court, dismissing all unnecessary officials and instituting an administration more in keeping with his frugal lifestyle. He was tolerant in religious matters (except in a hatred for Jesuits) and founded his actions upon Biblical teaching, though he was given to immoderate drinking and fits of uncontrollable fury. He remained faithful to his allegiance to the Emperor, assisting the Hapsburgs against France in the War of the Polish Succession (1734–35), but an improvement in Franco-Imperial relations led to estrangement between Prussia and Austria. His internal administration was splendid; not only were his father's debts discharged, but the state became prosperous and a full treasury was left for his successor, and equally important was his acquisition of Swedish Pomerania with its port of Stettin and a tough population which fitted in well with its new Prussian masters.

The economic strength of the state and the industries encouraged by Frederick William I not only made Prussia largely self-sufficient, but permitted the construction of a splendid army. As much as four-fifths of the annual revenue was spent on military affairs. Thus, upon Frederick

William's death, the 83,000 troops represented the fourth largest army in Europe, though the state was but thirteenth in population. The quality was equally impressive, though Frederick William's methods of recruitment were somewhat bizarre. Judging people primarily by their physical stature, his pride was his guard regiment of 'giant grenadiers', of whom the smallest was over six feet tall and the largest nearer eight feet. To recruit such immense men even kidnapping was employed, so that any unusually tall traveller in Europe became a target for forcible impressment. Even more eccentric was the King's acquisition of the 6th Dragoon regiment, which was taken from Saxon service in 1717, reputedly being swapped for a cabinet of fine porcelain – hence the regiment's nickname of *Porzellan-Regiment*!

Despite such eccentricities, the King's construction of the army was of far greater significance than any reforms instituted by his son, and it was Frederick William I's army which enabled Frederick the Great to wage war so successfully. Frederick William forged an especially close bond between monarchy and officer corps, established the first effective light cavalry and reformed a native-based armaments industry, patterns of weaponry remaining virtually unchanged throughout the century. In 1718, he made a deliberate break with the fashions and attitudes of French-influenced Europe, introducing a sober and restrained Prussian uniform more in keeping with his austere philosophy of life. Though this radically changed the appearance and attitudes of the Prussian army and state, it was also the cause of immense friction between the King and his heir, resulting in Frederick the Great enjoying a quite wretched early life.

Crown Prince

Frederick the Great was born on 24 January 1712, in the final stage of the reign of his grandfather; he became Crown Prince when barely a year old, when his father succeeded to the throne. His mother, whom Frederick William I had married in 1706, was Sophia Dorothea of Hanover, daughter of the future George I of England. Although stories exist of the child Frederick playing with his drum in preference to other toys, and despite the austere and militaristic atmosphere in which he was raised, it was obvious from his early years that he was the opposite of his father.

Among the strongest influences of his early life was that of his French governess, Madame de Rocouilles, who had tended Frederick William I in his childhood. As a result, the infant Frederick was raised with French manners, styles and education, and for the rest of his life Frederick spoke and wrote French as a first language. (When, for example, he wished to read the works of the philosopher Christian Wolff – whom Frederick William I had expelled, having little time for anything which resembled intellectualism – the books had to be translated into French before a German king could fully understand a German philosopher!)

Family Misery

Consequently, Frederick's preferences could not have been better chosen to arouse his father's ire. Frederick's only ally among his family was his elder sister Wilhelmine; his mother never expressed much affection and his other brothers and sisters (August William, Henry, Ferdinand, Ulrike and Amalie) were much younger. Wilhelmine alone took her brother's part against the oppression of their father, though 'oppression' is too mild a term for the King's conduct. Frederick delighted in French literature, poetry, elegant clothes and above all music, the playing of his flute remaining his chief amusement throughout his life. To the King, whose sole 'intellectual' exercise at this time was the so-called 'Tobacco Parliament' (a regular meeting of his army commanders to talk military affairs, smoke and drink), such French-style pastimes were effeminate and not calculated to produce a ruler of Prussia; he stated, 'Fred is a poet, a fiddler and will spoil all my labour'.[1]

To prevent this despoilation of what he regarded as Prussia's destiny, Frederick William behaved with what can only be described as barbarity. In 1728, by which time the King had already begun to humiliate Frederick in public and beat him with his cane in an attempt to knock out of him his artistic taste, Frederick William took his son on a state visit to Dresden, capital of Saxony-Poland, where the court of Augustus II was renowned for its immorality. A measure of the depravity of Dresden was the presence there of Countess Orzelska, Augustus' favourite mistress but also his illegitimate daughter. The young Frederick was somewhat smitten by the lady (who was herself in love with another of Augustus' illegitimates, and hence her half-brother), and to prevent the transference of the lady's favours Augustus made a bargain with the young Prussian prince: if he abandoned Orzelska, he could have instead a woman whom Augustus showed him reclining naked in one of the palace's reception-rooms. After a month in such decadence, Frederick William's austere tastes were thoroughly affronted and he dragged home the bemused Crown Prince.

Cruelty at Court

Frederick made an attempt to pacify his father, even joining the 'Tobacco Parliament' for drinking bouts (the highlight of which was sometimes that the King and his cronies pitched Baron Gundling, the King's intellectual adviser, into the moat; great hilarity once resulted when they forgot the weather and Gundling bounced on the ice). Into this crude society Frederick could never fit, and sought solace in his

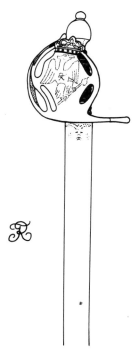

Prussian cuirassier broadsword of the 1732-pattern, its brass basket-hilt bearing the crowned eagle of Prussia with the cypher FR (Fredericius Rex) upon its breast.

103

French culture, his flute and the friendship of a few close associates. Such friendships, together with Frederick's dislike of female company and a loveless, childless marriage, raised questions of homosexuality. The matter is unresolved, though conceivably Frederick sought nothing more than a modicum of friendship from those of similar interests, as a contrast to the treatment he received from his father.

This treatment had now progressed from bullying to attacks of murderous ferocity, until finally after one severe beating and being dragged around the room by his hair, the King wrapped a curtain-rope around Frederick's neck and attempted to strangle him. A chamberlain dragged the King away; but this determined Frederick to flee. Aided by his closest friends, Lieutenants von Katte and Keith, he planned to slip abroad in disguise. But the scheme was discovered, Frederick was arrested, and the King only just restrained from killing him on the spot. Instead, Frederick was condemned to two years' imprisonment in the fortress of Cüstrin, deprived of books, paper, his flute and even a fork with which to eat his spartan food (though a kindly governor smuggled in enough to make the imprisonment bearable). The final cruelty was the beheading of von Katte under Frederick's window.

Apprenticeship

The execution of his close friend broke Frederick's spirit, and he begged his father's forgiveness and resolved to follow the King's wishes. The conditions of his imprisonment were relaxed, and he spent about fifteen months in Cüstrin undergoing a thorough tutoring in war, government and agriculture so as to fit him for kingship; gradually he began to win back his father's favour. But Frederick never forgot: when finally quitting Cüstrin he remarked on those who had taken his father's side in their quarrel, that one day 'I will heap burning coals upon their heads'.[2]

By 1732 Frederick had been 'reformed' to such an extent that the King gave him the colonelcy of a regiment. In the following year, he obeyed his father's will and married Princess Elizabeth Christina, daughter of the Duke of Brunswick-Bevern, a loveless marriage which brought Frederick neither happiness nor children; for much of his life he seemed to forget that his wife even existed. Frederick was given the estate of Rheinsberg, where he lived until he succeeded to the throne, and where he was free to devote some time to his own interests of literature and music.

Although much of his time was occupied by military matters, only in 1734 did he experience actual war, when he accompanied a Prussian contingent serving with the Imperial forces against the French, where Frederick created a great impression upon the veteran Eugene of Savoy. Eugene affirmed that Frederick showed all the intelligence, courage and skill to become the greatest soldier of his time, and this recommendation so impressed Frederick William that he appointed Frederick as

Major-General. (At this time Frederick made an unusual experiment, which almost caused physical damage, of trying to accustom himself to going without sleep and so double his 'active' life; despite constant draughts of coffee, he collapsed after four days!)

By the closing months of the life of Frederick William, Frederick had so rehabilitated his reputation that the King accepted him as a worthy successor:

Has not God been very kind to me in giving me so good and noble a son? [and, embracing the Crown Prince] My God! I die in peace, as I possess so worthy a son and successor![3]

Thus mellowed by age, Frederick William I died on 31 May 1740, and his eldest son became King Frederick II. He inherited not only the crown, but the army built by his father, which was to win Frederick his sobriquet: 'the Great'.

The metal-fronted Prussian grenadier mitre cap was one of the most distinctive items of equipment, each of Frederick's regimetns having a distinctive design to the brass or white-metal front. This brass-fronted cap (with yellow cloth rear and scarlet head-band) is in the design of infantry regiment No. 21, known by the name of its colonel (J.D. v. Hülsen 1756 to 1767; C.M. v. Schwerin to 1773; and Carl Wilhelm Ferdinand von Braunschweig thereafter).

'Enlightened Warfare'

At the start of Frederick's reign, the essential features of warfare in the mid-eighteenth century had changed little from the campaigns of Marlborough and Eugene. There remained, overall, the concept of 'limited

war' as befitted the philosophy of the Age of Enlightenment – that war should be conducted with the minimum of unpleasantness to all except those actually engaged; and whilst the process of actually hacking an enemy to pieces remained as terrible as it always had, it was expected to be achieved with 'honour'. To modern eyes this may appear a hideous paradox, yet it was a code which controlled the conduct of many armies in the mid-eighteenth century.

Frederick himself, who it might be argued was the cause of untold misery and the deaths of countless thousands, so vigorously objected to the death of individuals that on one occasion, he ordered one of his marksmen out of a ditch in order to prevent him lying in wait to kill an enemy soldier. Furthermore, Frederick himself was once saved when a French general refused to countenance his assassination by a sniper, though presumably he would quite willingly have seen him killed in a fair fight.

A change occurred gradually, however, when the concept of honour shifted from that of the individual to that of the state; patriotism began to predominate over the sense of honour emanating from a personal code of loyalty to the individual's good name. National partisanship to the Prussian state was largely responsible for the change. It now appears strange that the code of 'honourable war', by which civilians (especially women, children and the elderly) and personal property were regarded as inviolate, should co-exist with the appalling effusions of blood which occurred among the soldiery. And whilst atrocities still occurred, a degree of admiration cannot be suppressed for the gentlemanly way in which war was *supposed* to be waged. It is a concept, which, had its values remained unchanged, would have prevented many of the obscenities associated with twentieth-century wars.

Musket and Drill

By Frederick's accession military equipment had evolved little from the days of Marlborough. The gradual decline of the cavalry as the chief fighting force continued, with the infantry's importance increasing. The infantry weapon remained the smooth-bored flintlock musket, the

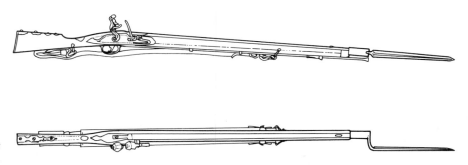

The Prussian infantry musket of Frederick the Great's army.

Frederick is cheered by the Anhalt-Bernburg regiment, which had just restored its reputation shortly after his criticism.

accuracy of which had not improved. However, the adoption of an iron ramrod was a considerable advance, ensuring that the infantryman would no longer be rendered harmless by the breaking of a wooden ramrod.

Greater importance was placed on drill, including the adoption of marching in step. This especially characterised the Prussian army and set the standard for an inculcation of discipline so rigidly enforced that the soldier would act almost as an automaton, sublimating the more natural reactions of panic and flight under fire.

Artillery continued to grow in importance, lighter carriages increasing mobility (including the advent of mobile horse artillery), though in Frederick's case the importance of artillery was recognised only grudgingly.

In organisational matters, perhaps the most influential figure was the French Marshal Maurice de Saxe (1696–1750), a natural son of Frederick Augustus I of Saxony, whose writing *Mes Rêveries* (published posthumously) contained much good sense and advice on 'modern' war. Saxe experimented with 'legions', corps of more than one 'arm' – combined forces of infantry, cavalry and artillery, which adumbrated the development of mixed divisions and semi-independent *corps d'armée*

107

capable of operating without support. Nevertheless, there still remained no universal system of army organisation in anything larger than a regiment. In fact, the previous tactical scheme remained: infantry aligned in one or two lines, cavalry on the flanks and artillery sited in advance of the front line (by necessity, as high-angle fire over the heads of friendly troops remained virtually impossible, despite the existence of howitzers capable of such fire).

Light Troops

A noted development was the increasing use of light troops, both cavalry and infantry, who instead of fighting in closely-packed masses were capable of operating in extended order, skirmishing, patrolling, raiding the enemy, covering advances and retreats. Much of this development came from Austria–Hungary, whose Balkan and Slavonic tribesmen, whilst too indisciplined to make ideal 'line' soldiers, could thus utilise their natural skills as hunters and bandits.

The Imperial Croats and Pandours formed the model for the light troops of other nations, who attempted to reproduce the natural skills of the Pandours in other ways. German armies, for example, found that foresters and huntsmen skilled at woodcraft made ideal *Jägers* or riflemen.

In the cavalry, light regiments were usually styled upon the Hungarian hussars, originally mounted tribesmen who made ideal light cavalry. So eager were other nations to emulate these wild individuals that it was usual for all hussars to wear a uniform which was a formalized version of Hungarian national dress – complete with tight breeches, fur caps and furred pelisses (over-jackets) – and to grow Hungarian-style moustaches and generally adopt the swaggering air, which characterised the original hussars.

The majority of such developments occurred before Frederick ever took the field as a commanding general, most of the progress in the Prussian army being inherited from his father; so Frederick saw little reason to change what already existed. Apart from disbanding his father's 'giant grenadiers', the army, its weaponry and even the uniforms remained largely unaltered throughout his reign. Frederick's developments were more in the manner in which the army manoeuvered. It was in the two Silesian wars – early stages of the War of the Austrian Succession – that he gained the necessary experience to enable him to win such fame in the later Seven Years War.

Prussian grenadiers' sabre with brass hilt and slightly-curved blade bearing an engraved crown and Frederick's cypher FR.

First Silesian War

By the nature of his position, Frederick enjoyed an advantage over

108

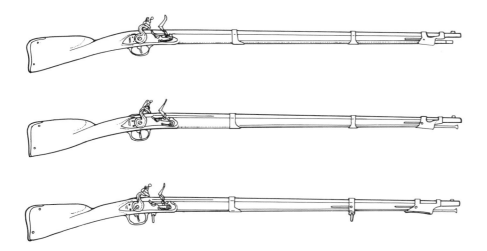

French infantry muskets used in the period of the wars against Frederick the Great: (top) 1728-pattern (middle) 1746-pattern; (lower), 1754-pattern (note the addition of sling-swivels on the latter).

other generals, which might be described as 'unity of command'. In other words, as head of state, reigning monarch and commander–in–chief, his will was absolute and unchallenged. The term 'enlightened absolutism' might be used to describe those of Frederick's ilk: monarchs who whilst exercising total authority regarded themselves as protectors of their subjects and put their responsibility to their subjects above everything. That, at least, was the ideal of the philosopher–king.

The first months of Frederick's reign seemed to demonstrate such an idea, as he relaxed the more brutal aspects of his father's regime; but shortly after his accession he plunged Prussia into war. The fact that he was the architect of much of this conflict little affected public perception of him as the ideal enlightened monarch. His extensive use of mercenaries was regarded as evidence of his wish to shield his own people from the worst effects of war. No matter how bitterly his campaigns were waged, he always regarded his opposing sovereigns as his brothers or sisters, members of the wider 'family' of annointed royalty irrespective of nationality. Admirable though these sentiments were, it is perhaps unfortunate that similar consideration was not given to the many thousands whose lives were taken or ruined in pursuit of his foreign policy.

Frederick's first campaign precipitated the War of the Austrian Succession (1740–48). The death of the Emperor Charles VI in October 1740 and the accession as Empress of his daughter Maria Theresa caused the rival claimants to dispute the succession – Philip V of Spain, Augustus III of Saxony and Charles Albert of Bavaria; they supported the idea of male heirs only. Frederick recognised the right of Maria Theresa to the throne, and offered his support against her rivals, but announced that in return he would occupy Silesia until an old Brandenburg claim to the territory was resolved. Although an Austrian province, Silesia would be a

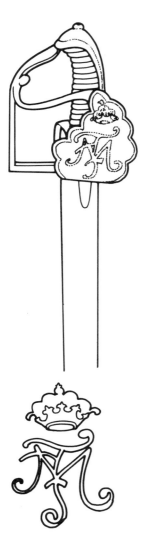

Austrian cavalry broadsword, with a semi-basket hilt bearing the cypher of Maria Theresa – in this case with the addition of the letter J for her son, Joseph, who became co-regent in 1765.

valuable addition to the Prussian state: 14,000 square miles with a population of 1,500,000, many of who were German Protestants, with a well-developed trading and industrial base. Its union with Prussia (at that time numbering only about 2,500,000 people) would have immediately increased the importance and resources of Frederick's state, which was justification enough for him to invade (the Brandenburg claim was actually tenuous in the extreme). For Prussia to attempt to seize part of the Empire might appear absurd, but Frederick's army was in a state of immediate readiness (thanks to the efforts of his father) and his treasury was full; and Austria was correspondingly unprepared.

On 16 December 1740 Frederick marched into Silesia at the head of some 27,000 troops, which by general consent were among the best-drilled and best-equipped in Europe. Meeting little opposition, Frederick consolidated his hold on the province and besieged the towns holding Austrian garrisons, primarily Neisse and Glogau. Putting his army into winter quarters, Frederick maintained the sieges and on 9 March 1741 Prince Leopold Max of Anhalt-Dessau, son of 'the Old Dessauer', captured Glogau by escalade. By the beginning of April, however, the initiative had swung towards the Imperial camp, as Field Marshal Adam Neipperg invaded Silesia with the army he had gathered in Moravia. Neipperg not only relieved Neisse, but also cut off Frederick's main army from his route to Prussia. It was a dangerous position, resulting partly from the lack of flexibility of the perhaps over-drilled Prussian army, and partly from Frederick's bowing to the advice of his senior commander, Kurt Christophe von Schwerin (1684–1757), a native of Swedish Pomerania who had served in the Dutch and Swedish forces before entering Prussian service in 1720. A gourmet who indulged in a somewhat lavish lifestyle, Schwerin was Frederick's military tutor at this early stage of his career. He was a brave and pious disciplinarian whose influence on the Prussian army had been beneficial; but in this instance he erred in allowing Neipperg to take and maintain the initiative. To stabilize the situation, a pitched battle had to be fought.

The Lesson of Mollwitz

On 10 April 1741, Frederick and Schwerin commanded about 21,600 troops against 19,000 Austrians at Mollwitz. Their slow deployment from column of march prevented any surprise, and though outnumbered, the Austrian superiority in cavalry almost immediately drove Frederick's right wing from the field in confusion. The fighting became intense and as the Prussian infantry milled around in confusion, Schwerin feared the worst and persuaded Frederick to quit the battlefield. Frederick, alarmed at his first pitched battle and the prospect of defeat, probably needed little persuasion and galloped away, almost being captured by Austrian hussars in the gathering dusk. He was considerably despondent until receiving a message from Schwerin. This announced not the expected defeat, but the fact that the magnificently-disciplined Prussian infantry had held firm and under Schwerin's direction had pushed the Austrians out of Mollwitz. This, Frederick's first victory had been achieved by Schwerin, for which, some said, Frederick never forgave him! Although his losses had exceeded those of the Austrians, the strategic situation had been saved; defeat would not only have restored Silesia to Imperial control but would have captured Frederick and his entire army. Frederick acknowledged three errors he had made: allowing the Austrians to catch him unprepared; permitting them to cut off his line of retreat and thus force him to fight when he had no wish to; and making heavy weather of his battlefield deployment. He determined never again to be caught thus.

Maria Theresa

Although Frederick's army remained unengaged after Mollwitz, the war widened alarmingly as Bavaria (with French military support), Saxony and Savoy entered the war against Austria, whereupon Britain and Holland declared their support for Maria Theresa; and Sweden, ostensibly supporting Prussia but influenced by France, took the opportunity to attack Russia which had also supported Maria Theresa's claim.

Frederick continued to rely upon his father's generals, notably 'the Old Dessauer' and his sons, the princes Leopold Max, Dietrich and Moritz. (Moritz, though, was a difficult subordinate, having grown up entirely uneducated – an experiment of his father's to see what would happen! – and almost totally illiterate.) However, a new generation of commanders was beginning to emerge, especially Frederick's hussar general, Hans Joachim von Zieten, an unimposing middle-aged officer from the lower gentry. Zieten's skill in light cavalry tactics was such that his hussars led the way for the total regeneration of the Prussian cavalry, which had been neglected in favour of the infantry.

By October 1741 Frederick's hold on Silesia was consolidated, and faced with mass opposition Austria acceded to the secret Truce of Klein Schellendorf, by which Frederick was left in control of Silesia in return for a cessation of hostilities. However, by December Maria Theresa was sufficiently confident of defeating her enemies that she revealed the terms of the Truce to embarrass Frederick, compelling him to resume the war or lose his anti-Imperial allies. Frederick immediately marched into Bohemia to co-operate with Franco-Bavarian forces, but an Austrian invasion of Bavaria forced the troops of that state to withdraw, which as the French were not strong left Frederick virtually isolated. Despite sending his vanguard of hussars ranging to the outskirts of Vienna, Frederick was compelled to withdraw to protect his communications, pursued by the Austrian army of Prince Charles of Lorraine.

Zeiten shown in his 'dress' uniform.

Manoeuvre at Chotusitz

On 17 May 1742, Frederick and Leopold Max of Anhalt–Dessau encountered Charles' superior Austrian force at the village of Chotusitz. Initially, the Prussian cavalry overthrew the Austrian left wing, but pausing to rally were themselves over-ridden by a counter-attack, and the Prussian right wing disintegrated. Frederick, commanding the Prussian right-centre infantry, kept them inactive whilst Leopold vainly attempted to cling on to the village of Chotusitz with his own wing of the Prussian army. Fighting in the village was intense and confused, the Prussian defence being led by the field–clergyman Seegebart, until Austrian pressure became insupportable and Leopold evacuated the village to reorganise his shattered troops. By now it was about 10.30 a.m., and Frederick put his own infantry into motion, having had them concealed in a hollow. As he manoeuvred unexpectedly against the Austrian flank around Chotusitz, the Imperial troops recognised the threat to their line of retreat and began to withdraw. Under pressure from Frederick's superb infantry the battle was over by 11 a.m., with the Austrians in near rout. Although Frederick's cavalry had behaved better than previously, they were still disordered. Pursuit with infantry alone would be fraught with hazard, so the Austrians were permitted to escape and were able to reform their forces within a few days.

The Prize of Silesia

Chotusitz brought to an end Prussian participation in the early part of the War of the Austrian Succession. Both Frederick and Maria Theresa were anxious for an accommodation. Frederick mistrusted his allies and fearing that a separate peace might leave Prussia isolated, he believed that he had done enough for the coalition. For her part, Maria Theresa, having seen her attempt to reoccupy Silesia end in defeat, had more important enemies to fight. By the Treaty of Breslau on 11 June 1742, Silesia was ceded to Prussia in return for Prussia's cessation of hostilities, though undoubtedly Austria intended to again attempt its re-conquest when the situation was more auspicious. Partly by good fortune as well as his own skills and his developments in his forces, Frederick's first war had ended with his aims achieved and the Prussian state strengthened both in territory and prestige.

Second Silesian War

During Prussia's absence from the war, Austria and her allies made very considerable progress against Frederick's erstwhile friends. By August 1744, Frederick had become greatly concerned at the triumph of Maria Theresa. Realising that she still intended to re-take Silesia, Frederick concluded an alliance with Louis XV of France and again took the offensive against Austria, advancing into Bohemia with some 71,000 men.

Bohemian Fiasco

Three Prussian columns, the largest under Frederick and the others led by Schwerin and Leopold Max of Anhalt-Dessau, converged on the Bohemian capital of Prague which surrendered on 16 September 1744. Frederick wished to bring about a major battle, in which he was confident of success, but unwisely allowed himself to be influenced by his French and Bavarian allies, who preferred that he ranged through Bohemia, reducing the many small garrisons. Frederick learned that Saxony had allied its forces with those of Austria, and that the combined army was advancing, so in his inexperience presumed that the battle he sought would result. It did not: instead, he was outmanoeuvered by the old Austrian Marshal Otto von Traun. With his communications threatened and as winter drew on, Frederick had to quit Bohemia with his army ravaged by desertion and deprivation; perhaps as many as 17,000 of his troops deserted to the Austrians, and it is possible that as few as 18,000 fit men were left at the end of the campaign, once dysentery had run its terrible course through the army.

This campaign, Frederick's first reverse, had a profound effect upon him. No longer over-confident, his military skill was being acquired by bitter experience, though his principal aim remained to bring about a pitched battle, in which he was confident that his magnificent infantry would win no matter what the odds.

In January 1745 a 'Quadruple Alliance' was formed officially between Austria, Britain, Saxony and Holland against France, Prussia and Bavaria. Furthermore, the Treaty of Füssen in April 1745, which made peace between Maria Theresa and the Elector of Bavaria, left Frederick virtually on his own, for his remaining French allies seemed uninterested in collaboration and pressed the war only in Flanders. The situation was inauspicious, especially as the treasury Frederick had inherited from his father was almost exhausted. Nevertheless, he was able to keep his army in the field by loans, though a major success was needed badly.

Hohenfriedberg

Success came in early summer, when Frederick rejoined his army after spending the winter at home; in March he had laid the foundation-stone for his new house near Potsdam, which was to become the famous Sans-Souci, probably the only place apart from his army's encampment where Frederick felt truly comfortable. Opposing Frederick's 59,000 men was Prince Charles' Austro–Saxon army of about equal size, and though it was the Austrians who took the initiative, on this occasion it was they who were outmanoeuvered. Frederick

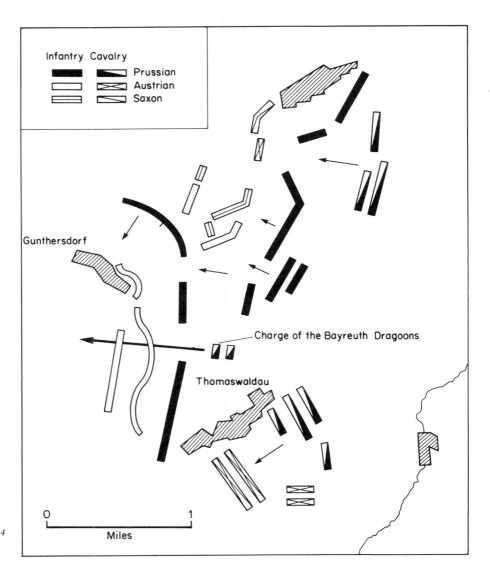

Legend:
Infantry Cavalry
Prussian
Austrian
Saxon

Gunthersdorf

Charge of the Bayreuth Dragoons

Thomaswaldau

0 — 1
Miles

Battle of Hohenfriedberg, 4 June 1745.

kept his main force as concentrated as the logistics of eighteenth-century warfare permitted (some dispersal was always necessary to provide horses' fodder, for example), and succeeded in concealing his location from the Austrians by judicious use of the terrain. Prince Charles thus camped near Hohenfriedberg on the evening of 3 June without realising that Frederick's whole army was within easy striking distance.

Frederick put his army into motion in the early hours of 4 June 1745, concentrating his first attack upon the Saxon wing of the combined army. Surprised and assailed by half Frederick's army coming out of the dawn, the Saxons made a stout resistance but were routed amid great slaughter, so that by about 7 a.m., a third of the allied army had been crushed. Now Frederick turned upon the Austrians, who were in motion but too late to help their allies; and in the classic way of 'defeat in detail', Frederick beat them in turn, despite a brave stand by the Austrian infantry after the cavalry had been overwhelmed. The final blow was struck by the Bayreuth Dragoons, the most celebrated of Frederick's cavalry. They made an impromptu charge, which destroyed what cohesion the Austrians had left, so that only three Austrian regiments remained to cover the flight of the rest. By 9 a.m., the fight was over, and a victory of major proportions achieved by the growing skill of the Prussian king and by the superb discipline of the Prussian troops, which was becoming legendary even among their enemies. The discipline that Frederick instilled was to characterise Prussian – and later German – armies for the next two centuries.

Hohenfriedberg was probably the most decisive battle of the war; after Frederick's aggressive pursuit with half his army (the remainder being left to mop up Austrian irregulars), Prince Charles was unwilling to risk another pitched battle.

Soor

Frederick conducted some months' inconclusive manoeuvering along the upper Elbe in north-eastern Bohemia, but then began to withdraw towards Silesia, followed by the Austrians. The latter were emboldened by the Prussian withdrawal, and Frederick's reconnaissance was again at fault. Thus, he was considerably surprised when on 30 September 1745 some 39,000 Austrians under Prince Charles approached Frederick's 22,000 at Soor.

Forced to fight to protect his communications, Frederick swung his army into the attack upon the Austrian left, the Prussian cavalry pushing back the Austrians. As the Prussian right advanced, the left and centre (intended as a reserve) assailed the Austrians in their front. The fighting was confused and, as Frederick admitted, was the most severe he had witnessed, but by noon the Austrians were in full retreat.

The victory of Soor was testimony to the excellence now attained by the whole army: their speed of reaction to the first surprise had been amazing, and the resolution they showed in storming the slopes of the Austrian position in the teeth of heavy fire confirmed the excellence of their discipline and morale.

Confirmation by Treaty

Believing that Soor had ended the war, Frederick left for Berlin; but late in the year learned that an Austro-Saxon force was attempting to invade Prussia itself. One advance was out-manoeuvred by Frederick and withdrew after the tireless Zieten's advance-guard of hussars defeated a Saxon force at Katholisch-Hennersdorf on 23 November. On 14 December, the second enemy advance was defeated decisively by 'the Old Dessauer' at the head of the Prussian army from the Elbe, at Kesselsdorf. This finally broke the Austrian resolve, and on 25 December 1745 the war was ended by the Treaty of Dresden, by which Silesia was finally recognised by Austria as a Prussian possession, whilst in return Frederick recognised Maria Theresa's husband as Emperor. The Treaty of Aix-la-Chapelle which ended the War of the Austrian Succession in October 1748 confirmed Frederick's right of possession.

Frederick and his Army

The conclusion of the Second Silesian War established Frederick as the leading military personality in Europe, a position he was to hold for the remainder of his life, and he came to be almost worshipped by those who approved of his aims and mien. He was, however, a most un-prepossessing figure – once the plump and comfortable-looking Crown Prince had given way by 1745 to a lined, weatherbeaten and almost emaciated veteran of only 33 years of age.

The Man

Frederick remained throughout a strange paradox. In the field, he shared without complaint the worst privations of the army, and appeared to relish the world of camp-fires, marches and combat, being nowhere as happy as when surrounded by his ordinary soldiers. Conversely, when away from the army he was a genuine intellectual of great mental capability, not a dilettante like so many examples of eighteenth-century 'enlightenment', who paid only lip-service to the philosophy of the time. His palace of Sans-Souci was a gem of good taste, where he could relax, write and converse (on equal terms with so eminent a personality as Voltaire), play his beloved flute, and conduct the business of the state. His work rate was prodigious, beginning at daybreak and toiling until noon; the afternoon was spent in study and music (though he admitted that even when composing for the flute his mind was often working on affairs of state); and the evening ended with a final bout of official correspondence. Retiring at about 10 p.m., he was awake for the next day's routine at four in the morning.

In appearance and lifestyle, Frederick was the antithesis of the typical eighteenth-century monarch. Although a dandy in his youth, as an adult he was renowned for the disgusting state of his clothes, surroundings and personal hygiene. Usually wearing a plain military coat, he sometimes went to bed without even removing his boots. Indeed, the story that he had no wardrobe or spare clothes, but carried on his back all he possessed is perhaps not very exaggerated. Frederick's lunches were an ordeal for his guests; the food was so hotly-seasoned as to be scarcely edible by normal palates, the conversation was usually a diatribe by the King into which little could be interposed, and his table-manners were revolting.

With Frederick's pet greyhounds allowed to foul the royal apartments unchecked, the contrast between his court and those of the other European sovereigns could hardly have been greater. Frederick was an unimpressive figure, about five-feet eight-inches tall, round-shouldered and with his head permanently inclined to the right (from so much flute-playing!), which together with his shabby and even disreputable appearance caused him to be mistaken; in one case a French prisoner-of-war addressed him as 'corporal'!

He had no home life, for his Queen was a stranger; she never once visited his palace of Sans Souci, and on the rare occasions Frederick dined with her in her own palace in Berlin, although he treated her with scrupulous courtesy, they never conversed.

Frederick retained the friendship of certain military favourites, but fell out completely with his hero Voltaire, using the philosopher as a sounding-board for his own ideas ('we squeeze the orange and then throw away the peel').[4] He even caused Voltaire's *History of Doctor Akakia* to be burned by the public hangman under the author's nose. Voltaire responded by speading scurrilous gossip about the king. Such soured relationships, and the genuine distress Frederick experienced when seeing the physical effects of warfare, caused him to write of the human condition: 'We run through the world to perform our bloody tragedies as often as our enemies permit us . . . We, poor fools, who have but a moment to live, render that brief space as mutually distressing as we can, and find pleasure in the destruction of every masterpiece which time and labour have produced, leaving behind us nothing but so many memorials of the havoc, desolation and misery which we have wittingly occasioned'.[5] Perhaps for more than one reason Frederick carried a little gold box upon a ribbon around his neck, containing a lethal dose of opium to end the 'tragedy' of his life.

The General

Despite his artistic capabilities, his most effective rôle was as a general. He was personally brave, frequently exposing himself to enemy fire to stiffen the morale of his men. He was a tireless rider, but with a somewhat eccentric style of equitation. He wore no spurs, but urged his horses by hitting them between the ears with a stick; and sometimes he fell off when concentrating upon other matters.

Short sight hindered him in the field, but what was never lacking was his rapport with his men, which resembled that attained by Napoleon. His men might regard him (as one said) as 'God in a blue coat', but they also called him 'Old Fritz' and spoke to him with a freedom which belies the stereotyped perception of the iron-disciplined Prussian regime. In camp, Frederick shared the bivouacs of his men and sat around their camp-fires; he talked to them in their rough German (instead of the French which he regarded as his first, civilized tongue), and shared their jokes. He gave his handkerchief to wounded men to bandage their injuries; he cajoled them and behaved like a father when he had to reprimand them, such as the famous incident when he questioned a deserter who admitted to running away because things looked black: 'Come, come', said Frederick, 'let us fight another battle today; if I am beaten, we will desert together tomorrow'.[6] When on one occasion he strayed into the line of fire, his infantry called: 'Get out of the way, Father, we want to shoot!'

This rapport with his men was the essence of Frederick's leadership; how much of it was genuine, however, is debatable. It was necessary to acquire their support as Frederick admitted: 'Prussians, I have ventured on the present war with no other allies to sustain me than your gallantry and devotion'.[7] The 'friendship and confidence of the private soldier', he noted, 'may prove of the highest advantage',[8] to achieve which one should become an actor, always concealing one's true feelings, he wrote. As to the soldier's welfare, it was necessary to keep them happy, but 'there is no necessity for attending to a soldier's grumblings, who is naturally never content'.[9] His real feelings for his troops are difficult to determine; he admired their bravery, but had limited sympathy once their usefulness was over. Invalids from the Prussian army were given scant regard, foreigners being expelled from Prussia and natives being granted a beggar's licence. A lucky few received a pittance, and when in a good mood Frederick might throw them a coin, but on other occasions would order his guards to 'Drive away those scum'. Whatever the true case, such cavalier treatment of those who had bled for him might raise the question as to whether his rapport with his troops was nothing more than an opportunist sham.

Frederick expressed the belief that a general should 'dissimulate', to conceal his true thoughts. Certainly, he hid his own gloomy outlook, which unlike that of his father was not sustained by any very deep religious belief. One attitude to religion is evident from his instructions to his officers: 'If we are in a protestant country, we wear the mask of the protector of the Lutheran religion, and endeavour to make fanatics of the lower order of people, whose simplicity is not proof against our artifice. In a catholic country, we preach up toleration and moderation, constantly abusing the priests as the cause of all the animosity that exists between the different sectaries . . .'.[10]

Whatever his failings, Frederick's military skill made him a consummate general, though it must be admitted that he profited greatly from his father's legacy. His subordinates were a mixed bag, some greatly skilled and others inept (one general was nicknamed 'the anvil' because he was beaten so often!), and though Frederick discovered generals of great talent – the hussar Zieten and the redoubtable Seydlitz are examples – he was fortunate in having relatives upon whom to lean, and his service also attracted very many princes from the other Protestant German states. Frederick's brother-in-law (a prince of Brunswick) was killed at Hochkirch, as were two Margraves of the royal house of Brandenburg, and all three of his younger brothers served as generals, of whom Prince Henry was the most successful. His brother August William was summarily dismissed and humiliated for incompetence and died a broken man the following year, believing that Frederick had used him as a scapegoat for his own failings. Not even his kin could escape Frederick's wrath if he felt it justified.

In the officer corps Frederick insisted upon as much discipline as among the ordinary soldiers, but this restriction was offset by the inculcation of fellow-feeling between the King and all commissioned ranks. No rank-distinction existed in officers' uniform, so that the lowliest lieutenant could pride himself on wearing the same coat as his monarch (though generally cleaner than Frederick's own coat!). The personal bond which thus existed between him and his officers was of the greatest significance. Nevertheless, Frederick wished the officer corps to be largely a noble organisation; middle-class officers had limited chance of advancement and were sometimes dismissed for no more reason than their lowly birth. Unjust though this appears, Frederick himself was arbiter of what constituted 'nobility' and could create nobles by granting deserving men the privilege of putting 'von' before their name. Thus, an ordinary musketeer was ennobled for heroism at Prague in 1744.

Like his father, Frederick seems to have distrusted educated officers, resulting in a lack of intellectual expression within the army; Moritz of Dessau was far from unique in being almost totally illiterate among the higher command. Though Frederick actively discouraged officers from writing (even of military treatises), fortunately there remained a core of intellectuals within the army, including the celebrated poet Ewald von Kleist (killed at Kunersdorf), and Field-Marshal Keith, a great linguist.

Literary Accomplishments

In contrast, but only to be expected of a philosopher-king, Frederick's own creative urge produced a vast outpouring of writings and musical compositions of considerable talent. The writing encompassed history, philosophy and poetry, but the most influential were his military writings, originally published for the guidance of his officers.

The first two major works were *Instructions* for commanders of infantry and cavalry (1748), of which lieutenant-generals received a copy of each but major-generals only that applicable to their own branch of service. The works were treated as secret documents, and not until sets were captured in 1760 did they receive wider circulation; within a short time translations were freely available throughout Europe.

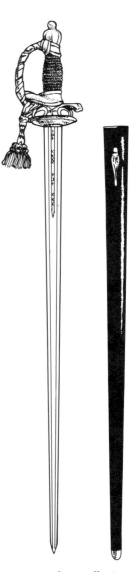

Prussian infantry officer's or general's sword (Degen) of the Frederickian period, with gilded hilt and the characteristic silver lace sword-knot with interwoven black thread, including black zigzags on the 'bell' of the tassel.

These books, together with the 1753 work *General Principles of War* (updated as *Elements of Fortification and Tactics* in 1771), distilled Frederick's military thought and remained popular even after the Napoleonic Wars had brought about a supersession of classic 'Frederickian' warfare. A new edition was published in Britain in 1818, for example. However, though Frederick's *Instructions* reveal many of his methods and military philosophies, they did not cover the workings of the army as a whole, being more concerned with the management of detachments. The result, perhaps deliberately on Frederick's part, was to restrict or discourage the initiative of his subordinates.

Frederick's *Instructions* emphasized the merits of 'limited war' in the enlightened style: 'terminate every business prudently and quickly . . . it is better one man perish than a whole people',[11] and never cause death needlessly: 'to what end serves the art of conquest, if we are ignorant how to profit by our advantage? To shed the blood of soldiers when there is no occasion for it, is to lead them inhumanly to the slaughter'.[12] Nevertheless, Frederick was not so gentlemanly as to act against his own best interests: when requisitioning provisions: 'we are justified in not being over nice with respect to the peasantry',[13] and his method of sending spies into the enemy camp appears barbaric: 'We find out a rich citizen who has a large family' to be used as a spy; 'he is to be threatened also at the same time, that if he does not return after a certain period . . . his house shall be burned, and his wife and children hacked in pieces. I was obliged to have recourse to this scheme . . . and it succeeded to my wish'.[14] Similarly, a guide 'may also every now and then be threatened to have his brains blown out if he dares to conduct the detachment into the hands of the enemy'.[15] Nevertheless, he stressed that 'the true point of honour alone may prove the foundation' of an officer's fortune, and that 'he should therefore regard it as the main-spring of all his actions';[16] that an officer 'should possess an equal share of sobriety and reserve';[17] and 'That man certainly deserved to be well rewarded, who risks his neck to do you service'.[18] Unfortunately, he did not generally follow his own advice in the latter regard.

Mercenaries
Frederick continued his father's policy of recruiting a large number of foreigners into the Prussian army, whom he regarded as mercenaries to be expended before risking the lives of his native-born subjects. More than a third of his army were foreigners, and though half of these might be expected to desert at the first opportunity, savage discipline held them together, and the policy enabled a state of such small population as Prussia to maintain so large an army. The enlisting of prisoners of war was a particularly unsuccessful method of recruiting, but was used extensively.

As many as a sixth of the generals were foreign, including Huguenot

Frederick and his dragoons on the march: 'Straight on children, straight on'. 'Straight on, Fritz, straight on', replied his men.

French (such as Frederick's great friend La Motte Fouqué), many from smaller German states, Russians and even Austrians. Among the most eccentric must have been Charles Guichard, alias Quintus Icilius (named after a Roman centurion) and Scipio von Lentulus, who actually claimed descent from ancient Roman nobility. Such foreign soldiers lacked Prussian national fervour, but were not necessarily any less soldiers from their inability to speak German. Perhaps the most famous Frederickian anecdote arises from this fact, concerning Frederick's three standard questions when interviewing troops:

'How old are you?'

'How long have you been in my service?'

'Are you satisfied with pay and conditions?'

One young French soldier, unable to understand the German which Frederick spoke to the common soldiers, was drilled by his officer to give the appropriate answers parrot-wise; but when Frederick *did* speak to him, for the first time ever he varied the order of his questions. Thus:

'How long have you been in my service?'

'Twenty-one years.'

'What? Well, how old are you?'

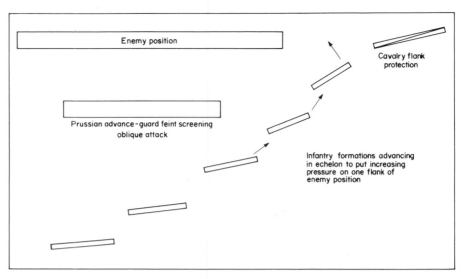

Enemy position

Cavalry flank protection

Prussian advance-guard feint screening oblique attack

Infantry formations advancing in echelon to put increasing pressure on one flank of enemy position

Diagramatic depiction of the 'oblique order' of attack.

'One year.'

'You or I must certainly be bereft of our senses.' To this, thinking it was the usual third question, the recruit replied, 'Both, an't please your majesty'.

'This is the first time I ever was treated as a madman at the head of my army', rejoined Frederick. It is reported that he was greatly amused, however, when the matter was explained to him![19]

Discipline of Command

The excellence of the Prussian army depended upon discipline. This was enforced brutally, ranging from beatings by officers and N.C.O.s to imprisonment, branding, hanging or running the gauntlet, a systemised beating under which men could die. Desertion was ever the bane of Frederick's army. As he admitted, the foreigners 'only wait for a favourable opportunity to quit a service to which they have no particular attachment'.[20] Thus, strict discipline was necessary to hold them in the ranks as well as to produce an army which would manoeuvre and fire as if on parade – even under the slaughterhouse conditions of combat. Even on the weariest of marches Frederick insisted upon the maintenance of order: 'Exact, children, exact' he would call to them; they would reply: '*Exactly*, Fritz'.[21]

A British traveller remarked that the discipline 'on a general view is beautiful: in detail it is shocking'.[22] Yet with so much of Frederick's army not susceptible to the call of patriotic feeling, it was a necessity. Interestingly, though, under Seydlitz's influence, corporal punishment was virtually eliminated in the cavalry.

Battlefield Tactics

Frederick's infantry continued to fight in the style of his father's reign, manoeuvering in closely-packed battalions, marching in column but fighting in line, when all muskets could be brought to bear. The Marlburian 'rolling volley' – the platoons comprising a line firing in succession, rather than different ranks firing simultaneously along the whole line – was copied by the Prussian army.

What was innovative, however, was Frederick's higher tactical plan which became known as the 'oblique order'. Simply, instead of arraying his army in one continuous line, his preferred deployment was in echelon, so that one flank of his troops came into action first. The others, arrayed obliquely alongside, progressively came up either to second the attack or cover the retreat if it were repelled. Thus, by concentrating his efforts against one of the enemy's flanks, he could bring massive superiority to bear upon a part of the battlefield, and roll up the enemy's line in detail, the most practical counter to the numerical inferiority under which Frederick usually suffered.

The plan could go terribly wrong if the supports were unco-ordinated (as at Zorndorf), but this most characteristic Frederickian

Seydlitz (left) and Zieten (right) portrayed together with their troops.

The Prussian Order of Merit, founded in 1665 but converted by Frederick on his accession into the decoration Pour le Mérite. *It became Prussia's principal military decoration and was nicknamed the 'Blue Max'. Worn at the neck, it comprised a blue-enamelled cross with gilt edging, eagles and lettering (a crowned F, Pour/le Mé/rite) with a black ribbon bearing a silver stripe near the edges.*

tactic had a profound effect at the time and on military thought in the immediate aftermath of the Seven Years War.

With cavalry, Frederick emulated Gustavus Adolphus and Marlborough in relying upon the charge with the sword, not glorified skirmishing with firearms. Under skilful commanders like Seydlitz and Zieten, the Prussian cavalry came to be among the finest in Europe. The rapidity of the charge also, noted Frederick, compelled the coward to be 'hurried away, and obliged to do his duty as well as the bravest . . . the whole depends upon the spirit of the attack'.[23]

Although Frederick was an enthusiastic supporter of Zieten's hussars, he was not enamoured of light infantry, believing that taking aim against an individual was a dishonourable way of fighting; as he told one of his own sharpshooters, waiting in a ditch to snipe at the enemy was no better than being a footpad, and that he should stand in the open and behave like a Prussian! Consequently, most of the army's skirmishing capacity resided in the 'Free Battalions', *ad hoc* organisations of irregular light infantry which were disbanded at the close of a campaign, whom Frederick regarded as villainous scum only fit for assassins. That some of the Free Battalions *were* evil rabble was largely his fault for not putting their organisation on a more regular basis! When, in his later career, Frederick began to evolve the Napoleonic-style tactic of 'softening' the enemy line by a combination of artillery and skirmish fire, his army was too stereotyped and his subordinates too deprived of initiative for it to be a success.

Artillery was Frederick's least favoured arm, and despite his innovative horse artillery, he never accorded the arm the same respect as the infantry and cavalry. Sieges were also not favoured, Frederick's entire strategy being directed towards bringing the enemy to a pitched battle where the discipline of his troops would prevail, and if for no other reason than protracted campaigns would allow his enemies to mass their inevitably larger forces against him. To offset the huge imbalance in numbers, Frederick *had* to be aggressive, and was probably the most offensively-minded of all the great captains. 'Battles determine the fate of nations',[24] he wrote, and that it was important to take the initiative and fight on one's own terms, and hence the constant emphasis on attack. It also meant that he laid himself open to more defeats than a less-aggressive general.

Frederick was advanced in logistical matters, refusing to be bound by the rigidity of fixed magazines and slow-moving convoys, but endeavouring to provide provisions along his route. A considerable part of his *Instructions* concerned the importance of regular food and drink, 'an indulgence which the poor fellows richly deserve';[25] 'the first object in the establishment of an army ought to be making provision for the belly, that being the basis and foundation of all operations'.[26]

A further prime concern was his insistence on personal reconnais-

124

sance: 'Every thing should be examined by our own eyes, and no attentions of this nature treated on any account as matters of indifference',[27] followed by what was termed *coup d'oeil*, the ability to exploit every feature of the terrain, which Frederick possessed in abundance. Finally, he warned against the slavish copying of history: 'we tread in the steps of our ancestors without regulating matters according to the nature of the ground';[28] and he laid much emphasis on keeping the enemy deceived and not fighting on his terms: 'In war, the skin of a fox is at times as necessary as that of the lion, for cunning may succeed where force fails'.[29]

A Position of Strength

With his military skill perfected and his army recovered from the Silesian Wars, the treasury replenished and the bulk of the state's resources diverted towards the army, Frederick was ready to fight the Seven Years War. It is a testimony to the resilience of his military system that Prussia was able to survive that war. As the British observer Philip Yorke noted, the army ran like clockwork because Frederick superintended everything himself. But vital as were Frederick's contributions, he admitted the chief reason for Prussia's success: 'With troops like these the world itself might be subdued . . . Let them be but well supplied with provisions, and you may attempt any thing with them'.[30]

Front and side views of a metal-fronted, Prussian artillery cap. It is in the style of a grenadier's mitre, but is much lower and squatter in shape, like that worn by infantry fusiliers. The inscription around the base of the cap is abbreviated to read 'KONIG. PREUSS. ARTILLERIE'.

The Seven Years War

The Seven Years War (1756–63) was a complicated affair, with campaigns ranging from North America to India, where Britain and France were already in conflict. However, the basic operations in Europe were to curb the perceived threat from Prussia and her intention of territorial expansion.

Austria still wished to recover Silesia, and having abandoned the British alliance, Maria Theresa was turning towards France and Russia for allies. Fearing a swamping by Russia and Austria together, Frederick concluded an alliance with Britain by the Treaty of Westminster (27 January 1756). This so outraged the French that sixteen months later they formally joined the Austro–Russian alliance, into which also came Sweden and Saxony. It was an alliance in which all except France had designs on Prussian territory, designs which if successful would have reduced Prussia once again to a minor principality.

Thus, by spring 1757 Frederick was at war with virtually all of continental Europe, and with Austria mobilizing many of the smaller German states over whom the Empire had suzerainty, his sole ally was Britain, much of whose military effort was directed towards the New World.

'The Old Dessauer' had died in 1747, and a new generation of subordinate commanders had arisen. Schwerin was somewhat out of favour, but a reliable substitute was the Scotsman James Keith, recently in Russian service. However, the most shadowy influence was that of Hans Carl von Winterfeldt, an ambitious and somewhat untrustworthy Pomeranian who acted as Frederick's adviser, chief of staff and (perhaps) his spy upon the other commanders, and who was thus mistrusted by many.

Capture of Lobositz

To forestall the coalition against him, Frederick decided to strike first, using his cardinal rule of rapid attack and defeat of his enemies in detail. At the end of August 1756, he marched over the Saxon border with 63,000 men, leaving more than that number protecting the northern and eastern frontiers. On 10 September he occupied the Saxon capital of Dresden and the Saxon army fell back to await assistance from the Austrian army of Marshal Maximilian von Browne. The Prussians ran into 34,000 of these, under von Browne, almost by accident on 1 October 1756 at Lobositz. Although the Austrians had chosen their position well and slightly outnumbered the Prussians, Frederick took the initiative. His first cavalry probe was mauled; but Frederick's deputy, the reliable and intelligent August William, Duke of Brunswick-Bevern, exhorted the infantry to charge with the bayonet and then directed howitzer fire onto the Austrian defenders of Lobositz village. As at Mollwitz, Frederick (perhaps angry at being deceived into fighting when he hadn't realised the Austrian strength) left half-way through and told Bevern to finish the battle. With the capture of Lobositz, Browne called off the action and withdrew, leaving Frederick as nominal victor.

The result was spectacular; the entire Saxon army surrendered, and Frederick coolly announced that the whole lot was to be incorporated into the Prussian army, not split up but in its own regiments. This act proved to be a complete failure. Not surprisingly, the Saxons deserted in droves, and by the end of the following year Frederick had only three Saxon infantry regiments and a grenadier battalion left – and these were mainly composed of men recruited individually and not dragooned *en masse*. Nevertheless, one of his enemies had been knocked out of the war at a stroke.

Jubilation at Prague

In April 1757, Frederick resumed the offensive; by now he had perhaps 175,000 men under arms, over half of whom protected Prussia's borders (assisted by an Anglo–Hanoverian army), whilst the remainder, under Frederick, Schwerin and Bevern, prepared to invade Bohemia. With the coalition now massing against him, Frederick needed more success to throw his enemies off-balance. In four detachments, some 113,000 Prussians crossed the Bohemian border, Frederick's own column uniting on 6 May with those of Moritz of Anhalt-Dessau and Schwerin near Prague, to where the Austrian forces had retired.

Intending to roll up the Austrian line from the right, Frederick began a march around their position, and Zieten's hussars fell upon the Austrian cavalry's flank and routed almost all. However, the Austrians realised the threat and began a re-alignment, countering the attempted flank-attack. Winterfeldt made a rapid but unsupported attack to disrupt the Austrian manoeuvre; it was massacred and Winterfeldt was knocked from his horse by a musket-ball in the neck. As the Prussians began to give way, old Schwerin seized the colour of his own regiment and rode forward calling 'Come along, children!'; as he fell dead, literally riddled with canister-shot, his troops broke and fled. But the sacrifice of the gallant infantry in their impossible attack was not in vain. As the Austrian army re-aligned, a great gap opened in their centre, through which Frederick hurled eighteen battalions. The Austrian army was split asunder, and with Frederick's brother Prince Henry urging the army forward (falling in a stream in the process), the Austrian lines crumbled and the whole mass poured back to the sanctuary of Prague.

The victory was Frederick's most convincing to date. He had evicted an army of about equal size from strongly-prepared positions, and although his 14,000-plus casualties were slightly higher than those of the Austrians, it was a remarkable achievement. The army was jubilant, but Frederick was almost incoherent with grief at the death of old Schwerin and the pride of the Prussian infantry.

Disaster at Kolin

The Austrian Marshal Leopold von Daun massed some 54,000 men to

relieve the survivors of the battle, now besieged in Prague. Frederick left Keith to conduct the siege and took about 35,000 men to meet Daun. They clashed on 18 June 1757 at Kolin, where the Austrians had established a strong position.

Frederick intended to repeat the Prague manoeuvre, beginning his attack with one wing and gradually increasing the pressure until the Austrian line crumbled; but it went wrong from the outset.

The initial attack went in with great style, but Moritz hung back with the supports, and the intended flanking-manoeuvre foundered. On the opposite wing, the Prussian cavalry showed great passivity and was swept from the field by the Austrians, who then assailed the Prussian centre from its rear. All order collapsed; Zieten was laid unconscious by a canister-shot and only the superbly-disciplined 'parade-ground soldiers' of Frederick's own regiment – the First Battalion of the Guard – remained calm amid the carnage, covering the retreat of the rest of the army but being virtually destroyed in the process. Attempting to rally the army, Frederick himself grasped a colour and reputedly made his famous cry: 'Rogues, do you want to live for ever?'; but to no avail. Frederick's gamble of attempting to defeat a greatly superior enemy by audacious attack had failed completely.

Kolin itself was not the full extent of the disaster. The siege of Prague had to be abandoned, Frederick's younger brother August William had been out-manoeuvred with his force and was dismissed from the royal presence in disgrace. Sweden invaded Prussian Pomerania, the Russians were in East Prussia and the French had defeated the Duke of Cumberland's Anglo-Hanoverians at Hastenbeck on 26 July. On 30

July, Frederick's deputy in the east, Hans von Lehwald, was defeated by the Russians at Gross-Jägersdorf, and the road to Berlin was open.

Frederick evacuated Bohemia as the crisis deepened, but took a little comfort from the discovery of a new cavalry general, who had greatly distinguished himself at Kolin – Frederick William von Seydlitz. Aged only 36 and a notorious roué, his constitution weakened by syphilis, Seydlitz was the most stylish member of Frederick's entourage; he was never afraid to speak his mind, was universally admired, recklessly brave and a superb horseman.

Rossbach – the Cheap Victory

Frederick realised that it was impossible to hold all his territory, but

Battle of Rossbach, 5 November 1757.

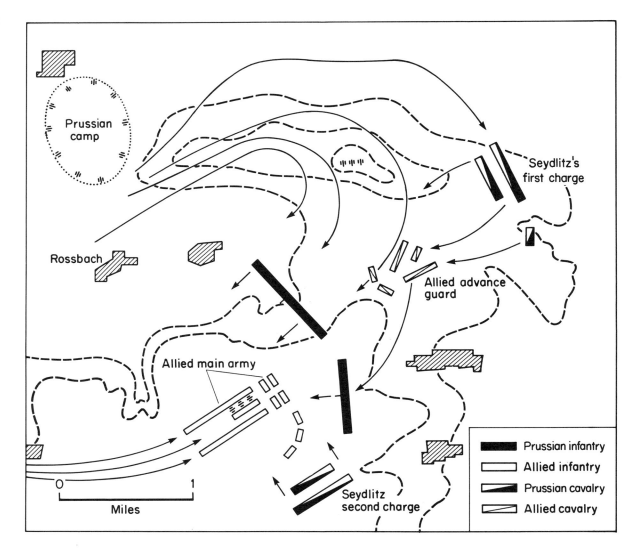

instead needed to defeat each allied force in turn before they could
unite to submerge him. He turned first upon the French–German army
advancing from the south, tentatively advancing through Saxony and
believing that Frederick's attention had been diverted by an Austrian
raid on the undefended Berlin.

This army, commanded by the French Duke of Soubise and Prince
Joseph of Saxe-Hildburghausen (commanding the German part, a hotch-
potch of minor German states mobilised by their allegiance to Austria
and glorified by the title *Reichsarmee*) was stretched out in column of
march when Frederick, his manoeuvres concealed from their view, fell
upon them at Rossbach, west of Leipzig, on 5 November 1757.
Seydlitz's cavalry scattered the allies' advance-guard, the Prussian infantry
wheeled into the path of the marching army; and Seydlitz made a final
charge which routed the Franco-Germans with appalling slaughter.

It was Frederick's cheapest victory – for 548 casualties he had destroyed a superior enemy, which lost 10,000 casualties and prisoners –
though the triumph was slightly less impressive when the mediocrity of
the opposition was considered. Nevertheless, it gave Frederick a
breathing-space.

The immediate aftermath of Rossbach brought only bad news. On 7
September, an Austrian force had overwhelmed Winterfeldt's troops
guarding the communications between Saxony and Silesia, Winterfeldt
being killed in the action (his being shot in the back raised a question
concerning his unpopularity). Then, if Frederick's devastation at the
news of the death of his friend were not enough, on 22 November
Bevern's army was routed at Breslau and Bevern himself was captured

whilst reconnoitering two days later. Too late, Frederick marched to Bevern's support but gathered up the remnants of his army, raising his strength to about 35,000; he faced Prince Charles of Lorraine and an immensely superior Austrian army which, having routed Bevern, was encamped near Breslau.

Leuthen – The Greatest Victory

Frederick was undaunted, and threatening his regiments with dire consequences should they flee, he determined to attack despite the odds. His army approached the enemy camp in the dawn of 5 December 1757 and the Austrians drew out in line of battle about half-a-mile in front of their bivouacs, near the village of Leuthen. The massed ranks could hardly credit that the small Prussian force was advancing, and christened Frederick's army 'the Berlin watch-parade'. Frederick made a show of deploying before the Austrian right, which drew in the Austrian reserves, whilst his main advance, screened by low hills, made for the Austrian left.

Executing his 'oblique attack', Frederick's troops fell upon the Austrian left wing, advancing as if on parade and supported by an artillery bombardment. By the time the Austrians realised that they had been deceived, their left had been destroyed, and though Prince Charles managed to patch up a new defensive line, the day was irreversible.

Frederick's infantry had brought up its ammunition-waggons and the Prussian artillery kept pace, so that an unending storm of lead and iron ploughed into the Austrian ranks. After a particularly vicious fight in the churchyard, the Austrians were evicted from Leuthen village. An attempted counter-charge by Charles' cavalry was itself taken in the flank by the Prussian horse, and the whole mass recoiled away and swept the tottering Austrian infantry from the field. The Prussians spontaneously raised the great hymn *Nun danket alle Gott* over the trampled and blood-soaked snow around Leuthen, signalling Frederick's greatest victory, a triumph of the oblique order and his magnificent army over a vastly-superior and experienced enemy.

Leuthen destroyed the Austrian threat for some time. For the loss of some 6,400 Prussians, Prince Charles lost in casualties and prisoners around 22,000, a third of his army, and the remainder were utterly routed. A further 17,000 were stranded in Breslau and capitulated before Christmas.

The Russian Threat

For the campaigning season of 1758, Frederick refused to invade Bohemia again, considering it 'little better than a desert'.[31] Instead, Frederick marched into Moravia, besieging the fortress of Olmütz, the major defence on the road to Vienna. The attempt was abandoned in the face of a Russian advance in the east; East Prussia had been over-run the previous year, and now the Russian Count Fermor returned and progressed onwards to attack Pomerania and Brandenburg. Only the

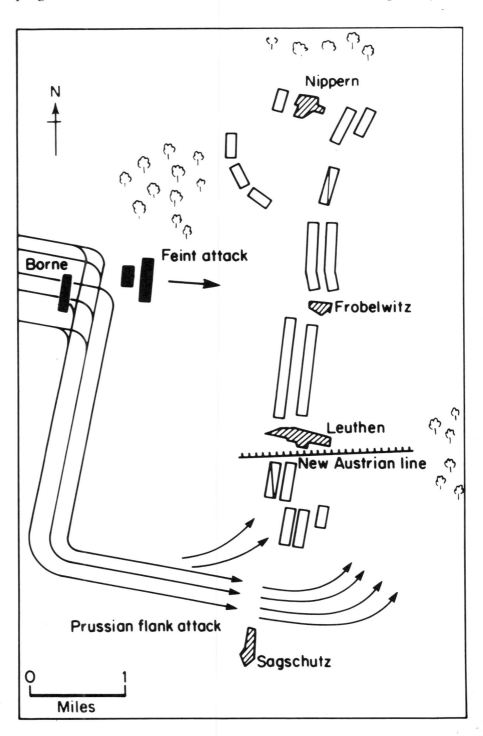

Battle of Leuthen, 5 December 1757.

The 'Berlin watch parade' at the Battle of Leuthen, 6 December 1757, showing the advance of the Prussian grenadiers.

western frontier was secured, by Frederick's general Duke Ferdinand of Brunswick, who drove the French over the Rhine and defeated them at Krefeld on 23 June.

Frederick moved to the north-eastern theatre, and at Zorndorf on 25 August 1758 attempted to repeat the manoeuvre of Leuthen, a circuitous march executed in the darkness of early morning to bring his oblique order into play against the Russian flank. Fermor, however, countered by changing his frontage, so that Frederick was forced into making a frontal attack which went wrong from the start. The left wing lost contact and its advance-guard, advancing with bands playing, went unsupported and suffered appallingly. By the time Frederick was able to galvanise the right wing into action in the late afternoon, the left had been all but destroyed. As darkness descended, both sides drew apart, both having fought to exhaustion.

Fermor pulled back on 27 August, leaving the Prussians nominally victorious, but at terrible cost. A third of Frederick's army had fallen, over 12,000; but at least the butchery of Zorndorf prevented further Russian operations, and Frederick was free to force-march to meet the next threat.

133

Slaughter at Hochkirch

In Saxony, the Austrian Marshal Daun was threatening the Prussian army covering Silesia. Whilst attempting to manoeuvre the Austrians out of Saxony, Frederick camped with 30,000 men at Hochkirch. Although his position was exposed, Frederick was unconcerned. Then, without warning, in the early morning of 14 October 1758, an immense Austrian attack descended upon the sleeping Prussians. The surprise was complete; hundreds were killed in their tents, and only when the camp came under intense bombardment did Frederick realise that it was more than a gang of marauding Croats.

Lack of reconnaissance cost Frederick dearly; Moritz of Anhalt-Dessau and Keith attempted to hold the village of Hochkirch, where the Second Battalion of the regiment of Margrave Karl of Brandenburg–Schwedt was annihilated to a man attempting to hold the churchyard, and Keith died trying to stem the flood. Frederick's brother-in-law, Prince Frederick of Brunswick, was decapitated by a roundshot; Moritz was wounded and captured, and though released on parole never served again, dying of cancer eighteen months later, ending the invaluable influence of 'the Old Dessauer' and his kin upon the Prussian army.

By mid-morning the Prussian force was streaming away from Hochkirch, its artillery lost, and only ingrained discipline prevented total rout. The battle cost Frederick 9000 men, but by assembling reinforcements he was able to prevent Daun from exploiting the victory, and the year ended with an Austrian withdrawal back to Bohemia.

The year 1759 was a bad one for Frederick, as he found it increasingly difficult to replace the casualties suffered in the multiple attacks mounted against Prussia. Ferdinand of Brunswick's Anglo–Hanoverian army (with limited Prussian support) continued to secure the west, winning a great victory over the French at Minden on 1 August 1759, which demonstrated that the British infantry was at least equal to Frederick's own. But elsewhere the situation was desperate.

Frederick's greatest problem was the necessity of fighting on more than one front at once, and lacking capable deputies to command where he was absent. On 23 July, his newly-appointed commander in the east, the impressive-looking but inept Johann von Wedell, allowed his army to be utterly smashed by the Russians at Kay. The Russians then linked with an Austrian army to present Frederick with a two-pronged threat, from themselves in the east and Daun in Silesia. Leaving Prince Henry to watch Daun, Frederick marched eastwards.

The Miracle of the House of Brandenburg

Again Frederick's reconnaissance was imperfect. When his approach-march toward the huge Russo-Austrian army at Kunersdorf on 12

Battle of Kunersdorf, 12 August 1759.

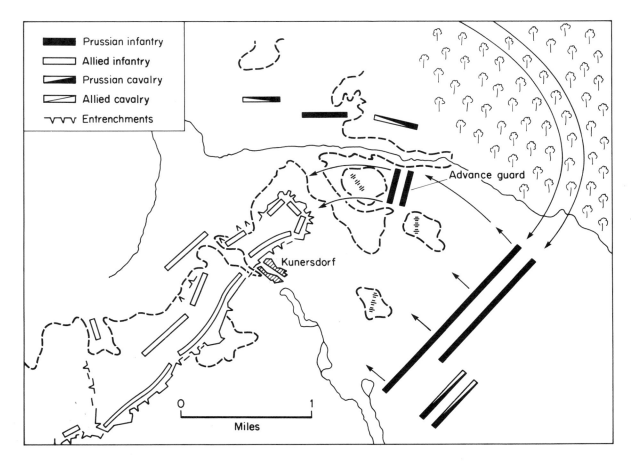

August 1759 arrived at what he intended as a position from which he could fall on their flank, he found the Russian Count Saltykov and his Austrian ally Gideon Loudon firmly across his path. Disordered by their long march and rough terrain, the Prussian attacks were unco-ordinated, their cavalry savagely mauled by strongly-posted enemy artillery and Seydlitz wounded, and when exhausted were routed by a Russo-Austrian cavalry attack.

With 19,000 casualties sustained, Frederick was able to rally only about 5000 men; but there followed what he called the 'miracle of the house of Brandenburg' – Saltykov declined to press home his advantage and destroy the remnants, thinking that Russian casualties had been heavy enough. It was this Russian withdrawal, not any skill of Frederick's, that probably saved Prussia.

However, Frederick's miserable year of 1759 had not yet ended. In Saxony, Daun captured the great base of Dresden on 4 September, and on 21 November a large Prussian force of 13,000 men was out-manoeuvered and forced to surrender at Maxen. Already weakened, the year had cost Frederick 60,000 men.

After 'The Miracle'

It was surprising that the Prussian army could still take the field in 1760, as the losses had been so great, especially in officers and in the most reliable elements. Nevertheless, Frederick (who usually disregarded motives like patriotism and idealism) was still content to enlist prisoners and mercenaries; the overall standard thus declined steadily, but the system was such that the armies were still able to resist.

In 1760, Ferdinand of Brunswick continued to hold off the French despite the odds, winning a sharp action at Warburg on 31 July, but elsewhere Prussia was sorely pressed. Prince Henry was sent to hold back the Russians whilst Frederick attempted to recapture Dresden, but suffered a bad reverse at Landeshut on 23 June when his friend La Motte Fouqué was overwhelmed and captured by an Austrian force under Laudon. The attempt on Dresden was abandoned as Frederick had to go to Silesia to assist Henry, and was soon faced by the combined forces of Daun and Loudon about 90,000 strong.

The Austrian commanders divided their forces for an enveloping manoeuvre against Frederick on the night of 14/15 August 1760 at Liegnitz, but the Prussian King was determined not to be caught again. Leaving Zieten in command of his first line, Frederick took the second line and formed to resist Loudon's attack. Having stood off three Austrian assaults, Frederick counter-attacked and demolished Loudon's force before Daun could move in support. Missing their golden opportunity to overwhelm Frederick once and for all – an error compounded by the fact that 30,000 Russians were within sound of the guns but did nothing – the allied armies continued to fumble. An Austro-Russian

Du bist verwundet mein So...

raid captured Berlin briefly on 9 October, but withdrew when Frederick turned towards the capital's relief, and no more was seen of the Russians for the remainder of the campaign. Daun concentrated the Austrians at Torgau, in a force about 53,000 strong.

On 3 November, Frederick divided his inferior force to assault Daun from two directions, Zieten from the front and himself from the rear. However, the astute Daun realised the danger and faced his army to meet Frederick head-on. Mistaking skirmish-fire for Zieten's attack, Frederick threw in his first assault at reckless speed and it was all but annihilated; and successive attacks were repelled with severe loss. Frederick was hit on the breast-bone by a canister-shot and winded, and was carried away from the battle. Another defeat was looming; but as dusk approached, and seeing that Frederick was making no progress, Zieten noted a weakness in the Austrian dispositions and threw in a heavy attack. The resulting noise emboldened Frederick's force to make another attempt themselves. The battle ended in darkness as the Austrian lines finally cracked, and the exhausted Prussian army was left in command of the field, though once again their losses had been appalling.

Thus, 1760 ended with the exhaustion of both sides, and for the campaigning season of the following year Frederick could muster barely 100,000 men, whilst the Austro-Russians assembled three times that number. Daun controlled much of Saxony, and the Russian general Alexander Buturlin held central Silesia. Such was the disparity in numbers that Frederick for once acted defensively, taking his forces into a strongly-defended camp at Bunzelwitz, situated on what is now the northern frontier of Czechoslovakia. Buturlin eventually made off for Poland with the bulk of his army, but the relief of pressure on Frederick was offset by the Austrian capture of the Prussian depot of Schweidnitz on 1 October. The depot had sustained Frederick in the Bunzelwitz camp and its loss was compounded by the Russian capture of Kolberg on the eastern Pomeranian coast on 16 December 1761. The news that Britain was declining to renew the subsidy to pay for Frederick's war effort completed his cup of misery, and the army spent a wretched early winter, bereft of provisions, morale and even hope.

Peace in Exhaustion

January 1762 brought about a miraculous transformation. The death of the Empress Elizabeth of Russia on 5 January brought to the throne the simple-minded Czar Peter III, who admired Frederick immensely. The military situation was transformed totally by Peter's breaking the Austrian alliance and joining his army to Frederick's. At last, the war in Silesia was on terms of reasonable parity, and the Treaty of Hamburg on 22 May 1762 brought peace between Prussia and Sweden, allowing Frederick to concentrate all his resources against the Austrians. His western flank was still secure, the irrepressible Ferdinand of Brunswick's Anglo-Prussians defeating the French at Wilhelmstal in Westphalia on 24 June.

Frederick manoeuvred against Daun, but having reached a position to attack, found his plans overturned by the news of the deposition and murder of the Czar. Peter's successor, his wife Catherine, broke off the alliance but did not revert to outright opposition of Prussia. Frederick persuaded the Russian commander to allow his force to stay on for a few days as reserve, and immediately attacked Daun at Burkersdorf on 21 July, which had the effect of evicting the Austrians from southern Silesia. The recapture of Schweidnitz on 9 October 1762 ended the war in Silesia; and on 29 October Prince Henry and Seydlitz defeated the Imperial *Reichsarmee* at Freiberg.

An armistice was called in November; so in less than a year Prussia and Frederick had come from the brink of collapse to what passed for victory. As both camps were by now totally exhausted, the Treaty of Hubertusburg on 15 February 1763 (which ended the Seven Years War) was welcomed by all parties. European territorial borders were re-established as they had been in 1756; in other words, the European theatre of the Seven Years War had killed perhaps half-a-million troops and had achieved hardly anything, save the continued existence of Prussia.

Final Years

The Seven Years War was Frederick's last real military services as the War of the Bavarian Succession (1778–79), between Prussia and Austria over the perceived Imperial wish to annex Bavaria, saw only unimpressive and desultory manoeuvres.

In the intervening years, Frederick had restored Prussian economic and military strength, and the partition of Poland in 1772 had added West Prussia to the kingdom, at last achieving the link between Pomerania and far-flung East Prussia.

In his private life, Frederick continued to pursue his joint passions of music, literature and the army; though his declining years were ones of sadness as his health gradually deteriorated and his old companions – those few close colleagues who had survived the war – gradually passed away. Perhaps surprisingly given his lifestyle, Seydlitz survived until 1783. Old Zieten, a frail shadow of the dashing hussar he had been, once fell asleep at Frederick's table but the King refused to have him wakened, saying 'Let him sleep; he watched long enough over us'.[32] Zieten died on 26 January 1786, upon which a saddened Frederick remarked, 'Our old Zieten has shown himself a good general even in death. In the wars he always commanded the advance guard; he has taken the lead now, too. I used to bring up the main body; I'll follow him'.[33]

In his last years Frederick stoically bore ill-health and appeared older than his years, a shrunken, fragile figure in a snuff-stained blue military coat. Afflicted by a cough and unable to lie down, he spent his last days and nights in a chair at his beloved Sans-Souci, quipping to the Duke of Courland that if he needed a watchman, 'I am a famous hand at keeping awake all night'.[34] He continued to be actively involved with the army to the very end. Even when unable to ride, he still inspected his troops, unwilling to give up his link with his glorious past. In 1785, he had some Pomeranian regiments march past him, and asked for them to march past yet again, removing his hat to them; probably he saw not only them, but the men of Leuthen, Rossbach and Hochkirch – Winterfeldt, Keith and Seydlitz. Still deprived of any family life (he was succeeded by his nephew), Frederick's lonely old age ended on 17 August 1786, and with it his era.

Legacy of the Great

Frederick's legacy was two-fold, partly as the founder of Prussian militarism, but in the narrower sense, his true military legacy was a slavish study and imitation of his methods. His campaigns were dissected and his military organisations emulated by all those who admired him.

The King in his declining years – Alte Fritz – on the terrace at Sans-Souci.

Nowhere was this admiration better demonstrated than in Britain where many of Frederick's most ardent admirers resided. When the British Army issued its first official drill-book in 1792,[35] its author Sir David Dundas (1735–1820), who had twice attended the vast manoeuvre-camps maintained by Frederick, was totally convinced of the rightness of the Prussian system and his book authorised its introduction. British experience in the American War of Independence eventually prevailed and Dundas' system – which earned its author the sobriquet 'Old Pivot' after the pivot on which the manoeuvres depended – was superseded by a modified and more practical system which included light troops, as little regarded by Dundas as by Frederick himself. As an experienced Scottish colonel remarked in action in Holland, 'I say, David, whaur's your peevots noo?' In Prussia, however, no such modification occurred, Frederick retaining the old uniforms and almost the same tactical style until the end of his life. It was, thus, essentially a Frederickian army which opposed Napoleon in 1806, and which was totally and crushingly defeated by 'modern' methods.

However, Frederick had his detractors. Macaulay wrote that: 'The evils produced by his wickedness were felt in lands where the name of Prussia was unknown'.[36] Yet nothing could erase Frederick's legacy and the shadow he cast over Europe, both in his time and upon Germany after his death: the name 'the Great' is rightly shared with Alexander. The text used for his funeral oration, 'And I have made thee a name like the name of the great that are in the earth', from I Chronicles accurately reflected his influence on his own kingdom. But as his biographer Kugler remarked, more telling was the reaction of a Swabian peasant to the news of his passing: 'Who is now to govern the world?'.[37]

References

Note: *the translations used have been the earliest to appear in English, such as Foster's version of Frederick's* Instructions *and Kugler's biography.*

1 Kugler (see Bibliography) p. 40.
2 *ibid.* p. 97.
3 *ibid.* p. 138.
4 Kugler, p. 275.
5 To his confidant Francesco Algerotti, March 1760; Kugler pp. 432–33.
6 *Frederick the Great: His Court and Times* (ed. Thomas Campbell) 1845, III p. 138.
7 On the opening of the First Silesian War: Kugler p. 162.
8 Frederick's *Particular Instruction* (see Bibliography) p. iii.
9 *ibid.* p. 75.
10 Frederick's *Military Instruction* (see Bibliography) p. 66.
11 *Military Instruction* pp. 128–29.
12 *ibid.* pp. 120–21.
13 *ibid.* p. 14.
14 *ibid.* p. 61.
15 *Particular Instruction* p. 38.
16 *ibid.* p. ii.
17 *ibid.* p. v.
18 *Military Instruction* p. 62.
19 Dialogue concentrated from *A Book of Naval and Military Anecdotes*, anon., London 1824.
20 *Military Instruction* p. 1.
21 Kugler p. 451.
22 *A View of Society and Manners in France, Switzerland and Germany*, Dr. J. Moore, London, 1780, II p. 144.
23 *Military Instruction*, p. 137.
24 *ibid.* p. 125.
25 *ibid.* p. 14.
26 *ibid.* p. 7

27 *ibid.* p. 43.

28 *ibid.* p. 27.

29 *ibid.* p. 52.

30 *ibid.* p. 6.

31 *ibid.* p. 14.

32 Kugler p. 585.

33 *ibid.* p. 605.

34 *ibid.* p. 607.

35 *Rules and Regulations for the Formation, Field-exercise and Movements, of His Majesty's Forces*; initially published as *Principles of Military Movements* in 1788.

36 *Critical and Historical Essays*, T.B. Macaulay, London 1864, II p. 253.

37 Kugler p. 612.

Chronology of Events

1701   18 JANUARY Foundation of Prussian royal house when Elector Frederick III of Brandenburg becomes Frederick I, King in Prussia.

1712   24 JANUARY Birth of Frederick, eldest son of Crown Prince Frederick William.

1713   25 FEBRUARY Death of Frederick I and accession of Frederick William I.

1730   2 SEPTEMBER Exile of Crown Prince Frederick to Cüstrin.

1731   30 NOVEMBER Frederick's rehabilitation; appointment to regimental colonelcy.

1733   12 JUNE Marriage of Frederick to Princess Elizabeth Christine.

1740   31 MAY Death of Frederick William I; accession of Frederick II.

1740   16 DECEMBER Frederick's invasion of Silesia.

1741   10 APRIL Defeat of Austrians (Neipperg) by Frederick and Schwerin at Mollwitz.

1741   9 OCTOBER Truce of Klein Schellendorf between Prussia and Austria.

1742   17 MAY Defeat of Austrians (Charles of Lorraine) by Frederick at Chotusitz.

1742   11 JUNE Treaty of Breslau ends First Silesian War.

1743   27 JUNE King George II of England defeats French at Dettingen.

1744   2/6 SEPTEMBER Capture of Prague by Frederick.

1745   8 JANUARY Formation of Quadruple Alliance.

1745   4 JUNE Defeat of Austrians (Charles of Lorraine) by Frederick at Hohenfriedberg.

1745   30 SEPTEMBER Defeat of Austrians (Charles of Lorraine) by Frederick at Soor.

1745   23 NOVEMBER Defeat of Austrians (Charles of Lorraine) by Frederick at Katholisch-Hennersdorf.

1745   14 DECEMBER Defeat of Austro-Saxons (Rutowski) by 'the Old Dessauer' at Kesselsdorf.

1745   25 DECEMBER Treaty of Dresden between Prussia and Austria.

1748   18 OCTOBER Treaty of Aix-la-Chapelle ends War of Austrian Succession.

1756   29 AUGUST Prussian invasion of Saxony precipitates Seven Years War.

1756   1 OCTOBER Defeat of Austrians (Browne) by Frederick at Lobositz.

1757   6 MAY Defeat of Austrians by Frederick at Prague.

1757   18 JUNE Defeat of Frederick by Austrians (Daun) at Kolin.

1757   30 JULY Defeat of Prussians (Lehwald) by Russians (Apraksin) at Gross-Jägersdorf.

1757   5 NOVEMBER Defeat of Franco-Germans (Soubise and Saxe-Hildburghausen) by Frederick at Rossbach.

1757   6 DECEMBER Defeat of Austrians (Charles of Lorraine) by Frederick at Leuthen.

1758   25 AUGUST Defeat of Russians (Fermor) by Frederick at Zorndorf.

1758   14 OCTOBER Defeat of Frederick by Austrians (Daun) at Hochkirch.

1759   1 AUGUST Defeat of French (Contades) by Ferdinand of Brunswick at Minden.

1759   12 AUGUST Defeat of Frederick by Austro-Russians (Saltykov and Loudon) at Kunersdorf.

1759   21 NOVEMBER Defeat of Prussians (von Finck) by Austrians (Daun) at Maxen.

1760   23 JUNE Defeat of Prussians (La Motte Fouqué) by Austrians (Laudon) at Landeshut.

1760   15 AUGUST Defeat of Austrians (Daun) by Frederick at Liegnitz.

1760   9 OCTOBER Berlin raided and temporarily captured.

1760   3 NOVEMBER Defeat of Austrians (Daun) by Frederick at Torgau.

1762   5 JANUARY Death of Empress Elizabeth of Russia.

1762   15 MAY Treaty of St. Petersburg, ending Prusso-Russian war.

1762   22 MAY Treaty of Hamburg, ending Prusso-Swedish war.

1762   21 JULY Defeat of Austrians (Daun) by Frederick at Burkersdorf.

1762   29 OCTOBER Defeat of Austrians (Serbelloni) by Prince Henry and Seydlitz at Freiburg.

1763   16 FEBRUARY Treaty of Hubertusburg ends Seven Years War.

1786   17 AUGUST Death of Frederick.

1991   17 AUGUST Frederick's coffin ceremonially re-interred at Potsdam, following German re-unification in 1990.

George Washington

FATHER OF HIS NATION

Washington as the victor at Princeton, with captured enemy canon and colours. Charles Wilson Peale's painting also shows British troops on Nassau Hill in the background.

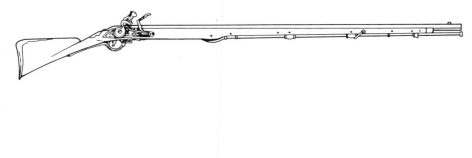

The weapon most often ranged against Washington's forces — the standard arm of the British Army for over a century the 'Brown Bess' flintlock musket, which existed in several patterns. The 'Long Land Pattern' had a 46-inch barrel; the succeeding 'Short Land Pattern' a 42-inch barrel. The nickname 'Brown Bess' was probably a term of endearment coupled with the 'browned' (rust-proofed) finish of the barrel.

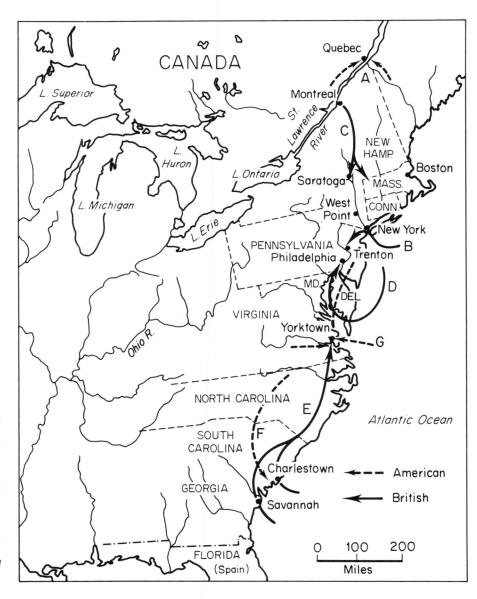

Principal campaigns of the Revolutionary War – the American War of Independence: (A) American invasion of Canada, 1775; (B) British offensive against New York, 1776; (C) British advance to Saratoga, 1777; (D) British advance on Philadelphia, 1777; (E) British operations in the south, ending at Yorktown 1780–81; (F) American counter-offensive in the south, 1781; (G) American three-pronged advance on Yorktown, 1781.

144

First in war, first in peace, and first in the hearts of his countrymen
John Marshall, 1799 (also ascribed to Henry Lee).

Strategist of Independence

George Washington has not always been regarded by some as being among the first rank of military commanders. Whereas none would dispute the ascendancy of Frederick the Great or Marlborough, Washington's claim to martial greatness could be challenged on the grounds that he never commanded armies of any significant size – that is, when compared to military operations in Europe.

Equally, Washington was no great tactician and his lack of experience made him vulnerable in the smaller sphere. Yet his strategic overview was very great indeed.

Despite their interference, he overcame his critics in Congress and the army, realising that the War of Independence would be a protracted struggle, and that rash offering of battle could undo the entire attempt for independence. The criticisms of his inactivity are, thus, largely unfair. Indeed, the unwillingness to fight unless he was confident of the possibility of victory was, in fact, a demonstration of his good sense and strategical skill. With Congress and the army both divided into quarrelling factions, Washington served as a unifying medium. He realised the necessity of building a professional army, with a skilled officer corps, and thus supported his foreign experts against all he criticisms of Congress, which viewed them as mere adventurers.

In training and reorganization of the American forces, Washington laid the foundations for the slow but steady victory he envisaged; and at Yorktown he demonstrated the breadth of his skill. He grasped immediately the implications of the naval aspect, and the chance to score a decisive victory; and having decided upon a course of action, he acted immediately and without hesitation. That he had the forces with which to perform this was equally his responsibility.

His perseverence and not inconsiderable skills were a major contributory cause towards American victory. Without him, independence would probably never have been won.

Early Life

George Washington was born on 22 February 1732 (old style, 11 February) at Bridges Creek, Westmoreland County, Virginia. His family had been domiciled in America for three-quarters of a century; their origin was as English country gentry, being connected to the Washingtons of Sulgrave, Northamptonshire. As Sir John Fortescue took pains to indicate, Washington was a 'gentleman' and put considerable store by the fact; which, by implication, gave him an inherent authority over the ruder settlers of the colonies. However true this may be, Washington did come from a 'good' family, with the advantages such birth would have conferred upon him had he lived in England: social position and the ownership of land.

The Washingtons first appeared in Virginia in 1658, and built considerable estates. George Washington's father, Augustine (1694–1743), was twice married and produced ten children. George was one of the six by Augustine's wife, Mary Ball, whom he had married in 1730. Upon his death, Augustine left one estate (Hunting Creek, later known as Mount Vernon) to George's elder half-brother, Lawrence; his other estate, on the Rappahannock, near Fredericksburg, he left to young George, who was placed under Lawrence's guardianship.

Of George's early life, little is known, save that he lived at Mount Vernon from 1735 to 1739. The best-known story of his childhood – his felling of a cherry tree and admitting the fact because 'I cannot tell a lie' – is almost certainly apocryphal and invented by 'Parson' Mason Weems. In fact, Weems' biography of Washington (1800, expanded 1806) contained much fiction, but it was most significant in influencing the public perception of Washington. George's education was elementary and defective in all but mathematics (being self-taught), but he developed a good command of English despite never being a wide reader. Although much of his later military career had a connection with France, he never learned that language.

Washington left school in 1747 and lived with his brother and guardian Lawrence at Mount Vernon. Lawrence's father-in-law was William Fairfax (of the same family as the great Parliamentarian generals of the English Civil War), with whom Lawrence had served at Cartagena in 1741, when that port (in what is now Colombia) was besieged unsuccessfully by Admiral Edward 'Old Grog' Vernon. Lawrence's admiration for the admiral resulted in the naming of the estate as Mount Vernon. Furthermore, his association with 'Old Grog' supposedly resulted in an appointment as midshipman in the Royal Navy for young George, an idea still-born due to the opposition of George's mother. (There is no proof of the veracity of the tale.)

In 1748, by the influence of Thomas, Lord Fairfax, head of the Fairfax family, the 16-year-old George was appointed surveyor of the

Fairfax property. For the next three years he worked on this duty, spending much time on the western frontier. It was this work which gave him a insight into the potential wealth of the territory, from which his later investments profited. In 1751, he went to the West Indies with Lawrence Washington, where it was hoped the latter might recover from consumption; but Lawrence died the following year, making George residuary heir to the Mount Vernon estate. It duly passed to him in 1761.

The French and Indian War

Anglo–French rivalry in North America had caused much conflict over the previous half-century, generally conforming to the period of the Wars of the Spanish and Austrian Successions. Basically, the French held the northern colonies (Canada) and the British the southern. The expansion of both nations inevitably led to friction, and in October 1753 Governor Robert Dinwiddie of Virginia appointed George Washington as his agent to warn off the French from their new posts on the Ohio in western Pennsylvania. This Washington accomplished during a somewhat hazardous winter journey, and after his return he was appointed lieutenant-colonel of Joshua Fry's Virginia Regiment.

The military forces of the American colonies at that time consisted of militia or volunteer regiments, raised from among the settlers and normally embodied only in time of war. Fry's regiment was briefly split into independent companies in 1754, and re-formed in 1755; Washington assumed command as colonel in September 1755. Such corps were styled 'Provincial' regiments, regularly-organised and disciplined; and like the ill-disciplined and desertion-prone militia, were more likely to be used to the realities of warfare in the north American wilderness than were the troops of the regular British Army.

From this very early period of his military service, Washington's good sense is evident. It was intended that the Virginia Regiment would wear civilian clothing, but he insisted that uniforms be provided, as the recruits were 'loose, idle persons that are quite destitute of House and Home, and, I may truly say, many of them of Cloaths'.[1] Originally, they were provided with red uniforms, and from September 1755 with blue coats with red facings and silver lace, a smart and workmanlike dress. Perhaps the blue colour was chosen to differentiate them from the British regulars – or perhaps it had some association with Washington's confessed dislike of 'gaiety' in dress.

Braddock at Monongahela
In April 1754, Washington took two companies to the Ohio and

defeated a French and Indian force at Great Meadows (28 May). He built a post near there, called Fort Necessity, where he was attacked by the French. Forced to surrender after a stern defence, he was allowed to leave with the 'honours of war' and received the thanks of the House of Burgesses, the colonial parliament. The outbreak of this 'French and Indian War' in 1754 caused the British government to appoint a new commander in chief for North America, General Edward Braddock, who arrived in February 1755.

Braddock, then aged 60, had been forty-five years in the army and represented the best and worst aspects of the old style of warfare. Trained in the classical mode – which saw precision drill and immaculate manoeuvres as an end in themselves – he was a rough, uncompromising martinet, but a man of unshakable courage and complete devotion to duty. As a subordinate commander in European warfare, he would have been an ideal choice to undertake a hazardous attack. However, in the unique conditions of north American warfare – with the fighting in the broken and wooded terrain that was styled 'the wilderness' – he was hopelessly out of his depth.

Braddock determined upon a four-pronged offensive against the French. In retrospect, it was a fatal division of his forces. His own command, two newly-arrived regiments, detachments of sailors and artillerymen, plus 450 Virginian Provincials and Indian scouts, Braddock planned to lead against the French base of Fort Duquesne, at the confluence of the Monongahela and Alleghany rivers, the site of modern Pittsburgh.

Braddock's abrasive attitude and his insolence towards 'inferior' provincial troops caused difficulties; but he was happy to appoint George Washington as his aide, with the rank of colonel. Braddock's advance on Fort Duquesne was conducted in immaculate European style, with pioneers cutting a road through the forested wilderness and pausing, as Washington remarked, to bridge every creek and flatten every molehill. Thus, it was a painfully slow progress, and gave the French ample warning.

The garrison of Fort Duquesne was small, and under normal circumstances quite incapable of resisting the 1400 men whom Braddock led; but the wilderness was anything but normal for soldiers schooled in European methods. About 70 French troops were sent from Fort Duquesne, with some 150 Canadian militiamen and about 650 Indians; and on 8 July 1755 they ambushed Braddock's force just after it had crossed the Monongahela. Firing from the cover of the dense forest, the French and Indians were invisible to the British; but the British formed their line-of-battle and began to fire ineffectual volleys into the forest. Shot down in their ranks, the British continued to shoot at their invisible foe and even brought their artillery into action. For a moment, the French Indians almost gave way, but rallied by the French regulars, they continued to pour musketry into the hapless British. The Virginians alone realised that European tactics were suicidal; like the French, they took shelter behind trees and fought from cover. However, Braddock, raging along his line with immense courage (but no good sense), drove them back into formation with curses. The slaughter was insupportable. When Braddock fell, shot through the lungs, the British broke and fled, pursued by the Indians, whose shrieking and barbarous reputation had done much to undermine British morale.

All through the terrible fight, Washington had emulated his general by riding over the field, in clear view of the enemy, miraculously escaping injury. Now, he took command of the shattered remnants fleeing before the Indians and attempted to rally the troops at the ford of the Monongahela; but as he remarked himself, he might as well have attempted to stop the wild bears of the mountains. Eventually, about 80 men were rallied and, although Braddock pleaded to be left on the field, his few surviving officers (60 out of 86 had fallen) had him borne away.

Order was restored on the following morning as the remnants of the expedition struggled to safety. Of 1373 'other ranks', 459 were saved; the wounded had to be left where they lay, to be murdered in the most barbarous manner by the Indians. Throughout the withdrawal, Braddock tried to do his duty and remained in command despite his agonising injury. Before he died, two days later, he said with amazement: 'Who would have thought it?'; and, his dying words: 'Another time we shall know better how to deal with them'.[2]

The massacre on the Monongahela, or 'the Battle of the Wilderness', demonstrated the fallacy of attempting to fight a campaign in north America using the manoeuvres of European warfare. It was Braddock's disaster, but not really his fault. Brutal martinet he may have been, but his failings lay in his schooling in European methods rather than in any particular stupidity of his own. The experience taught the British Army a lesson; and it is inevitable that Washington learned much from it.

The French and Indian War ran into the Seven Years War, and its result was the total elimination of French rule in north America. The British took note of Braddock's defeat and ceased to disregard the effectiveness of their Provincial troops: corps like the Ranger companies fought 'irregular' warfare with even more proficiency than the French and Indians. Washington's part in the British triumph was not crucial, though valuable in its way. Despite his youth (23 years), upon his return from the Monongahela, he was commissioned as commander of the Virginia forces. For the next two years he defended a 350-mile frontier with only 700 somewhat insubordinate men, in itself a considerable achievement.

In 1758 Washington had the satisfaction of witnessing the capture of Braddock's earlier objective of Fort Duquesne, when he led the

Virginia contingent of the army under General John Forbes. His association with Forbes, and with Forbes' second-in-command Henry Bouquet, who commanded after Forbes fell ill, can only have been beneficial to Washington's military development. Both Forbes and Bouquet were among the best British commanders of the north American theatre. Bouquet, a Swiss who had entered British service from the Dutch army, was quick to appreciate the nature of 'wilderness' warfare. Rapidly, he recognised the need for new tactics, and learned to appreciate the value of Provincial troops experienced in the unique conditions of combat that were posed by the north American terrain.

Mount Vernon and Marriage

Washington resigned his commission upon the conclusion of the war in Virginia. Consequently, he was not in the service at the time of the greatest British triumph: the capture of Quebec in September 1759 was a result of the audacious expedition of the young General James Wolfe (1727–59), slain at the moment of his victory on the Plains of Abraham (13 September 1759). Washington's health had suffered (he had been ill in the winter of 1757), but he ended his military service with a fine reputation.

In January 1759, he married Martha Dandridge (1732–1802), widow of Daniel Parke Custris, and the addition of her wealth to Washington's own property made him one of the richest men in the colonies. He settled at Mount Vernon and spent the next fifteen years in a style which resembled that of an English country gentleman. He enlarged his plantations, was meticulous in his business dealings and spent much time on outdoor pursuits. Like other Virginia planters, he saw no particular ills in using slave labour, but treated his slaves as well as the system could allow. Although he was by then one of the leading figures in the colonies and serving in the House of Burgesses, Washington showed no inclination towards political leadership.

War for Independence

The American colonies did not burst into revolt overnight, but friction with the British government was a long-standing process. The colonists had justified grievances, especially over taxation, which the often superior or patronising attitudes of the British administration did little to assuage.

Washington sided with the radicals, opposing the proposal to petition the King (George III) and Parliament – not because he expected such appeals to be dismissed, but because he objected to begging for what were regarded as legitimate rights. He appreciated that the course

of action the radicals were considering would lead to a total break with the mother-country and to probable war; others had no such clear perception of what they were about.

As the tension mounted, he was appointed a delegate for Virginia to the first Continental Congress, which met at Philadelphia on 5 September 1774. After its adjournment, he returned to Virginia, urging the formation of military forces in preparation for the possibility of conflict. At this stage, however, he was not prepared to declare for total independence. After drilling personally the forces raised by Virginia, he went to the second Continental Congress (March 1775) as a recognised military expert: he habitually appeared in uniform and it was accepted that he would command the Virginian forces if hostilities began.

Concord and Command

On 18 April 1775, General Thomas Gage, governor of Massachusetts, sent a detachment of troops from the British garrison of Boston to capture munitions gathered by the colonists at Concord. Forewarned of the approach of the British, companies of colonist militia (or 'minute men', those who could assemble at a minute's notice) gathered at Lexington Common. Who fired the first shot is unknown, but there was much justification for Emerson's description:

American 6-pounder field-piece; ordnance typical of the War of Independence.

> Here once the embattled farmers stood
> And fired the shot heard round the world.[3]

Brushing aside the colonists, the British advanced to Concord and destroyed those supplies which had not been removed. However, in their return to Boston, the British were harrassed continually by the gathering American militia, using their skirmish tactics of firing from cover. Total British losses were over 270; the Americans lost less than 100.

With the outbreak of hostilities, the Continental Congress resolved to put the colonies into a state of defence, and offensive action was undertaken within a month. Organisation, however, was haphazard, and it was obvious that an experienced commander-in-chief was required if the colonies were to be able to make any serious opposition to the British. The unanimous selection of the Congress, on 15 June 1775, was the soldier with the highest reputation – George Washington.

His appointment was proposed by John Adams of Massachusetts, and was not based entirely upon military considerations; the New Englanders had been the moving force behind the revolution, but desperately needed the support of the southern colonists. Thus, the appointment of a Virginian as commander in chief was calculated to enlist the support of that important colony.

Contemporary engraving of a British light dragoon wearing the uniform worn in North America during the War of Independence.

Conditions of War

The war between Britain and her colonies involved a number of features which were quite singular to the North American continent. Although light infantry tactics and skirmishing had been undertaken in Europe, nowhere was the terrain more suitable than in north America. Additionally, in no other territory were there the experienced backwoodsmen who were used to the conditions and the 'irregular' mode of warfare epitomised by the operations of the British Ranger companies in the French and Indian war. Not even the Austrian border troops, the previous great exponents of light infantry tactics, could match the skill of the American frontiersmen. However, the case can be very much over-stated.

The concept of the War of Independence as a contest between hidebound British redcoats of the style of Braddock's expedition, versus homely American farmers armed with rifles of extreme accuracy, is almost wholly false.

The British forces which fought in the War of Independence were still the steady, disciplined body they had always been. However, the experiences of the French War in north America had led to a re-assessment of the priorities for campaigning there. In the later 1750s,

the British developed proficient light infantry which was capable of matching the skill of their erstwhile French and Indian enemies. Such light infantry was not restricted to 'irregular' corps like the Rangers, but had spread to the regular army, each battalion maintaining a company of light infantry.

However, it was not only their tactics which were a major development. Practicalities even spread to the modification of uniform. The long coat-tails, which were awkward in forested areas, were cut off; one-piece 'gaiter-trousers' or even Indian-style leggings replaced breeches and long gaiters, and unstable cocked hats were cut down or replaced by leather caps or brimmed 'round hats'. Equipment was improved and such items as tomahawks issued, important as tools as much as weapons for woodland service.

The British Forces

Despite the proficiency and steady conduct of the British troops, the royal war effort laboured under a number of troubles. In a tactical sense, the sea was Britain's ally, for British command of the ocean (at least until France entered the war) enabled British troops and supplies to be moved by the navy between the various areas of military operation. In the wider sense, however, the distance between the seat of war and Britain itself was a major problem. Another was the person of the Secretary of State for the colonies, Lord George Germaine (or 'Germain', 1716–85). It is possible to be too harsh in criticism of this man, who exercised much influence in the conduct of the war in America. Yet in truth, he had contemptible qualities and, typically of the times, was thoroughly loathed in some quarters as a coward and a suspected homosexual.

As Lord George Sackville, Germaine had commanded the British cavalry at Minden (1 August 1759) and had refused to advance when ordered. As a result he had been court-martialled and dismissed the service as 'unfit to serve in any military capacity whatever'. So thorough was his condemnation that the sentence was instructed to be entered in the Order Book of every British regiment. He changed his name to Germaine in 1770, which style he retained until he became Viscount Sackville in February 1782.

The symbol of the British monarchy with the Hanoverian motto Nec Aspera Terrent, borne upon the front-plate of the British 1768-pattern grenadier cap. Although varieties existed, the usual pattern was black-enamelled upon white-metal, polished on the highlights to show the design in white on black.

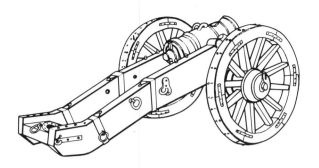

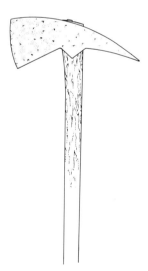

A weapon peculiar to the American War was the tomahawk or hatchet. Originally carried by frontiersmen as a tool-cum-weapon, in military service it was used not only by American militia and riflemen, but also issued to British light infantry.

Germaine was not an incompetent, however, and conducted much of the business of the American war with capability – although his interference in the planning of campaigns, impossible to achieve effectively from across the Atlantic, was a great hindrance to the commanders on the ground. It cannot have made for an easy relationship when British officers in North America realised that their directions were issued by a man whose ignominy was recorded in their regimental records. That apart, Germaine can be charged with most of the strategical errors made during the war. Although not as incompetent as he has sometimes been described, Germaine's presence had substantial relevance in the causes of American success.

A considerable proportion of the British military strength in the American War was represented by German mercenaries, who were hired from the smaller German states at considerable cost. In American history these almost 30,000 troops are often described as 'Hessians', though actually only some 17,000 came from Hesse–Cassell and 2400 from Hesse–Hanau; 5700 were hired from Brunswick, 2400 from Anspach–Bayreuth, 1200 from Waldeck and 1200 from Anhalt–Zerbst. Disciplined in the style of Frederick the Great, they were not overly effective in America; they had no loyalty whatever save that engendered by money, and were feared by the Americans as being unjustifiably cruel.

The Loyalists

Sometimes overlooked is the fact that Britain had much support from the American colonists. Many of them remained loyal to King George III and Britain throughout the war, and subsequently have been condemned in some American accounts as traitors. Styled Loyalists or Tories, they raised regiments in opposition to the rebel colonists. In fact, New York provided more troops for the British war effort than for the rebels.

From a white population of some 2,200,000, probably only about a third actively backed the revolution (though it was a much more 'popular' movement than suggested by some, who place the blame for the war upon a small band of New England activists); and at its conclusion,

almost 100,000 Loyalists left the colonies. Canada benefitted greatly from the influx of Loyalists leaving their native land, but many suffered great hardship for their adherence to their traditional allegiances. An obituary of an unexceptional Loyalist, John Chandler, exemplified the attitude of many:

... from his attachment to good order and peace of society, and affection to the British constitution, [he] left his native country, a numerous family, and affluent estate ... Fully convinced of the truth and propriety of an observation of an antient (sic) writer: 'Fear thou the Lord and the King, and meddle not with them that are given to change', he exemplified it by a pious and loyal, a peaceful and innoffensive conduct ... an honest man, a good member of society, and a pious Christian.[4]

The Colonist Forces

It is easy to put too great an emphasis upon the military character of the colonists as contrasting to that of the British. The idea that the American forces consisted of frontiersmen, all skilled with the Pennsylvania rifle, is entirely erroneous. A large proportion of the colonists were city-dwellers with no experience of frontier warfare. Equally, a considerable proportion *were* frontiersmen, some with experience gained in the French and Indian war.

The army organised to fight the British, however, was formed upon European lines, the men schooled in conventional tactics, and armed with smoothbored muskets very similar to those carried by the British Army. Indeed, in the American army's instructional manual (prepared by the Prussian Frederick William von Steuben), no consideration whatever was given to light infantry tactics or skirmishing. The nearest approximation to these were the directions that, on parade, the light company was not to get in the way of the exercise of the remainder of the battalion, and that when a march halted the advance- and rear-guards should establish a chain of sentinels (sentries) to prevent the main body from straggling! The fact that the colonists were armed mostly with muskets of no greater accuracy than those of the British resulted in very low casualties on some occasions; the poor shooting of the colonist militia in the Lexington–Concord skirmishes, for example, was

Among the many Americans who remained loyal to the crown were the Queen's Rangers, a unit recruited mainly in New York and Connecticut and later including British and Germans in its ranks. Their Regimental colour was blue, bearing the Union canton, a wreath of roses and thistles in natural colours and a crowned red shield edged gold and bearing the title 'Queen's Rangers 1st Amern.'

155

The Pennsylvania or Kentucky long rifle was a descendent of the German hunting rifle, produced originally by German gunsmiths settled in America. Although never used in great numbers in the War of Independence, it was a uniquely American firearm, and came to symbolize the frontier.

remarked upon especially, to the effect that probably only 1 in 300 American shots took effect.[5]

Riflemen

Those Americans (principally frontiersmen) who did use the Pennsylvania rifle were capable of quite astonishing feats of marksmanship. Their proficiency was described by George Hanger, a noted British marksman and advocate of 'rifle' tactics. On one occasion he was reconnoitering with Tarleton some 400 yards from an American position, a range which would normally have rendered a man totally immune from harm. Hanger, Tarleton and their orderly bugler were all mounted, the bugler three yards behind the two officers:

A rifleman passed over the mill-dam, evidently observing two officers, and laid himself down on his belly; for, in such positions, they always lie, to take a good shot at a long distance. He took a deliberate and cool shot at my friend and me, and the bugle-horn man . . . Colonel Tarleton's horse and mine, I am certain, were not any thing like two feet apart; for we were in close consultation, how we should attack . . . A rifle-ball passed between him and me: looking directly to the mill, I evidently observed the flash of the powder. I said directly to my friend, 'I think we had better move, or we shall have two or three of these gentlemen, shortly, amusing themselves at our expense'. The words were hardly out of my mouth, when the bugle-horn man, behind us, and directly central, jumped off his horse, and said, 'Sir, my horse is shot' . . . .[6]

By the standards of the ordinary firearms of the period, such marksmanship was awesome; yet, observed Hanger, the counter to corps composed exclusively of riflemen was how Sir Robert Abercromby opposed Morgan's riflemen:

. . . the moment they appeared before him, he ordered his troops to charge them with the bayonet; not one man of them, out of four, had time to fire, and those who did, had no time given them to load again: they did not stand three minutes . . . They never attacked, or even *looked at*, our light infantry again, without a regular force to support them . . . Surely a corps of British infantry and good marksmen besides, need by no means be alarmed at the attack of a fry corps.[7]

('fry corps' is Hanger's phonetic spelling for the German term *Freikorps*, i.e. irregular riflemen.)

Fighting the War

'Irregular' tactics were disconcerting to those trained in regular European methods. Before the battle of Monmouth Court House, Hanger commanded the British forward picquet, and the harrassment of the American skirmishers throughout a night of storms and thunder led Hanger to exclaim: 'Such a night of anxiety and danger I never since passed, and blessed my God when day began to dawn'.[8]

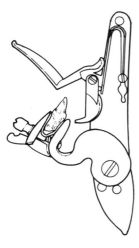

The mechanism of a flintlock.

156

Yet despite the successes of the American riflemen (the first units commissioned for the 'Continental Army' were rifle-armed), the contemporary preference for the musket was such that when the state of Maryland offered a rifle company to the Continental Army, the reaction was that whilst the men would be welcome, they would be of more use if armed with muskets, these being less prone to damage, quicker to fire and could accommodate a bayonet. Thus, the popular idea that riflemen played a large part in the American victory is false. It also explains, in part, why the British paid so little attention to rifle-armed troops, the only unit so equipped being a ranger corps formed by the Scottish officer Patrick Ferguson (1744–80), who invented the first breech-loading firearm used by the British Army.

Regarding the rifle, it is interesting to observe the contemporary standards of honour in evidence: before the battle of Brandywine, Ferguson had the chance to shoot George Washington, but declined to fire as it was regarded as totally dishonourable to shoot an enemy who at that moment was causing no offence![9]

Although riflemen came to be regarded as very much an auxiliary corps even in the American army, unable to take their place in the

Officer (right) and private (left) of the American army. The most notable feature of the uniform is the light infantry cap copied from the light troops of the British Army. It was a headdress more practical for skirmishing than the cocked hat. British caps often bore regimental devices, whilst political symbols were used in some American corps, in this case a skull and bones and 'Liberty' (signifying the popular motto 'liberty or death'). Others worn by American units featured regimental or state devices, such as the crescent badge of South Carolina, or 'COR' and Pro Aris et Focis worn by Congress' Own Regiment (2nd Canadian). Such caps were often provided with a peak.

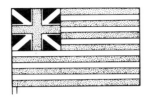

Raised by Washington upon taking command of the Continental Army was the 'Grand Union' flag, alternate red and white stripes (symbolizing the 13 colonies) with the British Union Flag in the upper canton; in June 1777 it was replaced by a similar deisgn but with 13 stars in the canton, the first 'Stars and Stripes'.

regular line-of-battle, Washington paid much attention to the significance of light infantry. Light companies (generally composed of the most experienced men) were formed in all American regiments, and kept up to strength despite the shortage of manpower in other companies. Such men could be detached from their units and formed into *ad hoc* light infantry corps for particular missions. Although the Continental Army's prescribed uniform was of the ordinary European style, Washington preferred a more practical costume as favoured by light infantry. Fabric smocks ('hunting shirts') and buckskins were used by a number of units, and Washington passed an opinion that, given the opportunity, he would like to see the entire army clothed in this manner – further evidence of his care for even the smallest concerns of his army.

Cavalry, which played so important a rôle in European campaigns, figured hardly at all in America. Much of the terrain was not suitable for the employment of cavalry, and the Americans had little facility for training them. Even Britain employed only two regular light dragoon regiments in America, though they possessed more in the form of Loyalist units.

Washington in Command

Upon his appointment to supreme command of the American forces, Washington declared that he did not regard himself as equal to the task; no mere rhetoric, but a belief genuinely held. To the end of his life, he may not have appreciated fully that no other commander in America could have achieved what he was to accomplish in the next several years.

Notwithstanding his wealth, it is a remarkable testament to Washington's personal qualities that he asked for no salary for his onorous position, but merely a defrayment of whatever expenses he incurred in the service. Throughout the war, he accepted no pay for what he must have regarded as no more than patriotic duty. So thinking, he set out at once to take command of the American troops attempting the besiege the British garrison of Boston.

Bunker Hill and the Boston Army

On 17 June (the day Washington's appointment was confirmed), the first battle of the war had been fought. The British had sallied out of Boston and stormed entrenched rebel positions at Bunker Hill (actually Breed's Hill, but the battle is generally known by the name of Bunker Hill). Two British assaults were repulsed bloodily; but as the rebels ran out of ammunition, the third drove them away. The action heartened the Americans, who believed that their undisciplined and shoddily-organised troops were thus proven to be the equals of the British. This was an over-confidence which almost had fatal results, and the action had proved again the amazing discipline and cold courage of the British infantry, whose success after suffering so terribly in the first assaults was truly remarkable.

On 3 July 1775, George Washington arrived at the camp before Boston to take command of the rebel army. He was an imposing figure, with a calm and dignified bearing which impressed all who met him. In his prime he stood 6 feet 3 inches tall, which alone marked him out among his contemporaries. Of fair complexion but rather florid, he weighed about 217 pounds, but was well-proportioned; Lafayette noted that his hands were the largest he had ever seen. It was the imposing and soldier-like bearing which was his most significant quality, however, with an air of dignity which discouraged even the possibility of familiarity with his subordinates.

The army of which Washington took command was, in truth, little more than a semi-organised rabble. At the time of his commission, the Continental Congress had decreed the formation of six rifle companies as the beginning of what was styled the 'Continental Army'. This term was used to differentiate between the new 'regular' army controlled by Congress, and the local militia formations controlled by their own state authorities. The militia units were normally only called out in time of danger, and irrespective of circumstances were enrolled for a specified period. For example, when Washington assumed command at Boston, the 17,000 militia he found there had enlistments which would expire at the end of the year, whereupon they would return home. That the troops went away upon the expiry of their enlistments was a problem which beset Washington throughout the war. Although generous bounties were offered to those who enrolled in the regular (i.e. Continental) army for the duration, the actual numbers of men available were usually a very great deal fewer than those who were supposed to be under arms. The initial Continental Army, for example, was set at 20,370 men in 26 infantry battalions, provided by only four of the thirteen colonies (Massachusetts 16 battalions, Connecticut 5, New Hampshire 3 and Rhode Island 2). By the end of 1775, only about 6000 men had been enlisted. Consequently, from December 1775 to January 1776, Washington had to call out the militia once again.

The organisation of the Continental Army changed progressively, with units being provided by the remaining colonies. In September 1776, the establishment was set at 88 infantry battalions, provided as follows: Massachusetts and Virginia 15 each; Pennsylvania 12; North Carolina 9; Connecticut and Maryland 8 each; South Carolina 6; New York and New Jersey 4 each; New Hampshire 3, Rhode Island 2; Delaware and Georgia 1 each.

Throughout the War, probably some quarter of a million men served

The 'Liberty Tree' flag of Massachusetts (also sometimes styled the 'New England Pine Tree Flag') existed in a range of designs and colours. The tree sometimes appeared in a white canton on a red or blue flag, with such mottoes as 'An Appeal to Heaven' or 'An Appeal to God'.

in some branch of the American forces; more precise calculations are impossible due to the limited periods of enlistment, some men enlisting for three or four terms in succession. The largest number of troops raised by Congress in a single year was 46,900 regulars and 42,700 militia in 1776; the greatest actual strength ever attained by the Continental Army (as different from the 'establishment' which existed on paper) was around 35,000. The largest force ever commanded by Washington was less than 17,000, inclusive of militia, and frequently very many fewer than that; in the Trenton campaign, for example, he had only about 4000 under his command.

The Other Commanders

The Americans possessed other capable commanders, but none who approached Washington's stature. Nathaniel Greene (1742–86) was a capable administrator and strategist who built his reputation on his campaign in the Carolinas, but he never won a major battle.

Horatio Gates (1728–1806) was English, and had served in the British Army and survived Braddock's defeat; but he was soured by his lowly background (son of the Duke of Leeds' housekeeper but godson of Horace Walpole) when compared with the patrician origin of Washington. Indeed, he conspired against Washington when it was suggested that Congress might appoint him in Washington's stead. Despite his victory at Saratoga, Gates was not a competent commander.

Charles Lee (1731–82) was also of English birth, and also a survivor of Braddock's expedition, and had served as a mercenary in the Polish army against the Turks. He was still drawing half-pay from his British lieutenant-colonelcy when he was appointed Major-General in the Continental Army, which was not regarded as the action of an honourable man. Unpopular in the American army (his 'dirty habits' and obscenities gave offence!), it was suspected that he hoped for Washington's defeat, so that he might become commander-in-chief himself, or that he was guilty of treason. Ultimately, he was dismissed by Congress.

Artemas Ward (1727–1800) was officially Washington's second-in-command, but their association was never easy. A mutual antipathy was fired by Ward's resentment at Washington gaining the senior position, though Ward was never an able general. On the other hand, Richard Montgomery (1738–75), an Irish-born, ex-British Army officer, was recognised even by his opponents as a brave and capable officer; but he was killed in the American attack on Quebec.

Perhaps the Americans' most capable commander, other than Washington, was Benedict Arnold (1741–1801). Though an unprincipled rogue, Arnold possessed very considerable military talent. The victory of Saratoga was largely his, but he is damned as the most heinous traitor in American history when he changed sides and was commissioned as a

Benedict Arnold, from an engraving published in 1781 by Fielding and Walker.

general in the British Army. (After a mixed career he moved to England in 1791 and died there. His descendents did much to resurrect the family's reputation. His son James Robertson Arnold (1781–1854) served in Egypt and rose to the rank of lieutenant-general in the British Army; his grandson, Capt. William Trail Arnold of the 4th Foot (1826–55) was killed whilst posting sentries in the advanced trenches at the siege of Sebastopol.)

With such commanders in the American army, Washington's value becomes even more apparent. Nevertheless, despite his obvious talents and his appointment as commander-in-chief, he was harrassed continually by the Congress. Congress quarrelled with the governments of the various colonies, both of which controlled parts of Washington's forces; both issued contradictory orders to Washington and countermanded his own; both appointed officers without his approval and disbanded troops which he required. Not until the situation became absolutely desperate did they accord Washington the powers which he might reasonably have expected to possess as commander-in-chief. With such hinderance from his political masters, it is a measure of Washington's capability that he was able to hold the rebel war-effort together as successfully as he did. It was a task beyond the capability of any other general.

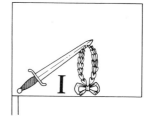

The design of many early American flags clearly demonstrated the colonists' ancestry, being stylistically very similar to flags of the English Civil War. None was more so that this, usually attributed to the 1st company of Webb's 3rd Connecticut Regiment: yellow with white sword and numeral, green laurel-wreach and red ribbon. Even the small size (36 inches) is akin to that of an English Civil War standard.

First Campaigns

The period from Washington's assumption of command of the 'Boston Army' and the British evacuation of Boston in mid-March 1776 was one of his most difficult yet most influential periods. His army's enlistment expired at the end of the year. Thus, his most pressing task was to create another army to replace it, to equip it, train it, arrange for provisions – all within the presence of the enemy and made up from a people deeply suspicious of 'professional' military establishments. Furthermore, he had to do it in the face of interference from Congress and from those who demanded immediate action despite the paltry resources at his command.

A General of Quality

Washington's initial reaction was one of disheartenment. He reported that such was the lack of public spirit and so great was the element of self-seeking, that had he realised the true case of the matter, nothing would have persuaded him to accept the command. However, since he had overcome the difficulties of the winter of 1775–76, he could surely overcome anything; and it is a measure of Washington's administrative and diplomatic skills that by February 1776 he was again in command of

about 16,000 men, provided with adequate ammunition and the artillery captured by the Americans at Ticonderoga in May 1775. No further doubts should have been entertained about whether or not the Americans had a general of quality.

The first campaign waged by the Americans had begun in September 1775, when Arnold and Montgomery invaded Canada. They were repulsed in their attempt to capture Quebec, Montgomery being killed on New Year's Eve. Although the expedition continued to the middle of 1776, the Americans posed no further threat to Canada. Washington had not been involved in this operation beyond in its planning (at a time when his energies were required more urgently on other matters), which left him free to pursue his own actions against Boston. The British commander, General Sir William Howe (1729–1814), evacuated the city on 17 March after Washington had opened his bombardment on 2 March. The British sailed for Halifax, leaving behind considerable stores and 69 pieces of artillery which were most welcome additions to the American resources. Massachusetts remained free of British troops for the remainder of the War.

Battle of Long Island

Washington began to transfer his army to New York, which he expected to be the most likely target for the British. This was indeed the case, and Howe had received considerable reinforcements from Britain. Washington was charged by Congress to hold New York, to which end he began the construction of fortifications. Before operations around New York began in earnest, the Declaration of Independence was signed on 4 July, putting a new perspective upon the war, and overcoming the reservations of some adherents to the American cause who had been uncertain of taking so irrevocable a step.

Howe landed on Staten Island on 2 July and began to build up his forces to an effective strength of around 25,000. Washington had about 13,000 men, whom he distributed widely. It was an action for which he may be criticised; for by disposing of them in this way, he left himself open to 'defeat in detail'.

In fact, that is exactly what happened. On 22 August 1776, the British began to cross from Staten Island to Long Island. Washington was not certain that this was the main attack, so although he sent reinforcements to General Israel Putnam, he did not take command personally.

Israel 'Old Put' Putnam (1718–90) was a brave and resolute (if almost illiterate) veteran who had served as an officer in Rogers' Rangers in the French and Indian War, and who would have made an ideal regimental commander; but as a general he was hopelessly mis-cast, with little aptitude for higher command. When Howe attacked on 27 August, the British completely out-manoeuvered the Americans, turning their left flank in overwhelming numbers. (Probably about 10,000

Brass regimental device from a British Army cartridge-box, an example of which was excavated at White Plains; the 15th Regiment of Foot was sent to America in 1776 and moved to the West Indies in 1778.

Americans, the major part of Washington's force, were on Long Island; of these, about 3500 were actually engaged. Howe had about 20,000 men). The Americans were routed with immense losses in proportion to the troops involved, probably over 1400, of whom over 1100 were captured. Howe lost less than 400.

The Battle of Long Island was the first full-scale action of the war, and demonstrated just how outclassed the Americans were, inexperienced and with incompetent leadership – and with a grievous failing of reconnaissance which prevented Washington from realising what Howe was about until it was too late.

Among the American commanders captured was William Alexander, Earl of Stirling (1726–83), the son of a Jacobite but who had served the British in the French and Indian War. Although his claim to the earldom of Stirling was never recognised officially in Britain, his presence in the rebel army serves to emphasize the very close links between the members of both armies. In this respect, it was virtually a civil war waged between factions of the same people.

Harlem Heights and White Plains

Having suffered severely for the fatal division of his force, Washington determined not to be defeated again by the more proficient and more numerous British forces. His entrenchments on Brooklyn Heights were still intact, and when Howe showed no inclination to launch an injudicious frontal assault of the Bunker Hill style, Washington decided to evacuate Long Island. This he achieved with considerable skill, abandoning the Brooklyn defences on 29–30 August; Washington was himself one of the very last to leave.

The demoralization of the Americans was considerable, and as on many other occasions Washington found his army dwindling as men left the ranks; and morale fell even lower when the decision was taken to evacuate New York (12 September). Washington withdrew slowly, leaving much of his artillery; 67 guns were captured by the British in New York. Yet, for the second time, Howe did not take advantage of Washington's dispersal of his forces in retreat to smash the American army.

On 16 September, Howe's advance-guard was repulsed by Washington's positions at the Battle of Harlem Heights; though styled a battle, it was little more than desultory skirmishing which cost each side only around 150 casualties. However, the British advance up the East River threatened Washington's communications and he continued to withdraw. Howe's pursuit was painstaking, but on 28 October he engaged an advanced American division at White Plains. At first, the rebel forces stood firm, but the British and Hessian advance was conducted with their usual steadiness; the American militia broke and were driven from the field. Washington himself was protected by his entrenchments, but on 1 November continued his retreat to an even stronger position across the Crotton river.

Instead of pursuing, Howe turned south to reduce the American strongpoints of Forts Washington and Lee. George Washington's inclination was to sacrifice these posts and save the troops who were in garrison; but he left the final decision to Nathaniel Greene, who decided to reinforce Fort Washington when he received an instruction from Congress that it should be held at all costs. The British attacked the fort with about 8000 men on 16 November. The Americans suffered few casualties but lost 3000 prisoners when the fort surrendered, together with a considerable amount of matériel. The British lost about 450 men.

Fort Lee was captured four days later, but the garrison escaped. These losses were severe blows to the American cause, but in the longer term they may be regarded as of considerable importance. By turning against the forts, Howe had abandoned his immediate pursuit of Washington's main army, and by failing to destroy the American forces had saved the American revolution.

Victory at Trenton

Washington's position was now deteriorating further, as he began to retire through New Jersey, pursued by the British General Charles, 2nd Earl Cornwallis (1738–1805), who had claimed that he would catch the American commander just as a hunter would 'bag a fox.' It appeared that his boast might not be unjustified when General Charles Lee, whom Washington had left to cover the retreat, allowed himself to be captured at Basking Ridge on 13 December. In fact, Lee had been so dilatory in obeying the instructions which he received from Washington that it might be suspected that he was so antagonistic towards his commander that he deliberately hazarded the American cause, perhaps hoping that a defeat of the troops under Washington's personal command might lead to Washington's dismissal and his replacement by Lee himself.

Washington, now reduced to a command of just over 3000 men, crossed the Delaware river into Pennsylvania. So great was the threat to the American cause that the Congress fled from Philadelphia to Baltimore. There, on 27 December, they granted Washington greatly increased powers in the hope that the revolution could be maintained by his efforts. These powers included the right to appoint officers under the rank of brigadier-general without reference to any higher authority; to purchase compulsorily anything needed for the army; and to arrest anyone who did not support the American cause. They were granted for a sixth-month period, and although Washington did not use the powers to the full, he was criticised by Congress for making citizens surrender the documents received from the British after accepting the British offer of protection. However, from the beginning of 1777 his new and very temporary authority allowed him effectually to reorganize

Lord Cornwallis in an engraving of a slightly later period than that of the War, but based upon a portrait from life.

the American forces. Yet so desperate was the appearance of the American cause that Howe went into winter quarters in New York. He had not waged the campaign with maximum speed, and it may be that his hesitation at this stage was to avoid the further effusion of blood, hoping instead for a diplomatic settlement. (As early as September 1776 an abortive peace conference had been called at Staten Island.)

At this moment, when the American cause looked to be on the point of extinction, Washington decided to move. With his army disintegrating from the shattering blows to morale dealt by the British victories, he determined to take the offensive with the few troops at his disposal, whose numbers might be halved by the end of the year when the enlistments expired. He had less than a week before his army might be expected to dissolve. The audacity of the plan, born of the desperate position of the Americans, was astonishing.

On Christmas night 1776, Washington crossed the Delaware river with some 2400 men carried in 'Durham boats' (shallow-draughted cargo-carriers resembling barges). The march of Washington's column was an epic in itself. In a night of bitter cold, a snowstorm and with the Delaware littered with grues of ice, many of his men were barefoot and reduced to wearing rags. Crossing the Delaware nine miles north of Trenton, Washington hoped to surprise the 1200-strong Hessian garrison of that town.

Although the Hessians had foreknowledge of the operation, thanks to their excellent intelligence, they believed it would be a minor raid, and that a skirmish on Christmas morning was the operation they expected. Consequently, Washington's attack at 8 a.m. was a complete surprise, and the Hessian commander, Johann Gottlieb Rall, an acknowledged drunkard, was unprepared. When roused, the Hessians put up a stiff fight, though the inclemency of the weather had rendered most of the muskets useless. Consequently, the action was largely one of hand-to-hand combat and artillery (Washington had brought 18 guns with him). Rall was mortally wounded, the Hessians' retreat was cut off, and the majority surrendered. The British force was effectively destroyed, but it is possible that the Americans suffered no fatalities save two or three who froze to death in the snow.

Washington had intended to continue his advance against the British garrison of Princeton, but as his planned supports failed to arrive, he had no choice but withdraw. Nevertheless, given the desperate situation in which the American forces had been, it was a stunning victory which greatly enhanced morale. Among the American wounded was William Washington (1752–1810), a distant cousin of the commander-in-chief.

Battle of Princeton
As Cornwallis moved after the Americans, Washington again decided

to take the offensive, and re-crossed the Delaware. By now his supplies were almost exhausted and the army's enlistment almost expired. Nevertheless, with the help of an unauthorised ten-dollar bounty and, no doubt, the force of his own personality, he persuaded many of the New Englanders to remain with the army for a short while longer. As a result, at the beginning of 1777, he was able to muster about 500 Virginians, 1100 volunteers who had temporarily renewed their enlistments, and some Pennsylvanian and New Jersey militiamen. Having learned from the failures caused by the division of his forces in the New York campaign, Washington now concentrated his small army.

Cornwallis believed that he had the Americans trapped, and so did not press forward in the sharp action which developed late in the afternoon of 2 January, but was prepared to wait until the morrow before destroying Washington. Certainly, the Americans could not have resisted a major attack by Cornwallis' greatly superior forces. So, rather than await the assault, Washington left his camp-fires burning and stole out of his camp in the early morning of 3 January, making a circuitous march around Cornwallis' flank in order to destroy the British supplies located in the town of Princeton. On his way there, the American vanguard encountered a British column *en route* to reinforce Cornwallis, and in a battle lasting only about a quarter of an hour routed it. When Cornwallis turned to strike belatedly at the Americans, Washington withdrew safely and took his barefoot, exhausted troops into winter quarters, encamping on the flank of the British advance in New Jersey. Cornwallis did not pursue.

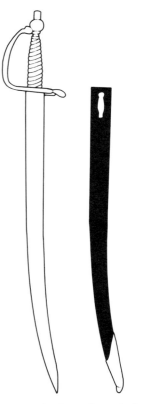

A typical infantry 'hanger' of the period, the hilt usually of brass and cast in one piece.

Ten Days of Triumph

The operation of Trenton and Princeton, though the numbers of troops involved were very small in comparison to European campaigns, was one of the most important of the war. With Washington's forces threatening their communications, the British garrisons in west and central New Jersey were withdrawn, but the outcome was more than just a matter of territorial advantage. The Americans cause had been on the verge of extinction, and from the operations around New York, their commander had appeared to be a very pedestrian general. The desperate gamble taken to advance against the British, at a time when the American forces were physically and morally nearing collapse, had paid immense dividends.

The ten days of operations around the turn of the year had proved that Washington was indeed a commander of considerable skill, and that the determination of the Americans was not to be overcome as easily as the British had believed. Even Frederick the Great admired the Trenton–Princeton campaign, but more than a military triumph alone, it is quite possible that it saved the American cause from destruction.

The War in 1777

Despite the brilliance of Washington's Trenton–Princeton campaign, on balance the war in 1776 had gone against the Americans, and in 1777 Howe continued to register British successes. Washington maintained his little army in existence, but his difficulties were still huge. There was a lack of support from both the public and Congress, and a continuing dearth of supplies. The American winter quarters at Morristown, New Jersey, formed a strong position against which Howe made no move. He has been criticized for not renewing the offensive against the Americans immediately, but in fairness a lengthy period of recuperation over winter was standard European campaigning practice.

The first half of 1777 was spent in inconclusive skirmishing, but in July Howe sailed from New York with some 15,000 men. Unsure of where this force would land, Washington held his army in readiness until he received news that Howe had sailed up Chesapeake Bay and disembarked at Head of Elk. He came to the obvious conclusion that the British were moving to capture Philadelphia.

Brandywine

Washington marched his army to cover Philadelphia, and took up a position behind Brandywine Creek, the first location from which he could effectually challenge Howe's march. It was not as strong a position as might have been expected, however, as there were numerous fords over which the British could cross. Although, on occasion, Howe had appeared a somewhat lethergic commander, at Brandywine on 11 September he conducted a skilful operation.

Washington had around 10,500 to 12,000 men, and Howe had no superiority in numbers, making a frontal assault impossible. Instead, he advanced in two columns, engaging the central part of the American force with his right column, and with his left column swung around to turn Washington's right flank. The British were steadier and more experienced than the Americans. Furthermore, Washington's subordinates were so careless of reconnaissance that Howe's left column, commanded by Cornwallis, was almost ready to fall on the American right flank before Washington was aware that they were there. When the threat became apparent, Washington acted with some skill, retiring his reserve to cover the right flank, and so prevented a complete destruction of his position when Cornwallis duly routed the original American right wing. The American forces initially withdrew in good order, but their retreat soon broke down in some confusion; but after the long flank-march, Cornwallis' men were not able to pursue. Washington lost around 1200 men (and 11 guns); Howe lost less than half that number.

Though defeated at Brandywine, Washington's army had not been destroyed, and he withdrew leaving a rearguard to blunt Howe's

Distinctive insignia maintained the regimental identify and ésprit de corps of the British Army. An example of this silver plate from an officer's shoulder-belt was excavated at New York; the 28th Regiment of Foot served at White Plains and Brandywine before moving from New York to the West Indies in 1778.

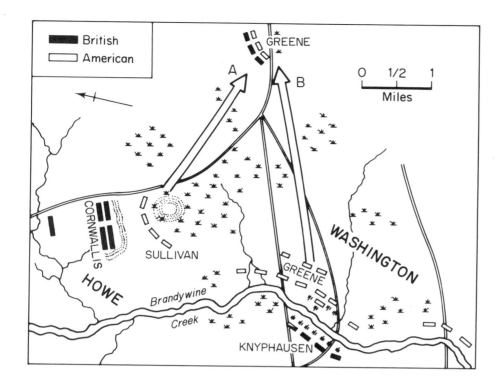

advance. This division, commanded by General 'Mad Anthony' Wayne (1745–96), was encamped at Paoli, Pennsylvania. There, on 21 September, they were surprised by a night attack conducted by the British General Charles 'No-flint' Grey (1729–1807). The nickname came from Grey's order that his troops were to remove their musket-flints, so that in the attack on Paoli they would have to fight hand-to-hand, and not be tempted to halt their rush upon the Americans by pausing to fire. Wayne's division was routed, losing about one tenth of his 1500 men.

Battle of Brandywine, 11 September 1777, showing (A) the rout of Washington's original right wing, and (B) the transfer of his original reserve to form a new right wing.

Germantown

In the immediate aftermath of Brandywine, Washington was out-manoeuvred by Howe. Marching some 140 miles in atrocious weather and with meagre supplies, the American army shrank to a strength of only about 6000 men. Fortunately, Washington was able to gather reinforcements. Philadelphia was evacuated, the Congress moving first to Lancaster, and then to York, Pennsylvania; and it again accorded Washington increased powers (for a period of six days!). Then, on 26 September, Howe occupied Philadelphia.

Reinforced to a strength of about 13,000, Washington attacked Howe's army at Germantown on 11 October. The plan was probably too complicated for the American army's limited experience, and it was also reported that some members of the army had imbibed rather too freely before the attack. A dense fog which descended in the early morning as the attack began was more of a hinderance to the Americans than to the better-disciplined British troops. The British 40th Foot, Howe's vanguard, retired into the substantial residence of a Mr. Chew, possession of which was a considerable obstacle to Washington. The defence of 'Chew House' was quite an epic, and resulted in the issue of one of the British Army's earliest medals, struck at the instigation of the 40th's Colonel Musgrave. Confusion in the fog, when one American formation fired upon another, disrupted the American attack, and their forces gave way. Losses (including prisoners) were about 600 on the British side and over 1000 on the American.

Germantown was a considerable defeat for Washington, for which he was not free of blame, for his plan of advance was so complex that even a well-disciplined British force would have had difficulty following it in the darkness in which the approach was made. Paradoxically, though it was a defeat, both Washington and his army thought that they had almost won, so that their morale actually improved as a result. Perhaps the fairest assessment might not be to criticise Washington for his poor tactics, but to recognise his courage and determination in making the attack at all.

A short time later, despite Washington's attempts to hold them, the American forts on the Delaware river were captured by Howe (with the assistance of the fleet of his brother, Admiral Lord Howe), Fort Mifflin on 16 November and Fort Mercer on 21 November. The Americans held them sufficiently, however, to disrupt the intended use of the Delaware as an avenue for British supplies.

Saratoga

As the campaigning season of 1777 in the Philadelphia region drew to a close, the British could be reasonably satisfied with their position, despite criticism of Howe for being overly cautious. However, in the north, British fortunes were more depressed. An expedition from Canada commanded by General John 'Gentleman Johnny' Burgoyne (1722–92) enjoyed initial success but suffered a series of defeats (Bennington, 16 August 1777; Freeman's Farm, 19 September; Bemis Heights, 7 October) at the hands of an American force commanded initially by Philip Schuyler (1733–1803) and latterly by Horatio Gates. Burgoyne was devoid of support, for the British commander at New York, Sir Henry Clinton (c.1738–95) made only a peripheral diversion to take pressure off Burgoyne. Thus, trapped with a greatly-outnumbered force of only 5700 men at Saratoga, Burgoyne surrendered on 17 October on the understanding that his troops could return home on parole; the Americans did not honour the agreement.

Saratoga was probably the war's turning-point, contrasting sharply with Washington's reverses in the central area of operations. British holdings in the north were reduced; the Americans were enormously heartened; and France recognised the independence of the United States. Yet though it benefitted the infant nation, Saratoga heaped even more trouble upon the already overburdened shoulders of the commander-in-chief.

The Cabal and Valley Forge

Of all the leaders of the American colonies, Washington was probably the one who appreciated the strategic situation best of all. He knew that to win independence, a protracted war would be necessary and that American resources would have to be husbanded. In contrast, Members of Congress favoured a more rapid and violent trial of strength, which, had Washington concurred, would almost certainly have resulted in British victory. Such misguided opinions served to undermine confidence in the commander-in-chief, and a clique of officers attempted to force the issue by having Congress replace Washington with Horatio Gates. The latter, an ambitious and jealous man, perhaps never really expected this to happen, but naturally took what advantage he could from his success at Saratoga.

Conspiracy
The plot against Washington is sometimes styled 'Conway's Cabal', after Brigadier-General Thomas Conway (1733–c.1800), an ambitious and pretentious Irish soldier who had served in the French army, who was used as the trigger for the plot by the New England Congress members trying to regain control of the revolution. Whether or not there was actually a plot is debatable. Perhaps it was merely an example of opportunist disaffection which got out of hand, conducted by semi-anonymous slander. When public exposure became likely, those involved retreated and left Conway to take the blame.

Whatever the case, the 'Cabal' failed completely, leaving Washington in a stronger position for having overcome the opposition to him. Conway wrote to apologise to Washington for having written anything or agitated in any way which could have prejudiced his career. Washington, knowing of Conway's attempts to undermine his position, declined to answer. Conway's friends in Congress abandoned him, so that when he complained about his lack of an active command, they took him at his word and accepted the token resignation he had offered. He returned to French service in 1779. Washington was then able to establish a reasonably cordial working relationship with Gates, and the threat to his position was ended.

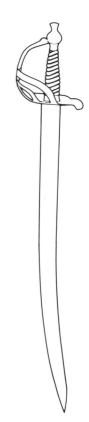

The so-called 1751 pattern British infantry hanger with brass semi-basket hilt. This was not an official designation and regimental patterns varied, being purchased privately from each unit's funds rather than being issued centrally.

171

Valley Forge

The winter quarters Washington established for the winter of 1777–78 were at Valley Forge, some twenty miles from the British at Philadelphia. The position was well-chosen for defence, but is synonymous in American military history for deprivation and hardship. No shelters were available for the troops until mid-January 1778, when wooden huts were constructed. As they received shelter, however, so their supplies of food and clothing virtually ran out. In the six-month winter quarters perhaps 2500 died of privation, about a quarter of the strength; yet there was no mutiny or mass desertion.

Given the atrocious conditions under which the army had to exist, this loyalty must have been due in a large measure to the confidence the army had in Washington's leadership. As the privation was due more to American corruption and mismanagement than to the weather or the British, it was something over which Washington could exert an influence, and even when struggling with the troubles of the Cabal, he made great steps to improve the wretched predicament of his troops. Clothing and provender was supplied by forced requisition from the local civilians, and by foraging-parties sent out under the command of Washington's most trusted subordinates. A major improvement was the appointment of Nathaniel Greene as Quartermaster-General (February 1778; he still retained his right to a field command) in succession to Thomas Mifflin (1744–1800), a supporter of (perhaps the instigator of) the Cabal, who regarded Washington with jealousy and hoped for preferment if Gates assumed the chief command. As Quartermaster-General, Mifflin had been incompetent, perhaps even dishonest, and Congress called an inquiry into his accounts; he was responsible to a considerable degree for the misery at Valley Forge.

Foreign Friends

A change began to take place in the American army at Valley Forge, due in large part to Washington's reorganisation and training programme. Washington was instrumental in this, though did not undertake it all personally. There was an in-built suspicion in the colonies of the concept of a 'standing army'; many had family memories of the influence of Cromwell's army on British politics. In spite of this, Washington realised that professional soldiers were needed to train and command the American forces. To this end, and against some resistance, he recruited experienced foreign commanders.

Probably the best-known of these recruits was the Marquis de Lafayette (Marie Joseph P.Y.R.G. du Motier, 1757–1834), a French aristocrat of little military experience before he volunteered for the American army. Despite his youth, in July 1777 he was commissioned as a major-general in the American army (when aged only 20!), and proved a most valuable friend and subordinate to Washington. Motivated by an idealism which in due course led him to support the early stage of the French Revolution, he showed considerable military skill and, even more important, helped to facilitate the eventual French entry into the war. He expended vast sums of his personal fortune on the American cause, and became such a symbol of Franco-American collaboration that a squadron of American pilots who had volunteered to serve in the French Air Force during World War I was titled the *Escadrille Lafayette*.

Another valuable foreign professional was Johann Kalb (1721–80), a Bavarian who had served in the French army and who was known in America as Baron de Kalb. Originally a volunteer for the American army like Lafayette, he too was commissioned as major-general. Having decided to go to America in the rôle of professional or mercenary soldier, he became caught up in the idealism of the War of Independence and was a genuine American patriot when he was killed in 1780. A reliable and capable officer, Kalb was worthy of higher command but had no political influence; his advice was ignored disastrously by Gates in the Camden campaign of 1780.

Washington's personal flag, as flown at Valley Forge with a blue ground bearing thirteen white stars.

Steuben

More significant than all the other helpers was the presence of Baron von Steuben. Friedrich Wilhelm Ludolf Gerhard Augustin von Steuben (known in America as Frederick William Augustus von Steuben, 1730–94) was the son of a Prussian engineer and had served Frederick the Great in the Seven Years War, most importantly in the general staff. He left Prussian service in 1763, and after a period as chamberlain to the court of Hohenzollern-Hechingen (where he gained his barony), was so deeply in debt that he had to return to the profession of arms. Failing to secure a commission in the French, Austrian or Baden forces, he was recommended to Benjamin Franklin as a man who might be of use to the American service. Franklin (who was an effective recruiting-officer for foreign personnel) in turn recommended him to Washington as a lieutenant-general of the Prussian army, which Steuben certainly was not. However, his offer to serve as an unpaid volunteer (drawing only expenses, like Washington himself) doubtless impressed the Congress; in February 1778 he joined the camp at Valley Forge. Trained in the Prussian system of painstaking and immaculate drill and unbendable discipline, Steuben formulated a programme of training which Washington approved.

Steuben's personality probably contributed to his overall effect. Speaking no English, he cut a somewhat eccentric figure in his immaculate uniform and with his German style of command. It was even said that his American aide, with whom he communicated in mediocre French, was at times instructed to swear on Steuben's behalf when his pupils were not performing as he wished!

Steuben's effect on the American army was profound. It was far greater than merely an influence over the men he drilled in person; his methods spread throughout the army, and were authorized officially in the manual *Regulations for the Order and Discipline of the Troops of the United States*, to which Congress provided the preface in March 1779:

Congress judging it of the greatest importance to prescribe some invariable rules for the order and discipline of the troops, especially for the purpose of introducing an uniformity in their formation and manoeuvres and in the service of the camp: Ordered, that the following regulations be observed by all the troops of the United States . . .

The *Regulations* are remarkably clear and concise, and though comprehensive ran to only some 150 pages. The introduction of a uniform drill for the entire army was significant, pre-dating by a decade the equivalent British manual; and it specified that when assembled in line, units should be formed in two ranks, unlike the prevalent European practice of three-rank lines. In this, Steuben was considerably in advance of many other military theorists: in British service, for example, the more effective two-rank line only became accepted around 1800.

Steuben's *Regulations* and his presence in the American service had a major effect on the professionalism and discipline of the American army. However, this is not to suggest that the American troops overnight became as well-drilled and steady as the British and German regulars whom they faced. Disciplined firing by volley remained the preserve of the British; but the improvement in the American army was immense. Washington was a prime mover in the process of reforming the army, but probably they never achieved the level of discipline and professionalism he desired. Despite the improvement, bad officers remained in position, some from political influence. Nevertheless, the overall standard had improved greatly from Washington's early command, when he had expressed the belief that officers should be gentlemen, not (as was frequently the case in the early stages, at least in his opinion) men unfitted to be shoeblacks, with others elected by their men and with such an air of equality that the rank and file had no more respect for their superiors than for a broomstick!

Upon Washington's recommendation, Steuben was appointed Inspector-General of the American army in May 1778, but enjoyed only a brief field command, at Yorktown, where his knowledge of European siege-warfare was put to good use. He became a citizen of his adopted country in 1783 and remained there for the rest of his life, assisted by a governmental pension and help from his friends. Although he remained improvident to the end of his life, he is duly revered as the first professional instructor of the American army. Perhaps his influence has been overestimated on occasion. After all, his raw material was not the armed mob with which Washington had to contend initially, but rather a nucleus of campaigners of some experience. Yet whatever the argument, Steuben's involvement and effect was certainly of the highest importance.

The War in 1778–79

The most significant development in the year following the Valley Forge winter was the alliance between France and the United States. In February, a treaty of friendship was concluded between the two, with a military alliance to take effect if war occurred between Britain and France. Such a war duly came about in June 1778, and considerable French resources were henceforth at the disposal of the American camp. Of especial strategic significance was the presence of the French fleet, as prior to French entry into the war the British domination of the sea was unchallenged, the Americans having no naval forces larger than frigates or privateers.

Sir Henry Clinton, in an engraving of about 1782.

During Washington's winter at Valley Forge, Howe made no attempt to attack him. Perhaps he considered it would have been wasteful to exhaust his army by a winter campaign, when the American army might be destroyed by privation. Alternatively, perhaps he realised that without a large reinforcement and with Germaine's continual interference, the chance of concluding the war successfully was small.

Monmouth and Charles Lee

In May 1778, Clinton succeeded Howe in chief command of the British forces in North America. With resources more limited than those upon which Howe could draw, little could be accomplished in the north. Philadelphia was evacuated on 18 June in order that British forces could be concentrated in New York.

Washington set in motion his army of 15,000 men to pursue and intercept Clinton. He hurried on his advance-guard under the command of Charles Lee, who had rejoined the American army in mid-May 1778 after an exchange of prisoners. Lee was supposed to attack the British rearguard in the flank and hold it until Washington could arrive with the main body. He failed miserably in his task, and by virtue of his conduct even aroused suspicions of treachery.

On 28 June, Lee engaged Clinton's rearguard at Monmouth, but his troops were thrown back and pursued by part of the British force. They retreated in confusion for some three miles until they ran into Washington's main body. Washington took personal command of the action and formed a line which checked the British pursuit. The action ended with nightfall, and Clinton resumed his march without further molestation. It was an intensely disappointing action for the Americans, for Washington might have expected to win a considerable victory against an army on its line of march and encumbered with baggage.

Lee's incompetence had deprived Washington of even the possibility of a victory. It was said that when the first stragglers from Lee's command met the main force, Washington refused to believe that Lee was in retreat; and that when Lee arrived in person in the midst of his disorganised and exhausted troops, Washington gave him a most awesome tongue-lashing. Despite this, however, it appears that Washington intended to take the matter no further until Lee wrote him a sequence of letters claiming that he had been treated unjustly. Thereupon, Washington charged him with disobedience of orders, misbehaviour in the face of the enemy, and with writing disrespectful letters. Inevitably, Lee was found guilty of all charges, though it might be suspected that only the third was proven and the other two verdicts given as guilty as a result of the grossly-insulting letters. He was suspended from duty for a year. When the sentence expired, Lee suspected that Congress was considering dismissing him from the army completely. He wrote them so insulting a letter that that is exactly what happened.

The casualties in the Battle of Monmouth were around 350 on each side, as many as a fifth of these being deaths from sunstroke, the action being fought in the most appalling heat. A further 600 (mostly Germans) deserted from the British army, probably as a result of connections they had established in Philadelphia and which they were loath to break.

Although the war had four more years to run, the Battle of Monmouth was the last major field action in which George Washington commanded. It is unfortunate that he was let down so badly, but his personal reputation was unaffected by Lee's ineptitude (or worse). Clinton reached New York in safety, and Washington, taking up a position at White Plains on 30 July, blockaded him there.

Guerrilla War in 1779

In the northern section of operations, the British forces were not sufficiently strong to make a serious challenge to Washington's army, though much desultory (and very savage) guerrilla activity went on throughout. Clinton attempted to draw Washington from his positions and the British captured the post of Stony Point in the lower Hudson valley (31 May 1779); on 15–16 July it was repossessed by an audacious American attack led by 'Mad Anthony' Wayne.

Most operations were concentrated in the south, which had seen two years of guerrilla-style warfare but no major operations. A French expedition collaborated with an American force in an attempt to recover Savannah, which the British had taken at the very end of 1778. This Franco-American assault, launched in October 1779, was beaten off with such loss that the French admiral, Comte Charles H.T. d'Estaing (1729–94), refused to maintain the siege and sailed away. In June 1779, Spain entered the contest by declaring war on Britain.

The War in 1780–81

The defeat of the Savannah expedition caused American morale to wilt and their confidence in the French to decline. In December 1779, Clinton was ordered to leave the northern operations and proceed with part of his army to conquer the Carolinas. He left the New York garrison under the command of Baron Wilhelm von Knyphausen, who had served as a general in the Prussian army.

Clinton's expedition landed near Charleston, which was besieged and captured on 12 May 1780, together with over 5000 American troops and a considerable quantity of *matériel*. Leaving Cornwallis to complete the campaign in South Carolina, Clinton returned to New York.

In the winter of 1779–80, Washington's winter quarters were at Morristown, New Jersey, most of the troops actually encamping at Jockey Hollow, about three miles from Morristown. As at Valley Forge, a town of log huts was built, but the weather was more severe; the commissariat again failed, and the army once more faced death from bitter cold and starvation. Although there was some unrest among the army – for example, two Connecticut regiments tried to go home in May 1780, having been unpaid for five months and short of food for weeks – there was no widespread disturbance. The blockade of New York was maintained by Washington, but no offensive was mounted.

In July 1780, a French army landed at Newport, commanded by Jean Baptiste Donatien de Vimeur, Comte de Rochambeau (1725–1807), but the proposed Franco-American operation against New York was forestalled by superior British naval strength.

Banastre Tarleton of the British Legion. This engraving of 'Bloody Ban' was published by Walker in 1782.

Treachery

In September 1780 came the infamous treason of Benedict Arnold, who commanded at West Point, a vital post on the Hudson Valley. Arnold intended to turn it over to Clinton, but the plot miscarried when Arnold's British contact, Major John André (1751–80) was captured carrying the documentary proof of the treason. Arnold escaped, to be rewarded with a British commission; André was hanged as a spy. His death was regretted by all, even by his enemies, but it is unfair to criticize Washington for refusing to accede to André's request for an honourable death by firing-squad. He could not be seen to weaken in the face of the most serious treason of the war, despite the fact that it must have been extremely painful for him to confirm the sentence.

'Bloody Ban', Gates and Kalb

Cornwallis' 'pacification' of the Carolinas grew into a particularly vicious guerrilla war. Especially reviled by the Americans was Banastre Tarleton (1754–1833), a British cavalry leader of great skill, whose Loyalist British Legion was an extremely proficient light corps. It was this Legion's uncompromising methods (greatly exaggerated) that led to the nickname 'Bloody Ban' and the term 'Tarleton's quarter', the latter indicating a refusal to accept the surrender of a defeated foe.

The situation in the south was grim for the Americans. Although Washington was still commander-in-chief, Congress appointed Horatio Gates as commander of the 'Southern department', without Washington's sanction and not under his control. Although Washington was known to oppose their selection, Gates' reputation from Saratoga was sufficient for Congress to disregard the commander-in-chief. It was a serious error.

Gates had been disparaging about the country of his birth. After Saratoga, he had written: 'If Old England is not by this lesson taught humility, then she is an obstinate old slut, bent upon her ruin!'.[10] Then, on 16 August 1780, Gates was defeated so comprehensively at the Battle of Camden that the action has been described as the most catastrophic ever to involve an American force. By a strange quirk of fate, Gates was defeated by Cornwallis, who was the nephew of the officer to whom Gates had acted as A.D.C. during his service in the British Army! Most of the blame was Gates', who abandoned his command and fled from the field on a racehorse. He had put too much trust in raw militiamen, who broke and fled. In contrast, it was the small body of Continental infantry, dispatched by Washington to South Carolina in support of Gates, who put up a most gallant defence until they were overwhelmed. Their commander, de Kalb, whose wise advice Gates had ignored, was mortally wounded. Two days later, Tarleton smashed the guerrilla force of Thomas Sumter, the 'Carolina Gamecock' (1734–1832), at Fishing Creek. American humiliation in the south was complete.

Morgan at Cowpens

After the disasters of 1780, Congress realised their error and returned control of the war to the commander-in-chief. Washington immediately appointed Nathaniel Greene to command in the south, on 14 October 1780. It was a wise choice, for though Greene never won a battle, he appreciated the strategic situation.

Reinforced by a small force of Washington's Continentals, Greene took the offensive at the end of the year. On 17 January 1781, his subordinate General Daniel Morgan (1736–1802) engaged Tarleton's command at Cowpens. Morgan, alias 'the old waggoner', was a frontiersman and cousin to Daniel Boone. He had served the British in the French and Indian War but his reputation had been founded on his command of Rangers (riflemen) in the War of Independence. At Cowpens, he defeated Tarleton utterly.

After some manoeuvering in the early months of 1781, Cornwallis engaged Greene at Guilford Court House on 15 March. Despite the British being numerically inferior, Greene was defeated, but retired in reasonable order. Cornwallis' victory was costly, however, and he decided that he had insufficient resources to hold Georgia and the Carolinas, so marched into Virginia. Greene continued to operate against the British garrisons left behind, aided by such guerrilla leaders as Sumter and Francis 'Swamp Fox' Marion. Though checked near Camden at the Battle of Hobkirk's Hill on 19 April, and at Eutaw Springs on 8 September 1781, British losses were such that by the end of the year only Charleston and Savannah were still British possessions in the south.

Final Victory

Moving to Virginia, Cornwallis was opposed by an American army under Lafayette, whom Washington had placed in command. He evaded the British attempts to engage him in a major action. Washington now began what was to prove his final campaign. He had three options for operations in 1781: attack New York, concentrate against Cornwallis in Virginia, or operate against Charleston.

Battle of the Cheseapeake
The favoured plan was apparently to move on Clinton in New York, but the colonies were dilatory in supplying the men he needed. What decided Washington was the news that Cornwallis, having overrun much of Virginia, had retired into the defences of Yorktown to await reinforcement; and that a French fleet under Comte François J.P. de Grasse (1722–88) was expected. Washington appreciated the strategical significance immediately. If the French fleet could sever Cornwallis' communications by sea, the British would be trapped in Yorktown. Washington determined to leave a small force to watch New York, and move swiftly against Cornwallis.

Arriving off Yorktown at the end of August 1781, de Grasse disembarked the reinforcements he had brought for Lafayette. The British fleet of Admiral Thomas Graves (c.1725–1802) hurried from New York. After an inconclusive action on 5 September in the Battle of the Cheseapeake (also known as the Battle of the Capes), Graves realised that he was unable to smash the French fleet, and retired to New York. As Washington had planned, Cornwallis was now isolated in Yorktown. In mid-September, Washington's and Rochambeau's armies arrived, mostly transported by sea in French ships.

Yorktown
The British fortifications on both banks of the York River, at Yorktown and Gloucester, were considerable: Cornwallis had some 7500 men, but with limited supplies. Washington, commanding about 9000 Americans and 7000 French, began the investment of Yorktown on 28 September 1781. Washington was in overall command of the three

forces: his own, Lafayette's and Rochambeau's, the French commander having unreservedly placed his troops under Washington's control. On 30 September, Cornwallis withdrew to his inner fortifications, and the American-French bombardment began on 9 October. Two redoubts were stormed and captured on 14 October, and a very spirited British counter-attack was repelled two days later.

Cornwallis' situation was now desperate in the extreme. Almost out of ammunition and supplies, and with almost 2000 of his men ill, his last gamble to evacuate part of his army across the York river was ruined by a storm. On 17 October, he had no option but open negotiations with

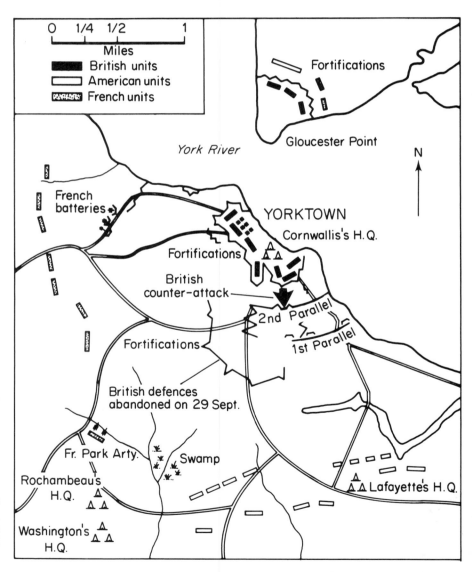

Battle of Yorktown, 28 September–19 October 1781, showing the American, British and French forces and fortifications.

Washington, who insisted on complete surrender. On 19 October, the British garrison marched out to lay down their weapons. Most appropriately, their bands played *The World Turned Upside Down*, an old royalist air perhaps better-known as *When the King Enjoys his Own Again*. From the British viewpoint, Cornwallis' surrender had 'turned the world upside-down.'

Clinton's reinforcement from New York, conveyed in Graves' fleet, arrived a few days too late. Washington's appreciation of the vital importance of sea power, and his concentration against Cornwallis, had virtually put an end to the war.

'It is all over'

Peace did not follow immediately after Yorktown, but the end was inevitable. Lord North, whose ministry had conducted the war, supposedly exclaimed: 'Oh God! It is all over!' when news of the disaster of Yorktown was received in London. In effect, he was right. In November 1781 Washington returned to the blockade of New York, leaving Rochambeau to winter in Virginia. North's ministry collapsed on 20 March and in the following month, negotiations were opened for peace. Undoubtedly, Britain could have continued the fight, but with the war having broadened into other spheres (the siege of Gibraltar 1779–83 was the most notable event, but threats were made against the valuable British possessions in the West Indies), it was simply not worth

Yorktown depicted shortly before the siege commenced. Although the engraving is Victorian, it is believed to be based upon contemporary material.

In 1782, Washington instituted the 'Badge of Military Merit', an embroidered heart in purple fabric to be worn on the left breast. Although the circumstances of its award have changed (it was reinstituted in 1932), the Purple Heart remains one of the oldest military decorations in existence.

the effort of sustaining a war quite without allies and which was, in any case, of highly dubious outcome.

Much criticism has been levelled at King George III (unfairly), and against his ministers, but the reasons for British defeat are more than simply the mismanagement of the war by the central government. That the British underestimated the determination and strength of the colonies is certain, and thus insufficient military forces were despatched at a time when the rebellion could have been crushed. The difficulty of conducting a war at long range was also significant. Had complete control been accorded to the general-in-chief in America, the situation would have been better. Certainly, Britain possessed some commanders of skill, and their army was as steady and reliable as ever. Yet more than that, and more than simply the fact that the colonists had a resolve equal to that of their British kinsmen and opponents, was the presence in the American ranks of a general of great skill – George Washington.

Preliminary articles of peace were signed on 30 November 1782 (the Treaty of Paris), concluded on 3 September 1783. In Britain's war against France, hostilities continued until the Treaty of Versailles (20 January 1783). The intervening period gave Britain an opportunity to regain control of the seas, accomplished by Admiral Rodney in his decisive victory over de Grasse at the Battle of the Saints (12 April 1782). The terms of the treaty signed with the United States provided for the total British evacuation of the Americas south of Canada. British forces left Charleston in December 1782, and almost exactly a year later the last British troops embarked at New York.

Saying Farewell

On 4 December 1783 Washington took an emotional farewell of his officers at Fraunces' Tavern, New York. Unashamedly in tears, he shook the hand of each officer present, raised his arm in a gesture of farewell, and walked out of his military career with as much dignity as he had entered it.

He has been styled 'the American Cincinnatus', an appropriate analogy to Lucius Quinctius Cincinnatus (born c.519 BC), one of the almost legendary heroes of ancient Rome, who was twice called from his farm to defend Rome. Having defeated Rome's enemies – in 458 BC he reputedly overcame the Aequians in a single day – without seeking personal reward he then returned to his simple life on his farm.

The association of American commanders known as the Society of the Cincinnati, originating in May 1783, was named after him. Its eagle insignia was the only foreign decoration permitted to be worn at the French court, by French officers upon whom it had been bestowed. Washington had no hand in the formation of the society, but became its first president. It is interesting to note that the town of Losantiville, Ohio, was re-named Cincinnati in honour of the association.

Father of his Country

Unlike Cincinnatus, Washington was not allowed to spend the remainder of his life on his estates, as he had intended. When the Federal Convention met in 1787 to draw up the present constitution, Washington attended (somewhat unwillingly) as a Virginia delegate. When elected as the first President of the Republic, there was no opposition, such was his immense popularity and so greatly were his qualities esteemed. He appears to have been as genuinely unsure of his capability for the job as he had been about the position of commander-in-chief. He began his inaugural address on 30 April 1789 thus:

> Among the vicissitudes incident to life, no event could have filled me with greater anxieties than that of which the notification was transmitted by your order . . . On the one hand, I was summoned by my country, whose voice I can never hear but with veneration and love, from a retreat which I had chosen with the fondest predilection, and, in my flattering hopes, with an immutable decision, as the asylum of my declining years . . . On the other hand, the magnitude and difficulty of the trust to which the voice of my country called me . . . could not but overwhelm with despondence one, who, inheriting inferior endowments from nature, and unpractised in the duties of civil administration, ought to be peculiarly conscious of his own deficiencies . . .[11]

Presidency

Washington was re-elected as President for a second term in 1792, and refused to serve a third, despite being sure of election had he made himself available. His term as President was not without its difficulties, and he became somewhat disillusioned by attacks on him from hostile politicians; but these were from a very small minority, and he never lost public confidence. Never an advocate of party politics, he held the two opposing factions apart, and gave the office of President a dignity and security which it might not have achieved in other hands. His presence and determination kept the United States neutral in 1793, when a considerable movement wished to support France in the beginning of the French Revolutionary Wars. The virulence of some of the attacks upon him at this time reputedly led him to remark that he would have been happier in his grave than in his present situation. Yet his was the voice of reason, honesty and decency, which was recognised by the American people, and thus their devotion never wavered.

The United States had some military problems during his presidency, notably against the Indians in the Ohio valley. Expeditions under Generals Josiah Harmer (October 1790) and Arthur St. Clair (November 1791) met with catastrophe. A new army was formed, and Washington appointed his old subordinate Anthony Wayne as its commander. On 20 August 1794, at Fallen Timbers, the Indians were crushed and peace was brought to the frontier.

George Washington retired from the presidency in 1797 and returned to the life he had desired at Mount Vernon, but in 1798 he

Washington reviewing his troops at Fort Cumberland, 18 October 1794.

resumed his position as commander-in-chief at a time of a threat of war with France. The Continental Army had been disbanded at the conclusion of hostilities with Britain, and a new army had to be formed; and the political allocation of commissions caused Washington much worry in this period. In December 1799, he contracted an infection of the windpipe, and died after only a day's illness on the 14th of the month. His faithful wife Martha lived until 1802; they had no children. His will contained a direction that his slaves be freed. It was a typical gesture.

First in the Heart

It has been said that a person's worth may be gauged by the opinions of his opponents. The British *Gentleman's Magazine* was a mirror of contemporary attitudes and uncompromising in its condemnation of Britain's enemies. For example, upon a French general its obituary ended: 'he was base, venal, ungrateful and cruel. His death was too honourable for his life'.[12] However, upon Washington, who had been responsible for the British loss of half an empire, it reported the death of 'the illustrious General':

His disorder was an inflammatory sore throat, which proceeded from a cold . . . His last scene corresponded with the whole tenor of his life. Not a groan nor a complaint escaped him, in extreme distress. With perfect resignation, and a full possession of his reason, he closed his well-spent life. His funeral was celebrated with every mark of honour and regret so justly due his virtues.[13]

Washington as the first President – the famous portrait.

Before he resigned the presidency, Washington had made a 'Farewell Address' to the American people on 17 September 1796. In his speech he warned against factionalism:

The name of AMERICAN, which belongs to you in your national capacity, must always exalt the just pride of patriotism more than any appellation derived from local discriminations.[14]

He also expressed an opinion on his own career. He said that he was 'too sensible of my defects not to think it probable that I may have committed many errors'. Instead he hoped that the Almighty would mitigate the results of such errors, and that his country might excuse the mistakes he had made in the 'forty-five years of my life dedicated to its service with an upright zeal', and that the 'faults of my incompetent abilities will be consigned to oblivion, as myself must soon be to the mansions of rest'.

He ended the address in a way which exemplifies his character, by renewing his affirmation in:

the benign influence of good laws and a free government – the ever-favourite object of my heart, and the happy reward, I trust, of our mutual cares, labors, and dangers'.[15]

Five days after Washington's death, a resolution in the House of Representatives, introduced by John Marshall of Virginia but attributed to Henry Lee, described Washington as 'first in war, first in peace, and first in the hearts of his countrymen'. Rhetoric apart, the description is not inaccurate: he was truly the Father of his Country.

References

1   *The Writings of George Washington* ed. J.C. Fitzpatrick, Washington 1931, I p. 32.

2   *History of the British Army* Hon. Sir J. Fortescue, London 1899, II p. 279.

3   *Hymn sung at the Completion of the Concord Monument* Ralph Waldo Emerson (1803–82).

4   *Gentleman's Magazine* October 1800, p. 1007.

5   For example, see 'The British Expedition to Concord' A. French *Journal of the Society for Army Historical Research* XV p. 29, London 1936.

6   *To All Sportsmen* Col. G. Hanger, London 1814, pp. 123–24.

7   *ibid.*, p. 200.

8   *ibid.*, p. 217.

9   Ferguson's own remark on the incident is recorded in *Cassell's*

Biographical Dictionary of the American War of Independence 1763–1783 London 1973, p. 364.

10 See 'From British Major to Rebel General' *Regimental Annual of the Sherwood Foresters 1926* ed. H.C. Wylly, London 1927, pp. 264–65 (It is a somewhat disparaging biographical note in the journal of his old (British) regiment, still bitter about his conduct after 150 years!)

11 *The Addresses and Messages of the Presidents of the United States* ed. E. Walker, New York 1841, p. 19. (This includes a useful compilation of Washington's most important speeches as President.)

12 *Gentleman's Magazine* July 1800, p. 693. (On Dubois Crancé.)

13 *ibid.*, January 1800, p. 84.

14 *The Addresses and Messages op. cit.*, p. 65.

15 *ibid.*, pp. 65–66.

Chronology of Events

1732   11 JANUARY   Birth of George Washington at Bridges Creek, Virginia.

1754   28 MAY   Defeat by Washington of French and Indian detachment at Great Meadows.

1754   3 JULY   Washington's surrender at Fort Necessity.

1755   9 JULY   Defeat of Braddock at the Monongahela.

1774   5 AUGUST   Washington appointed by Virginia convention as one of seven delegates to Continental Congress.

       5 SEPTEMBER   Opening of Continental Congress at Philadelphia.

1775   19 APRIL   Opening skirmish of the War of Independence at Lexington and Concord.

       15 JUNE   Washington appointed commander-in-chief of the forces of the 'United Colonies'; appointment confirmed 17 June.

       17 JUNE   Battle of Bunker Hill.

       3 JULY   Washington assumes command of the 'Boston army'.

       31 DECEMBER   Failure of American attack on Quebec; death of Montgomery.

1776   4 JULY   Declaration of American independence.

       27 AUGUST   Battle of Long Island.

       12 SEPTEMBER   Abandonment of New York by Washington.

       16 SEPTEMBER   Battle of Harlem Heights.

       28 OCTOBER   Battle of White Plains.

       26 DECEMBER   Major victory by Washington at Trenton.

1777   3 JANUARY   Victory by Washington at Princeton.

       11 SEPTEMBER   Defeat of Washington at Brandywine.

       4 OCTOBER   Defeat of Washington at Germantown.

       17 OCTOBER   Surrender of Burgoyne at Saratoga.

1778   6 FEBRUARY   Alliance between United States and France.

       17 JUNE   War between France and Britain.

       28 JUNE   Battle of Monmouth.

1780   16 AUGUST   Rout of American forces in the south at Camden.

1781   17 JANUARY   Defeat of Tarleton by Morgan at Cowpens.

       4 AUGUST   Cornwallis moves to Yorktown.

       5 SEPTEMBER   Battle of the Cheseapeake.

       28 SEPTEMBER   Investment of Yorktown by Washington, Rochambeau and Lafayette.

       9 OCTOBER   Opening bombardment of Yorktown.

       19 OCTOBER   Surrender of Cornwallis at Yorktown.

1782   12 APRIL   Battle of the Saints re-establishes British command of the sea.

       30 NOVEMBER   Treaty of Paris (peace between Britain and United States).

1783   20 JANUARY   Treaty of Versailles (peace between Britain and France).

       4 DECEMBER   Washington takes leave of army.

1789   30 APRIL   Washington elected President.

1796   17 SEPTEMBER   Washington's 'Farewell Address'.

1799   14 DECEMBER   Death of Washington.

Wellington

THE IRON DUKE

Arthur Wellesley, 1st Duke
of Wellington. Portrait by
T. Heaphy c. 1813.

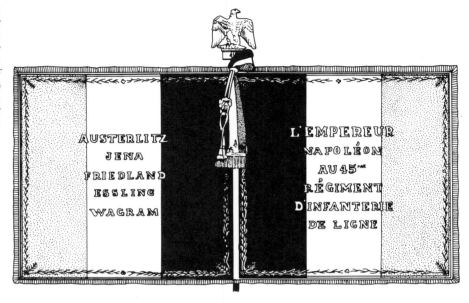

One of the most famous flags of the Napoleonic Wars, the 'Eagle' of the French 45th Line Regiment, captured by Wellington's forces at Waterloo by Sgt. Charles Ewart of the 2nd (Royal North British) Dragoons (Royal Scots Greys). The red, white and blue French tricolor had a gold fringe and decoration, including the regiment's battle-honours.

AUSTERLITZ
JENA
FRIEDLAND
ESSLING
WAGRAM

L'EMPEREUR
NAPOLÉON
AU 45ᵐᵉ
RÉGIMENT
D'INFANTERIE
DE LIGNE

Spain and Portugal at the time of the Peninsular War

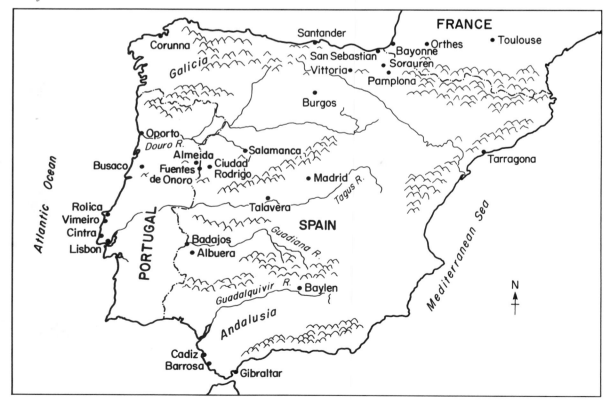

'Our Arthur'

On 16 May 1811 the British fusilier brigade advanced towards the heights at Albuera to save the battle which their commander, Marshal William Beresford, was in imminent danger of losing. The brigade marched into a tempest of fire and shot which reduced one of the three battalions, the 2/7th Royal Fusiliers, from 568 effective men to 85 in about thirty minutes; it was the most concentrated butchery of the Napoleonic Wars. As they advanced, Fusilier Horsefall of the 7th turned to his companion and remarked, 'Whore's ar Arthur? Aw wish he wor here'.[1]

It is testimony to the faith of the ordinary soldier that all knew 'our Arthur' would not have led them into such a position, and is the highest accolade which can be accorded a general, even one who was the greatest British soldier of his generation, perhaps of his age, and perhaps the greatest of all time: the Iron Duke.

Young Wesley

Arthur Wesley was born about 1 May 1769 – rival dates range as widely as 6 March and 30 April – probably in Merrion Street, Dublin (even the place of birth is disputed). He was a younger son of Garret Wesley, Second Baron and First Earl Mornington, a comparatively minor member of the Irish peerage. Earl Mornington died aged only 46 in 1781, leaving five sons and a daughter in not the most affluent of circumstances. In the usual practice of the time, the younger sons were directed towards careers in the church or army.

Young Arthur, a somewhat withdrawn boy of no obvious talents, was sent for his education to Eton in 1781, but the family's impoverished fortunes led to his being taken away in 1784, resources being concentrated on the more promising of the younger sons, Gerald and Henry. The eldest son, Richard, now himself Earl Mornington,

Regimental Colour of the 33rd (1st Yorkshire West Riding) Regiment, as carried at Waterloo. This was the regiment of which Wellington was commander early in his career, and whose name the regiment's successor bears to this day. White with a red cross, with the Union and wreath in proper colours, the central shield bears the regimental number in gold Roman numerals.

had forsaken his own academic career and saw no reason why more money should be expended on his dull brother. Even Arthur's mother, who showed him little affection, could imagine only one fate for her 'awkward son, the fool of the family': 'fit food for powder' and nothing more.[2] Thus to a military career poor Arthur was directed, via the Royal Academy of Equitation at Angers in Anjou, a French military school and wherein he learned little except a fluency in French.

At this period, the promotion of officers in the British army was dependent not upon experience or ability, but largely upon family influence or upon the cash to purchase commissions. So, on 17 March 1787, Arthur was gazetted an Ensign in the 73rd Highland Regiment. It is unlikely that for the next six years he performed any regimental duty whatever, as his time was spent as A.D.C. to the Lord Lieutenant of Ireland, a post secured by his family connections. During this time he progressed in rank through the 76th and 41st Foot, the 12th Light Dragoons and finally the 33rd (1st West Riding) Regiment whose major he became in April 1793 and its lieutenant-colonel commanding in September of the same year. There were many evils associated with the 'purchase' system of promotion, including the commissioning of children. However, the system's greatest defence is that it permitted the rise to high rank of young officers of talent such as Arthur Wesley, who without the purchase and 'influence' system might not have attained a battalion command until the age of 40, instead of at 24.

Wesley's sojourn in Ireland was diplomatic and administrative rather than military in character. As Member of Parliament for Trim in the Irish House of Commons – the Mornington family seat – he gained an insight into political affairs and the time was not wasted. However, he was still regarded as a dull fellow, but probably only because he spent much time in study rather than frivolity, and eventually forsook his violin (on which he had considerable skill) so as not to deflect his thoughts from his chosen profession.

It was in Ireland that he became engaged unofficially to Catherine (Kitty) Pakenham, daughter of Lord Longford; and where he first developed what may be termed his philosophy on life, which eschewed ostentation in favour of a sober and balanced outlook in which gambling, drinking to excess and smoking had no part. The scrupulous honesty and unbending fairness which characterised Wesley's dealings throughout his life were already in evidence: his brother paid for his lieutenant-colonelcy, but Arthur attempted to repay it as soon as his finances permitted, and it is proof of the friendship between the brothers that Richard refused to accept reimbursement.

In June 1794 the 33rd Foot was ordered on active service to the Netherlands, as part of the reinforcement for the Duke of York's Anglo-Hanoverian contingent of the Allied armies in Flanders. Britain had entered the war against republican France in the previous year, and their initial small military expedition (sent to the Low Countries largely for reasons of political solidarity) had been supporting the Austrian, Dutch and French royalist forces in opposing the 'steamroller' of the massed republican armies. The British army in the Netherlands was inexperienced but lacked nothing in courage, though their leadership was uninspired, despite the good intentions of the Duke of York. The 33rd Foot was noted as being one of the best British regiments – benefitting greatly from Wesley's attentions – but the campaign of 1794 was inauspicious from the beginning. It culminated with a retreat through Holland, into Westphalia and a final evacuation from Bremen in May 1795, the army being decimated by the brutal winter of 1794–95. The lack of warm clothing, provisions and transport was a scandal but one which occasioned no radical reforms of the military establishment. Young Lt. Col. Wesley's regiment was involved in three sharp actions during this campaign, at Boxtel (15 September) and at Geldermalsen (30 December and 5 January). In all three, both regiment and commander acquitted themselves well, but the campaign ended in disappointment if not total disaster. It provided young Wesley with his first experience of combat, and impressed on him the importance of logistics and supply in addition to tactical ability – and, as he said, at least it taught him 'how *not* to do it'. It was the only unsuccessful campaign in which he was ever to engage.

Officer's shoulder-belt plate of Wellington's old regiment, the 33rd Foot. It was silver with engraved design including the title 'First Yorkshire West Riding', the design probably worn throughout the Napoleonic period.

Sepoy General

Strangely, for an age dominated by the struggle against France, Wesley was not to face them again for some thirteen years, by which time his reputation had been established on the other side of the globe. After his return from the Netherlands, his military prospects appeared so unpromising that he considered abandoning his career for a civil position, simply as a way of earning a living. Fortunately, the 33rd found employment in Britain's eastern colonies, and it was to India that Arthur Wesley directed his steps in 1796.

The 28-year-old lieutenant-colonel was no longer the shy dullard of his youth, but was described as a most handsome man of military bearing, of medium height (around 5ft. 9 or 10ins.), a pale complexion, dark hair, clear blue eyes and a remarkably large aquiline nose which was to be the focal point for cartoonists and the origin of most of his nicknames – 'Nosey' or 'Beaky'. To India he took a library of diverse subjects, confirming his enquiring nature, and impressed most of those he met with his obvious intelligence, quick thought and rapid speech (with a very slight lisp). Although another of his nicknames, 'The Beau', came later in his career from his usual semi-civilian uniform of impeccable taste, it was probably appropriate for his demeanour even at this early period.

Shortly after beginning his Indian service he changed his surname following other members of his family, 'Wesley' being replaced by the earlier and more traditional spelling 'Wellesley', and it was as Wellesley that his name became celebrated.

The Company

British administration in the Indian subcontinent was not primarily directed by the government in London, but was dependent upon the Honourable East India Company, originally a trading concern but which had assumed the status of effective government over the British possessions in India. Administered by a Court of Directors in London, John Company (as it was known) by the late eighteenth century was in many respects like a sovereign state, maintaining its own army and the power of declaring war or making treaties with any of the indigenous Indian rulers. There was, however, a Governor-General appointed by the British government as the King's deputy in India, who collaborated with the Company and who was responsible for the British 'King's regiments', which served in India as a support to the Company's forces. In fact, the bulk of the European troops were those of the King's army, as the Company's forces included but few corps of European composition, mostly being sepoy regiments of native soldiers commanded by white officers.

The Company's army allowed British interests in India to be served without the expense of maintaining a large British army. For example, in 1796, only 10,718 British troops were in the subcontinent, little more than half the number employed in Ireland and less than six per cent of the entire British army. The influence of the European regiments, however, far outweighed their numbers.

War with Tippoo

In May 1798, a new Governor-General arrived in the person of Richard Wellesley, Lord Mornington, whose influence was to be crucial in the emergence of his brother Arthur Wellesley from a battalion commander into a commanding general.

The most troublesome of the indigenous rulers of India was Tippoo Sahib (or Tipu Sultan), ruler of Mysore, a man renowned for his cruelty and who had been defeated in the Third Mysore War (1789–92) which had cost him half his dominions. Tippoo was clearly intent for revenge and intrigued with France in the hope of gaining their assistance for a war which would, from France's viewpoint, help to occupy British resources and divert attention from Europe and elsewhere. The new Governor-General attempted to eliminate French influence by insisting that their advisers in the employ of the Maratha Confederacy (another large native power-block) be dismissed. When Tippoo refused to co-operate, Richard Wellesley sent two forces into Mysore, precipitating the Fourth Mysore War.

The general-in-chief was George Harris, and following the death in a duel of the officer responsible for equipping the field force, Arthur Wellesley was appointed to the task, which he accomplished with speed and skill. He was then placed in command of the allied force based upon the troops of the Nizam of Hyderabad, a loyal ally of the British.

The British forces converged on Tippoo's capital of Seringapatam, during the course of which Arthur Wellesley met with the only defeat of his career – albeit a minor setback – when he led a night attack on a defended post known as the Sultanpettah Tope. His advance became confused in the darkness and failed, but after some hours of great dejection he led a stronger force which carried the position without trouble next day. On 4 May 1799, Seringapatam was stormed and Tippoo killed in its defence, whereupon Arthur Wellesley was named as governor of the city, though he had taken no part in the assault. It was an appointment which raised charges of nepotism – though from his diplomatic and administrative experience there is no doubt that he was the best candidate for the post.

During this period of command, Wellesley learned many of the skills which were to benefit his country in future years, though it gave him an aggressive attitude which he had to curb when fighting European enemies. By the very nature of Indian warfare, aggression was the keynote of the British tactics. Faced with immense, but ill-disciplined, native armies, a rapid attack to rout the enemy quickly, irrespective of circumstances, was the safest way of redressing the vast disparity in numbers. Nevertheless, there was an equal necessity for careful admin-istration and organisation of supply, as Wellesley demonstrated when given his first independent command, in May 1800. With a small army of Company troops plus four King's regiments – 19th and 25th Light Dragoons and 73rd and 77th Foot – he was ordered to hunt down a troublesome and obnoxious bandit, Doondia Wao, who had several thousand followers. Not until 10 September was he engaged, Wellesley leading the cavalry charge which scattered the bandits and killed Doon-dia, demonstrating Wellesley's great capacity for coolness and heroism under fire. More valuable than his growing reputation was the experi-ence gained in managing an independent command and running his own system of logistics.

Sir Arthur and the Marathas

In 1802, civil war among the Maratha tribes resulted in the deposition of the British-supported Peshwa Baji Rao II. The new ruler, Holkar of Indore, was immediately attacked by a simultaneous operation in the Deccan and Hindustan in support of the Peshwa, planned by Richard,

The 1796-pattern light cavalry sabre was carried by British light dragoons and hussars throughout the Napoleonic Wars. Its hilt and scabbard were plain iron.

now the Marquess Wellesley. This Second Maratha War (1803–05) finally established the reputation of the Governor-General's brother, now Sir Arthur Wellesley, as a general of repute, for he commanded one column whilst General Gerard Lake led the other. Marching into the Deccan, Sir Arthur captured Poona on 20 March 1803 without opposition and restored the Peshwa, whilst the main Maratha army, commanded by one of the leaders of the Confederacy, Doulut Rao Scindia, withdrew before him.

Wellesley commanded some 11,000 of his own army (only 2,000 Europeans, the 19th Light Dragoons and 74th and 78th Foot), the 9,000-strong Hyderabad contingent (including one European regiment, the Scotch Brigade, later 94th Foot) and a host of Mysore and friendly Maratha cavalry of little combat value. On 8/11 August 1803, Wellesley stormed and captured Scindia's fort at Ahmednuggur in short order; as a Maratha chief remarked, 'These English are a strange people and their General a wonderful man; they came here in the morning, looked at the pettah-wall, walked over it, killed all the garrison, and returned to breakfast'![3]

Continuing his advance, Wellesley came upon the main Maratha army somewhat unexpectedly at Assaye on 23 September. Wellesley had only 7,000 men, only 1,500 of them Europeans; Scindia had 12,000 good, European-led infantry, over 100 guns and 20–30,000 cavalry. Wellesley had intended to operate with caution, but faced with such overwhelming odds decided to make an immediate attack before the Marathas could react to his presence. The fight was a desperate affair in which the 500 men of the 74th stood-off masses of Maratha horse, losing over 300 in the process, and Wellesley himself had two horses shot from under him.

Tactically, it was no masterpiece, but more a triumph of courage and solid discipline over the horde of Marathas; yet it was counted by Wellesley as one of his greatest successes, despite 1,584 casualties.

Still advancing, Wellesley came up with Scindia at Argaum on 29 November 1803. Again he attacked immediately despite his troops having been on the march for nine hours, and again despite the disparity in numbers (30–40,000 Marathas against Wellesley's 10–11,000) the Indians were totally routed, Wellesley's army suffering but 361 casualties.

Wellesley's campaign ended on 15 December with his storm and capture of the fort of Gawilghur, and Lake's successes in Hindustan confirmed the defeat of the Marathas (though a brief outbreak of fighting occurred again in the following year, in which Wellesley took no part). He sailed for home in March 1805, rewarded with the order of a Knight of the Bath – but though ranking as major-general and despite his great triumphs, in the fashion of the time 'sepoy generals' were largely discounted in Europe.

His reputation might have to be re-made in Europe, but the experience

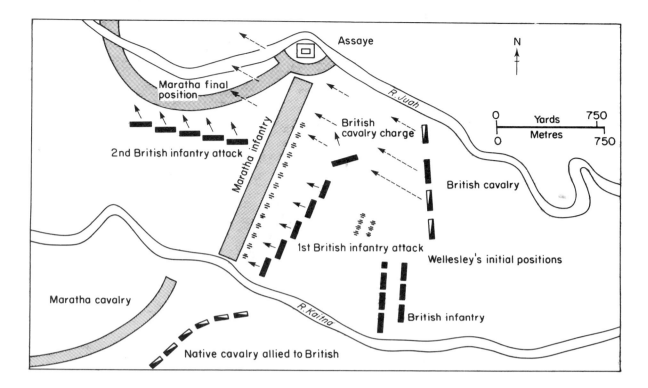

Map labels:
- Assaye
- N
- Maratha final position
- R. Juah
- British cavalry charge
- 2nd British infantry attack
- Maratha infantry
- British cavalry
- Yards 0 750
- Metres 0 750
- 1st British infantry attack
- Wellesley's initial positions
- Maratha cavalry
- R. Kaitna
- British infantry
- Native cavalry allied to British

Battle of Assaye, 23 September 1803.

he had gained was invaluable, and indeed he never forgot his Indian service. When questioned about his remarkable endurance and physical strength which allowed him to survive a phenomenal work-load and remain unexhausted even by Waterloo, he replied, 'Ah, that is all India'.[4]

Napoleonic Warfare

The wars of the French Revolution brought about the most radical change in tactics since the disappearance of the pike, though to some extent this was the culmination of a gradual process of change. The successes of Frederick the Great had tended to produce, in most armies, a concentration upon the severely-disciplined, automata-like drill in which troops were arrayed precisely and manoeuvered, fired and fought like machines, to the almost total exclusion of the system of tactics characterised by light infantry – those of fast-moving, quick-thinking skirmishers who took advantage of natural cover and harassed the enemy with well-aimed shots instead of the unaimed volley of the 'line–of–battle'.

Perhaps the best description of the failings of the post-Frederickian tactics is that given by Sir Henry Bunbury, who observed the Russian army in Holland in 1799 as 'stiff, hard, wooden machines' who appeared to have stepped from the pages of a history of the Seven Years War: 'they waddled slowly forward to the tap-tap of their monotonous drums; and if they were beaten they waddled slowly back again, without appearing in either case to feel a sense of danger, of the expediency of taking ultra tap-tap steps to better their condition'.[5]

Copying the light troops of the Seven Years War, several armies had developed light infantry in the post-Frederickian period, most notably the extremely proficient light troops employed by Britain in the American War of Independence. However, following the conclusion of peace, the more backward-looking military theorists had actively discouraged the existence of light troops in preference to the immaculately-drilled precision of the line. In Dundas' Prussian-inspired drill-book, sanctioned by the British Army in 1792, only 9 out of 458 pages were devoted to the skills of light troops and skirmishers. Consequently, no army was immediately capable of fielding sufficient light infantry to oppose the French revolutionary forces.

Revolutionary Sharpshooting

The French regular army was almost destroyed by the revolution, as aristocratic officers fled abroad. Huge numbers of volunteers and conscripts were swept into the army to oppose the confederation of states determined to crush the revolution and restore the French monarchy. So desperately were men required by the French republic that the time to train them in precision manoeuvres was not available. In addition, such discipline did not accord with the philosophy of 'liberty, equality and fraternity' which was the keynote of the republican system. The new recruits, fired with patriotic enthusiasm (itself a new concept in military theory) had little more skill than the ability to rush headlong at the enemy and attempt to defeat them with patriotic fervour. So, in order to harness this capacity, the *amalgame* was devised, by which each regular battalion was linked with two volunteer or conscript battalions, the regulars (still retaining much of their pre-Revolution discipline) fighting in line to use their drilled firepower, to cover the frenzied charges of the volunteers. From this developed the French tactic of *l'ordre mixte* (mixed deployment) which was used throughout the Napoleonic Wars, units in line providing covering-fire for alternate units in column, columnar deployment allowing much more rapid advances. Coupled with this was the tactic of preceding every attack (or covering every retreat) with vast numbers of men deployed as skirmishers *en débandade* (in open order), blanketing the enemy line with aimed sharpshooting. The men so employed were termed *tirailleurs* (sharpshooters) or *voltigeurs* (literally 'vaulters', i.e. the most agile men in a battalion), and though each French battalion ultimately had its own company of *voltigeurs*, the skirmish tactic was so deeply ingrained that on occasion entire brigades could be deployed in 'open order'.

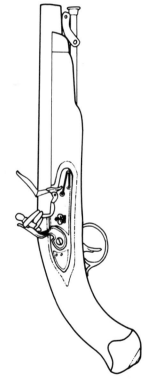

British 'New Land Pattern' cavalry pistol. It was equipped with a swivel-ramrod, which was attached permanently to the stock, ensuring that it could not be dropped when being loaded on horseback.

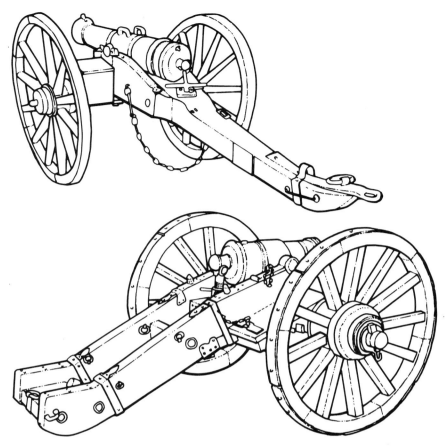

Against these tactics – unconventional for their time – the 'traditional' armies of Europe had little answer. Expecting to meet an enemy in the disciplined line of the past, which exchanged volleys until one withdrew, they were now faced with a damaging sharpshooting which killed their officers and broke up their ranks, to which massed volleys were an ineffective reply; and when thus disordered, the main French attack would erupt in column from behind the cloud of skirmishers and at a run would smash through and rout their opponents' line. Such tactics saved the infant French republic in the immediate period after the revolution, and when perfected with men who had been trained fully, were a major factor in the success gained by Napoleon over every enemy he encountered. The only effective counter to the French infantry tactics was to be that devised by Sir Arthur Wellesley.

The other 'arms' of an army, cavalry and artillery, played a subsidiary rôle in the earlier Napoleonic era, though the importance of both should not be under-estimated. Cavalry were now more clearly divided into light and heavy regiments, the 'heavies' being used in vast formations to inflict a hammer-blow upon the enemy on the battlefield. The 'lights' were equally adept at this (if lacking the impetus of armoured

During the Napoleonic Wars, the British Army employed two basic patterns of artillery carriage for field service. This howitzer has a double-bracket trail.

men on huge horses) and in addition were used for scouting, skirmishing and harassing the enemy's flanks and communications.

Horse artillery, first used effectively by Frederick the Great, was now truly capable of keeping pace with the cavalry to provide its fire-support; and together with the field or foot artillery, was used increasingly in massed batteries instead of, as before, being distributed piecemeal along the battle-front. By assembling a huge battery of guns to lay down a bombardment, it was found that an enemy's line could be shot to pieces at a certain point, which was then vulnerable to an attack by cavalry or infantry, the common maxim being that a massed battery was more effective than the sum of its parts.

The Corps

The co-ordination of the various elements was a factor even more vital in Napoleonic warfare than in the past, and the new system of organisation encouraged it. Previously, the largest permanent formation on campaign had been the brigade, the combination of two or more battalions into a tactical unit (though some armies, even into the early nineteenth century, did not even have this most rudimentary organisation). Now, it became increasingly common for brigades to be linked in divisions, and divisions to be combined with their necessary supporting services (cavalry brigades and artillery) to form *corps d'armées* or army corps. In effect, these corps were self-contained armies capable of operating independently of support.

With the huge increase in the numbers of men employed – Napoleon led more than half a million to Russia in 1812 – such organisation was vital in the facilitation of conveyance of orders and process of supply. However, the organisation had an equally-important strategical function which allowed Napoleon to confront two enemy armies at once, one of his detached *corps d'armée* holding off one army, whilst his main body overwhelmed the other, and then moved to support the isolated corps and deal with the second enemy force.

Lines of Supply

The final element in classic Napoleonic warfare concerned supply. Previously, armies had been shackled by their supply-lines and slow-moving convoys of waggons. Now, from the earliest days of the Revolutionary Wars, the French armies subsisted by a system of living off the land or, more bluntly, by plundering the terrain over which they marched.

Initially, such foraging was introduced from necessity; the French republic simply could not produce enough to feed its soldiers let alone get the supplies to them. However, in freeing them from dependence upon supply-lines it also gave the army a capacity for rapid manoeuvre unknown before, an immense advantage over armies operating with the old system of dragging their baggage and bakeries behind them. French armies living on plunder were often near starvation, but so rapid were their manoeuvres that campaigns were no longer the protracted affairs of the past. Nevertheless, by 1807 even Napoleon had to concede that as forces became ever more numerous, old-fashioned systems of supply had to be reintroduced to prevent literal starvation.

Wellesley in Europe

On his return from India, Wellesley had no obvious military employment for there had been no serious campaigning in Europe since 1799, the British presence in the Mediterranean involving only minor actions following the successful conclusion of the 1801 Egyptian expedition. Instead, Wellesley made some attempts to establish a political career, purely from a desire to defend his brother Richard's reputation, the Marquess' actions in India attracting considerable criticism.

Consequently, Arthur held the parliamentary seats for Rye (1806), St. Michael (Cornwall) in 1807, and Newport (Isle of Wight) from 1807 to 1809, and for two years was Chief Secretary to the Lord Lieutenant of Ireland.

Political Workhorse

Such political activity brought Wellesley into close contact with many members of the Tory administration – and cannot but have helped his military career when it is considered that many generals had a claim for employment before him by virtue of seniority. Most influential of these contacts was probably that with Lord Castlereagh, with whom Wellesley co-operated closely during Castlereagh's tenure as Secretary for War. Indeed, it was Wellesley who highlighted the lunacy of the plan for conquering Mexico, Wellesley who finalised the details for the expedition to support Sweden in 1808 (which aborted due to the instability of the mad King of Sweden) and Wellesley who formulated the plan for supporting Spain which became the Peninsular War. As Castlereagh's adviser he remarked that he was like a willing horse upon which everyone put a saddle, and that as in India his employment was 'in everything'! That he was given so many tasks is the greatest testimony to his ability.

Misguided Matrimony

More significant for Wellesley's personal life was his marriage to Kitty Pakenham, which he appears to have initiated out of a sense of honour, believing that she had waited for his return to the exclusion of all others (actually she had even become engaged during his absence), and this

Loading a canon as depicted in a Hill & Hopwood print, after James Green. A member of the Honourable Artillery Company rams home the charge down the barrel of a fieldpiece. That part of the rammer which protrudes from the barrel is a fleece-covered 'sponge' end; it was used for swabbing out the barrel, removing burned powder, after every shot.

despite the fact that throughout his entire service in India she had written to him not once. Nevertheless, believing that their unofficial engagement had to be honoured, Wellesley duly proposed and married her, an unfortunate alliance for them both; as throughout his life, Wellesley's sense of honour overcame all other considerations. Their relationship was cool, Kitty not being Wellesley's intellectual equal and a bad manager of finances, and giving him little of the expected companionship (though not from any reasons of malice). Sadly, the marriage was perhaps the most unfortunate aspect of Wellesley's life, and he once remarked that it was hardly credible that anyone should have been such a damned fool as to marry under such misguided circumstances!

Defeat of Denmark

Wellesley's military service at this period was limited to the briefest of commands (of an infantry brigade) in the abortive Ems–Weser campaign of 1805–06. Intended to liberate Hanover, it was virtually still-born following Napoleon's crushing defeat of the Austrians at Austerlitz. Nevertheless, Wellesley's political contacts doubtless contributed to his being given a further active command in the Danish expedition of 1807. This was launched upon the British government's learning of a secret clause in the Treaty of Tilsit (between Napoleon and the Czar, whose forces Napoleon had recently defeated), by which Napoleon intended to seize the Danish fleet and thus increase his naval forces to the extent that they might challenge Britain's domination of the sea. The British government decided to forestall any such plan by appropriating the Danish fleet themselves, necessitating a military landing and the capture of Copenhagen.

Wellesley was allocated a brigade of British infantry, but though only a subordinate commander, the conduct of the general-in-chief, Lord Cathcart, was so lifeless that his staff formulated the plan of campaign and Wellesley put it into effect. This involved the occupation of the whole of the island of Zealand and the investment of Copenhagen, in the course of which Wellesley marched away to intercept a Danish army moving to the city's relief. The Danish forces were little more than militia and no match for Wellesley's six British battalions and eight German Legion (Hanoverian) squadrons. At Kjöge, on 29 August 1807, Wellesley's small force met the Danes and routed them for trifling British loss, Wellesley directing his troops with the aggression generally restricted to British armies in India.

The action was comparatively small in scale but decisive in terms of the campaign, for with their army defeated and their capital bombarded, the Danes surrendered and the British expedition withdrew, taking the Danish fleet with them and neutralizing the potential augmentation of Napoleon's power. Most importantly, perhaps, Wellesley's reputation was enhanced by a European victory, so that his status was no longer that of purely a 'sepoy general'.

The Iberian Experience

The scene of Wellesley's greatest achievements, and Britain's most significant contribution to the war against Napoleon, was the Iberian peninsula, the beginning of that war occurring at the end of 1807.

Napoleon had organised a Continental System, by which British goods were prohibited from entry into European ports, in an attempt to destroy British commerce. The scheme was spectacularly unsuccessful despite French control or influence over most of the major trading centres on the European coast; and Portugal, Britain's oldest ally, steadfastly refused to be pressured into joining the Continental System. To compel compliance, Napoleon determined to invade that country via his ally, Spain, and to depose the Spanish royal family in order to cement his hold upon the Iberian peninsula.

Accordingly, 30,000 French troops under General Andoche Junot were sent through Spain to occupy Lisbon (1 December 1807), the Portuguese royal family fleeing to Brazil after appointing a Council of Regency which appealed to Britain for help. In March 1808, a further 100,000 French troops marched into Spain and the ineffectual Spanish king, Charles IV, and his equally useless heir, Ferdinand, were compelled to renounce the throne and were interned in France. A popular uprising in favour of the new legitimate King Ferdinand was suppressed by the French with appalling brutality, and as the new King of Spain pro-French factions 'elected' Napoleon's somewhat unwilling elder brother, Joseph Bonaparte.

Spanish resistance increased and regional governments or *juntas* were established to oppose the French, but given the lack of central direction and the wretched condition of the Spanish army, their task was impossible without help.

In response to their appeals, Britain decided to provide that help by the dispatch of an expeditionary force to co-operate with the Spanish troops in opposing the virtual French annexation of the country. Initial command of the British expedition was given to Sir Arthur Wellesley, recently promoted to lieutenant-general, but as the original 10,000-strong force was envisaged as being insufficient, the size of the expedition was increased. This required a change of command, for despite his influential friends in government, Wellesley's appointment could not have been justified for so large a force given his lack of seniority. The largest augmentation to the expedition was the force commanded by Sir John Moore, recently in command of the abandoned expedition to support Sweden. Although Moore was a capable general and a great trainer of men (his efforts were largely responsible for the re-creation of an effective British light infantry force), his Whig politics prevented the Tory administration from appointing him to overall command. Thus, the expedition was given to Lieut. General Sir Hew Dalrymple,

Joseph Bonaparte, King of Spain, in an engraving by L. Rados after J.B. Bosio.

governor of Gibraltar, with Sir Harry Burrard as his deputy. Both were aging, and both were equally inept.

Before their arrival, however, Wellesley was left in command of the expedition, to which was added an immediate reinforcement of 5000 men under General Brent Spencer, who had already been supporting the Spanish at the Cadiz area. Wellesley considered landing in Spain, but after reconnoitering at Corunna, where he learned of Spanish reverses, he settled on Portugal, disembarking at Mondego Bay in early August 1808, where he was certain of a friendly welcome from the stalwart Portuguese. Once his supplies were ashore, Wellesley determined to advance with his 14,000 men to capture Lisbon from Junot's occupation force. On 17 August 1808, he ran into a small French contingent under General Henri Delaborde at Roliça (known by a typographical error as 'Roleia' in British annals). Wellesley planned a combined frontal assault with double outflanking movement against Delaborde's position along a hill-crest. However, Delaborde withdrew and in the pursuit of one of Wellesley's battalions was somewhat mauled. Then a general attack drove away the French, producing Wellesley's first victory against them at trifling cost. He resumed his advance on Lisbon.

However, Harry Burrard arrived at this juncture and mistakenly ordered the advance to be halted until Moore's force had arrived. In deciding to spend the night of 20 August aboard ship, Burrard forfeited the opportunity of winning the victory which went to Wellesley. Burrard's decision was probably the most significant turning-point of Wellesley's career.

Vimeiro

Determined to defeat the British before they could be reinforced, Junot advanced from Lisbon with 13,000 men and 24 guns, intent on out-flanking the British position; but his manoeuvre was observed and Wellesley re-aligned his army along the crest of Vimeiro ridge early on 21 June 1808. Though outnumbering the French, part of Wellesley's army was composed of Portuguese of little experience and uncertain quality, so he let Junot take the initiative.

Junot made two assaults on Vimeiro hill at the right of the British position, which made some headway; but his co-ordination was poor and with this attack and his attempted outflanking of Wellesley's left both being driven off, he decided to withdraw after a severe mauling.

By now, Burrard had arrived, but remained out of action, allowing Wellesley to complete the battle he had begun. Despite the fact that casualties had been light and that a large part of the British forces had been entirely unengaged, Burrard prohibited any pursuit of the re-treating French. Wellesley knew that a pursuit would have captured Lisbon, but being over-ruled by his superior had no option but let the French escape – much to his disgust. As Burrard wandered off looking for his dinner, Wellesley remarked dejectedly to his staff 'with a cold and contemptuous bitterness', that 'You may think about dinner, for there is nothing more for soldiers to do this day'.[6]

'Dowager' Dalrymple joined 'Betty' Burrard next day, and though Junot's position was untenable and the British were poised for complete victory, they decided to treat with the French. As a result, they concluded the Convention of Cintra (22 August) by which Junot and his army were to be allowed to return home, with their arms and all the plunder of Portugal, in British ships. This disgraceful treaty – 'Here Folly dash'd to earth the victor's plume' according to Byron – was greeted with outrage throughout Britain, and all three generals were recalled to England to face a court of inquiry. As the victor of Vimeiro and a most unwilling signatory to the convention, Wellesley was completely exonerated; but both Dalrymple and Burrard were removed from command.

Corunna

In the meantime, command of the British forces in the Peninsula had devolved upon Sir John Moore, who in response to Spanish pleas and obeying the intentions of the British government, decided to advance from Lisbon into Spain to collaborate with the Spanish armies. But the Spanish were the most untrustworthy of allies, depriving him of intelligence and supplies, and after the defeat of their field armies Moore realised that he must withdraw. However, a plea for help from Madrid decided Moore to advance again; but typical of the Spanish lack of co-operation was the fact that Madrid surrendered without striking a blow the day after the dispatch of its appeal.

Thus betrayed, Moore's small army found itself opposing 150,000 French under Napoleon's personal command, and only a precipitate retreat could prevent disaster. The retreat to Corunna became synonymous for privation and horror, as much of the army's discipline broke down. Yet, at the end, the shattered, starving remnants turned at bay and won a victory at Corunna which allowed them to be evacuated by the Royal Navy. Moore was killed in the action and was buried on the ramparts at Corunna, 'left alone with his glory'.

With the death of Moore, Sir Arthur Wellesley was the only realistic choice for resuming the war in the Iberian peninsula, and being so junior a lieutenant-general he could always be superseded by the government if necessary without the appearance of a change in policy. He was therefore instructed to defend Portugal but not to enter Spain without permission from London.

He formally assumed command of the British forces in Portugal on 27 April 1809, facing a daunting task against vast numbers of French troops. To understand how he squared up to the task and to appreciate the events of the succeeding five years' campaigning, consideration must be given to the army which the future Duke of Wellington commanded – how his genius transformed it into 'probably the most complete machine for its numbers now existing in Europe',[7] and how that same genius was able to defeat an army which until that time had beaten every nation in Europe.

Wellington's Army

Unlike almost every other European army, Britain's depended entirely upon voluntary enlistment, resulting in the rank-and-file being drawn from the lower strata of society and giving the army a bad reputation: 'Whoever "listed for a soldier" was at once set down among a catalogue of persons who had turned out ill' as one Peninsular veteran wrote.[8] Men were attracted by the sizeable 'bounty' paid on enlistment – £23/17/6d. in 1812 for a lifetime enlistment – or entered the army out of poverty, to escape justice, or were seduced by the blandishments of recruiting-sergeants who promised rapid promotion and a life of ease. In reality, the soldier's lot was terribly arduous, with discipline enforced by the lash which was awarded for even minor misdemeanours, 1000 strokes of 'the cat' being a not uncommon punishment.

It was said, with much truth, that the best regiments (i.e. generally those with the best officers) had the fewest punishments. There were mercifully few officers who awarded the lash with what was regarded at the time as too great liberality, though the worst aspects are exemplified by the tenure of Col. Quentin of the 10th Hussars, who *on campaign* in the Peninsula had 21,555 lashes actually administered, out of 38,900 awarded, in a four-month period in 1813.

Pay was meagre, rations poor. Cooper of the 7th remarked that: 'When a man entered upon a soldier's life . . . he should have parted with half his stomach'.[9] The burden was heavy, for the soldier's equipment ranged from 59 to 75 pounds in weight, which had to be carried on his back. Yet despite what appears to modern eyes as a life of insupportable misery, the British private soldier was considerably better off than his average Continental counterpart, which fact seems to have been reflected in their performances on the battlefield.

The calibre of British officer was generally high and although the most wretched attracted perhaps more attention than their cases warranted, in general the rapport with their men was good. It was this rapport that played a very considerable part in the growing excellence of the army under Wellington's command, especially after the worst aspects of the purchase system had been eradicated so that (in theory) a regimental officer could less often rise above his capability.

Line and Square

The infantry was the backbone of the army, the indomitable 'thin red

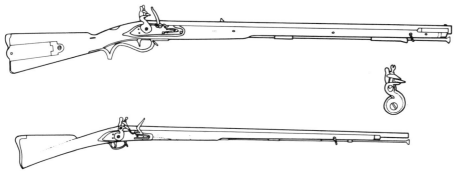

Ezekiel Baker's rifle (upper), which bore his name, was one of the best weapons of the Napoleonic period. It was capable of great accuracy in the hands of trained marksmen like those of the British 60th and 95th Foot. However, the principal weapon of the British Army in the Peninsular and Waterloo campaigns was the 'India Pattern' variant of the 'Brown Bess' (lower), which from about 1809 was equipped with a reinforced or 'ring-neck' cock (inset).

line' which was never once beaten on the battlefield during the Napoleonic Wars (those occasions when units were excessively mauled being largely the result of bad command). There existed in the British infantry more of a regimental identity than in other armies, so that pride in their unit might hold them together when others would have fled; hence the obeying of the call to 'Die hard, 57th' at Albuera and on scores of other fields.

The quality of weaponry had not improved over the past half century, the musket – known by the affectionate nickname 'Brown Bess' – still being appallingly inaccurate ('as to firing at a man at 200 yards with a common musket, you may as well fire at the moon and have the same hope of hitting your object').[10] Nevertheless, as before, in the terms of the warfare of the time, it was not necessary for muskets to be more accurate than to make a hit anywhere on a vast, tightly-packed mass of enemy troops. Despite the official regulations recommending that infantry fight in ranks three deep, by the beginning of the nineteenth century it was almost universal practice to fight in two-deep lines. By this system every musket could be brought to bear, giving an enormous advantage of firepower over a French column, in which only the first two or three ranks could use their muskets. British troops used the column only for manoeuvering, and when threatened by cavalry would form an impenetrable square bristling with bayonets on every side.

A major development was the emergence of a proficient force of light infantry, a number of complete regiments being converted and trained in the skills of the 'outpost': skirmishing, scouting and harassing the enemy. Although the basis of these skills existed before, Sir John Moore was to a considerable degree responsible for their perfection at his training-camp of Shorncliffe, so that he may fairly be regarded as the father of the resurrection of British light infantry tactics. Allied to these corps were the regiments of riflemen, green-jacketed marksmen armed with the rifled 'Baker' musket, a weapon capable of great accuracy. These troops – the 95th Rifles and the rifle battalions of the 60th (Royal American) Regt. (the latter largely German in composition) –

more than matched the French *tirailleurs*. Thus, much of the French tactical advantage was negated by the light company which existed in each British battalion, and by the fabled Light Brigade, later Division, which was the élite of Wellington's army in the Peninsula.

Horse and Gun

In contrast to the excellence of the infantry, the British cavalry was perhaps the weakest element of the army – not in quality of individual trooper or equipment, but in a lamentable lack of control, many cavalry officers seeming to believe that a charge at full gallop was all that was required of them: bravery without the discipline to re-form at the correct moment. Consequently, a number of disasters occurred when the cavalry got out of hand and charged too far, turning victory into defeat. Luckily for Wellington, the Iberian peninsula was not ideal terrain for the employment of massed cavalry, and he never had them in the same numbers as did continental generals. In light cavalry duties, scouting and skirmishing, the British (and especially the King's German Legion, a corps formed from George III's expatriate Hanoverian subjects) were as competent as any, the difference between 'light' and 'heavy' regiments being less marked in British services than in many others.

The artillery was extremely proficient and their equipment very good, but they never existed in sufficient numbers for the use of 'massed batteries': British forces were usually out-gunned by their opponents in numbers if not performance.

Command

The British Army was always short of commissariat and administrative personnel. In the Peninsula there were few commissariat troops (the Royal Waggon Train, and even these were regarded by the Treasury as an unnecessary expense), so that the army's provisions depended to a large extent upon mule-trains run by hired Portuguese civilians – though the system was sufficiently well constructed that provender and munitions were generally available when required. Wellington's staff was minute when compared with the vast numbers of officers employed by Napoleon. To a considerable degree this was due to the fact that Wellington attended to virtually *everything* himself; hence the excellence of his military system.

Few other commanders in history have been so vital to their army as was Wellington; he was commander-in-chief, diplomat, head of intelligence and policy-maker in one. Yet he was always greatly conscious of the fact that the army he commanded was effectively the only one which Britain could field. A single defeat would not only have led to his recall but might also have resulted in Britain's exit from the war, for the Whig opposition was often vociferous in its criticism of the Ministry's

conduct. It says much for Wellington's strength of character that he could bear this enormous responsibility *and* run the campaign with virtually no assistance.

The reasons for his success may originate in two characteristics which he possessed: the highest standard of moral rectitude which would allow him to do nothing which he regarded as in any way disadvantageous to his country; and a capacity for unremitting labour which is epitomised in his maxim to always 'do the business of the day in the day'. The volume of his work, which becomes apparent when his dispatches are examined and the breadth it covered, from the most mundane matters of supply to the planning of campaigns to diplomatic duties and meticulous reports to the government at home, is simply staggering.

Tactics and Strategy

His tactical and strategic genius is evident, though it was a process of continual learning. Whilst he was not proof against errors, he never made the same mistake twice. He compared his planning with that of the French whose schemes, he said, resembled a fine leather harness, which looked superb but when broken was useless. In contrast, the Duke's were like a harness made of rope, which appeared shoddy but when damaged, he could tie a knot and go on; such was the flexibility of all his planning.

British cavalry in action as depicted in an aquatint by M. Dubourg, after Denis Dighton. Corporal Logan of the 13th Light Dragoons (right) engages and kills Colonel Charmorin of the French 26th Dragoons at Campo Mayor, 25 March 1811.

209

His critics have described him as a 'defensive' general, one who sat on a prepared position and simply relied upon the excellence of his troops to beat off whatever attacks the enemy threw at him, but this is a fallacious argument. Certainly, his earlier Peninsula actions *were* defensive – having Britain's only army he could not risk it by hazardous manoeuvres – but within the defensive format his battles were offensive, vigorous counter-attacks being the culmination of the initial blocking of enemy advances. Wellington had a great capacity of being at the critical point whenever he was needed, and his personal direction of such movements was crucial in a number of actions.

If anything may be termed the classic 'Wellingtonian' tactic, it must be his 'reverse slope' deployment used throughout the Peninsular War as the most effective means of countering the French rapid advance in column. By drawing up his troops on the reverse slope of a ridge or hill-crest, Wellington protected them from the French preliminary bombardment and skirmish-fire, and concealed his whereabouts. The culmination of the rapid columnar attack was supposedly deployment into line, so that *all* the column's muskets could be brought to bear; but this would only be done when close to the enemy line.

Against Wellington, the French rarely knew where the target was, so when it appeared over the crest of the hill which the French were ascending, the attacking column was taken by surprise, shattered by a volley or more of British musketry; and before they could recover their composure, they were bundled back down the hill by a British bayonet-charge. This occurred time and again, and never failed to repel French attacks; yet no effective counter was devised to the reverse slope tactic and it was used by Wellington throughout. It required well-trained and stalwart troops and a general with what the eighteenth century termed *coup d'oeil*, an eye for the utilisation of features of terrain; and Wellington had both these in abundance. He was so far ahead of his opponents in skill that he once described the French attacks as coming on in the old style, and being beaten off in the old style; in other words, it was almost a matter of routine that Wellington's system would prevail.

The Allies

The contribution of allied troops was considerable; though their regular armies were generally wretched, Spain's main contribution to the Peninsular victory was their guerrilla activity, which wrought havoc with the most appalling brutality so that no Frenchman could ever feel safe once having crossed the Pyrenees. This occupied French resources and drained morale, and cost them many thousands of casualties. One estimate puts their loss to guerrillas at 100 *per day* throughout the entire Peninsular War.

Equally significant was the Portuguese army, which Wellington integrated entirely into his forces. From a wretched state in 1808, the

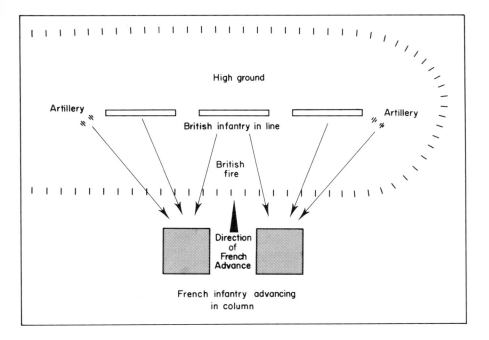

High ground

Artillery

British infantry in line

British fire

Direction of French Advance

Artillery

French infantry advancing in column

Portuguese troops were re-formed and re-organised by the Irish officer William Carr Beresford, seconded by Britain as Marshal of the Portuguese army, with a number of British officers being introduced into Portuguese regiments in important posts. The result was that the Portuguese became superb troops, 'the fighting-cocks of the army' as Wellington described them, and who were widely considered as reliable as their British comrades.

Wellington's deputies gave him little help, for he was given no choice in the appointment of divisional commanders. Some, like Rowland Hill (known as 'Daddy' from his concern for the welfare of his men) or Thomas Picton (an uncompromising Welshman) were excellent. Others, whom Wellington was forced to employ, were worse than useless, including incompetents, some generally regarded as cowards — and even one who appears to have been a certifiable lunatic (poor Erskine, who eventually killed himself).

The presence of so much 'dead wood' gave Wellington more problems than any general should have been asked to bear, and he even had to fight the administrators in London to keep officers of proven ability. As he admitted in 1810 to 'Black Bob' Craufurd, the stern commander of the Light Division, 'Adverting to the number of General officers senior to you in the army, it has not been easy to keep you in your command'.[11] With such constraints, it is amazing that Wellington was able to perform the prodigies he did.

The classic 'Wellingtonian' tactic: three British infantry battalions arrayed in line along a hill-crest, moving up to the very crest of the hill as the French advance approaches. The French infantry, in column each of 80 men wide, was thus able to bear 160 muskets per column, 320 muskets in all. The three British battalions, in a 2-rank line (say, about 600 men per battalion), were able to bring all muskets to bear. Thus, 1800 muskets, against the 320 of the French formation, was far superior in fire power.

Scum and Fine Fellows

The most basic element, however, remained the individual redcoat, drunken, rough fellow that he was. Wellington's most misunderstood remark concerns his men being 'the scum of the earth'. In this, he referred to their social background, and added, 'it is really wonderful that we should have made them the fine fellows they are'.

Just what 'fine fellows' they were is apparent from a story told by George Napier who was wounded in the Peninsula. An Irish private commanded by Napier, a drunken reprobate named John Dunn, walked seven miles to enquire after his health:

'Didn't I see you knocked over by the bloody Frenchman's shot . . . But myself knew you wouldn't be plaised if I didn't folly on after the villains, so I was afeard to go pick you up when ye was kilt . . . now I'm come to see your honour'.

Napier asked why Dunn was bandaged:

'Why sure it's nothing, only me arrum was cut off a few hours ago below the elbow joint, and I couldn't come till the anguish was over a bit. But now I'm here, and thank God your honour's arrum is not cut off, for it's mighty cruel work; by Jasus, I'd rather be shot twenty times'.

Napier then enquired of Dunn's brother:

'I seed him shot through the heart along wid me just as I got shot myself . . . but, captain, he died like a soldier, as your honour would wish him to die, and sure that's enough. He had your favour whilst he lived, God be with him, he's gone now'.

To walk seven miles without food or drink, immediately after an amputation, was typical, wrote Napier, so that 'whenever you see a poor lame soldier, recollect John Dunn, and never . . . pass him coldly by'.[12]

This 'scum of the earth' never regarded Wellington with the reverence they had accorded Marlborough, for he remained an aristocratic figure, cold and aloof in appearance if not at heart. But they trusted him implicitly never to sacrifice their lives uselessly, and always lead them to victory. 'The long-nosed b***** wot beats the French' – as he was affectionately known – never once betrayed that trust.

The Peninsular War – Defending Portugal

Upon his return to the Iberian peninsula, Wellesley's first action was to reorganise the army from its hitherto somewhat haphazard collection of brigades into divisions, by associating two or more brigades and allocating to the resulting formations their own commissariat and artillery detachments, so that each division was to a degree self-sufficient. He left the cavalry organised in brigades (divisions were established but the terrain was not suitable for them to act *en masse*), detaching squadrons or regiments to accompany infantry divisions as and when required; and he formed a central 'artillery reserve' for separate disposition on the battlefield.

At this time Wellesley's task was daunting. Though his army was good in quality, it was weak in numbers, very short of artillery, and the reorganisation of the Portuguese army was only beginning, so that their forces could not yet be counted as reliable. A great bonus, however, was Wellesley's appointment as Marshal-General of Portugal, which gave him complete control over all his forces without reference to the Council of Regency, a 'unity of command' which was vital (and was later extended to those Spanish regular troops who marched with his army). Although bound by instructions from London and dependent upon the government's support, at least in the field, Wellesley's word was law.

Oporto

On landing in Portugal on 22 April 1809, Wellesley had some 23,000 men under his command, but Portugal itself was as yet not secured. Two French armies were immediately threatening his foothold in the Peninsula: those of Marshal Nicolas Soult at Oporto and Marshal Claude Victor near the border-fortress of Badajos. The possession of Lisbon was the most vital factor for British success in the Peninsular War, for its harbour on the Tagus was the main supply-route from Britain. The Royal Navy's command of the sea ensured that as long as Lisbon was held, the army could receive all the munitions and provender it might require (very different from the French supply-trains which were continually harassed by Spanish guerrillas).

Leaving sufficient troops to hold Lisbon and watch Victor, Wellesley advanced toward Soult at Oporto; but the Frenchman, lacking immediate support and over-estimating the strength of his opponent, had already decided to withdraw. Soult believed himself protected by the width of the river Douro at Oporto, having cut all the bridges. However, on 11 May, Wellesley slipped his vanguard over the river on four wine-barges which had been overlooked by the French, the first troops removing their red jackets to prevent recognition. Taken completely by surprise, the French were hustled out of Oporto, Wellesley pursuing them for some ten days, costing Soult 4,500 casualties, and all of his guns and his baggage.

Reward of Talavera

Having expelled Soult from Portugal, Wellesley sought permission from London to advance into Spain, to collaborate with the Spanish army of General Gregoria de la Cuesta, Captain-General of Old Castile. The Spanish, however, proved to be unreliable allies; and the aged, infirm Cuesta an unwilling and incompetent collaborator who even kept the British short of supplies. Nevertheless, the combined Anglo–Spanish army concentrated and moved against Victor, knowing that Soult was too far to the north to assist. Cuesta's incompetence allowed Victor to escape, and return with the 46,000-strong army of King Joseph Bonaparte and Marshal Jean-Baptiste Jourdan. Thus compelled to fight by Cuesta's ineptitude, Wellesley assembled his 21,000 men along a defensive position at Talavera.

On the night of 27 July, the first French attack almost succeeded in driving the British from their key position, but Rowland Hill repelled the attack. Next morning Victor renewed the offensive, to be defeated by the reverse-slope tactic, but another assault in the afternoon was only thrown back by the most severe fighting. Cuesta's Spaniards remained inactive all day, leaving Wellesley to fight the French unaided. Although Victor urged further assaults, King Joseph abandoned the attempt and retired, having lost a sixth of his men.

Wellesley's army was fought to exhaustion and had lost 5,363 men. Though reinforced next day by 'Black Bob' Craufurd and his Light Brigade (after a phenomenal forced march), with the Spanish refusing to provide any more food and Soult now threatening his communications with Portugal, Wellesley began to retire. He left his wounded in Cuesta's care, who immediately abandoned them to the French. Clearly, co-operation with the Spanish armies was no longer possible.

Talavera was of vital significance in the conduct of the Peninsular War. It raised Anglo-Portuguese morale but demonstrated clearly that the original intention of collaborating with the Spanish in an offensive war had to be abandoned. Henceforth, the small British expedition must rely only upon themselves, and attempt to hold as much of Portugal as possible whilst they built up their strength and reformed the Portuguese army. It had one more effect: Wellesley was rewarded by the title of Viscount Wellington of Talavera. The style of title was selected, in his absence from Britain, by his brother William, who decided on 'Wellington' because it was a place near Wellesley in Somerset (from where the family originated), and because Richard already held the title Wellesley.

Building the Lines

In the immediate aftermath of Talavera, French victories at Ocaña on 19 November 1809 and Alba de Tormes wrecked any plans the Spanish *junta* had of a war of re-conquest. They were able to do little more than hold on to Andalusia in southern Spain, whilst Wellington had to defend Portugal alone.

Appreciating the vital necessity of protecting Lisbon, on 20 October 1809 Wellington initiated the building of the most comprehensive defence-works of the era, the 'Lines of Torres Vedras'. These comprised two chains of fortified positions running across the Lisbon peninsula, securing the city and its environs from French attack. The Lines (named after the largest position, at Torres Vedras) were not a continuous defensive wall but mutually-supporting strongpoints, fortified with artillery, which provided a field of cross-fire so that no French advance could progress without being raked from two or more forts.

Credit for the building of the Lines is usually accorded to the engineer who overlooked their construction, Richard Fletcher (one of Wellington's most valuable subordinates until his death in action) but the original document written by Wellington for his guidance is remarkable, instructing Fletcher exactly how and where to site his main defences. The plan of turning the Lisbon peninsula into a fortress was entirely Wellington's, and illustrates yet another facet of his military genius.

Upon the opening of the campaigning season of 1810, Joseph Bonaparte believed the war was won. Apart from the guerrilla bands, Spanish resistance was virtually confined to Andalusia, the *junta* having installed itself in Cadiz, the capital of free Spain, where it was replaced by a more effective Council of Regency, ruling in the name of the exiled Ferdinand VII. Wellington sent a small British contingent to Cadiz to stiffen the defence, and until mid-1812 some 60,000 French troops were tied down in an ineffectual blockade of the city, the security of which was never seriously threatened. Nevertheless, by spring 1810 some 325,000 French troops were in Spain, and their only opposing field army was the small band under Wellington's command in Portugal.

In May, a new French commander was installed as leader of their 'Army of Portugal', André Massena, an old comrade of Napoleon's from the Italian campaigns, and one of Napoleon's most capable subordinates (despite an unresistable penchant for looting and a preoccupation with his mistress who accompanied his headquarters dressed as an officer!).

Faced with enormous odds against him, Wellington realised that until the situation altered he could only afford to fight upon his own terms, and that the longer Massena's advance on Portugal could be delayed, the more complete would be the defences of Lisbon.

Busaco

The Spanish-Portuguese frontier was dominated by two fortified cities, Ciudad Rodrigo in the north and Badajos in the south, possession of which was necessary for an invader (from either direction). Wellington was so aware of his own weakness that he made no attempt to assist the Spanish garrison of Rodrigo, which surrendered to Massena on 9 July. The next French target was the Portuguese fortress of Almeida. Although Wellington's Light Division (commanded by the stern disciplinarian Robert Craufurd) administered a check at the bridge of the Coa, Almeida fell unexpectedly after a chance shell blew up the

215

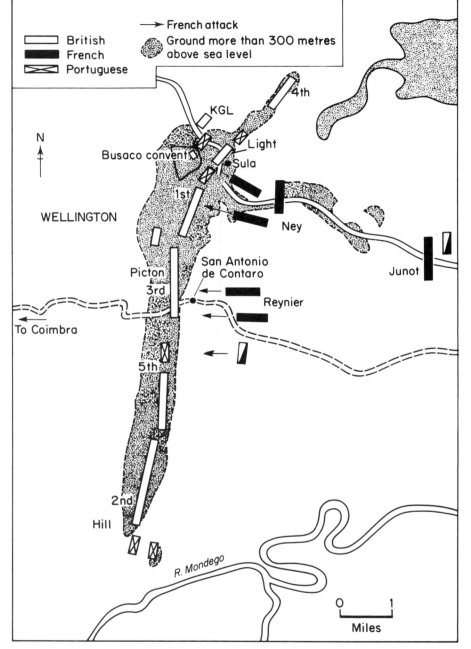

Legend:

- □ British
- ■ French
- ⊠ Portuguese
- → French attack
- Ground more than 300 metres above sea level

Map labels: 4th, KGL, Light, Busaco convent, Sula, 1st, WELLINGTON, Ney, Picton, 3rd, San Antonio de Contaro, Junot, Reynier, To Coimbra, 5th, 2nd, Hill, R. Mondego, N, Miles 0 1

magazine. Massena was free to advance into Portugal, and was met by Wellington in a superbly-chosen defensive position, the long, steep hill of Busaco, a short way from Coimbra.

The position could have been outflanked, for the Portuguese brigade instructed to block the route never received Wellington's orders.

However, with Wellington's army concealed as usual on the reverse slope, Massena's subordinate, the headstrong Marshal Michel Ney, decided that it must only be held by a small detachment and so launched a frontal attack on 27 September. (Massena himself appears not to have bothered to check Ney's assessment, being preoccupied with his mistress, Henriette Leberton, at that moment!)

Marshal Ney, Wellington's opponent at Busaco, Quatre Bras and Waterloo portrayed in an engraving after Gérard.

Massena had about 63,000 men; Wellington 26,843 British and 25,429 Portuguese. Two French attacks were launched, Ney against the British left and General Jean Reynier against the right. The latter attack ran onto the British 3rd Division, commanded by Sir Thomas Picton, a totally uncompromising, hard professional who had resigned as governor of Trinidad over allegations of using torture in interrogation, and who was renowned as an eccentric (he wore his night-cap at Busaco!). This tough character threw back Reynier's attack, whilst Ney, unaware of this French defeat, made a frontal drive up Busaco ridge. Ten yards from the summit, the French were amazed to see Craufurd leading his British infantry from the reverse slope. Taken completely by surprise and shattered by musketry, the French were sent streaming back down the hill in total chaos. Having lost 4,500 men and been thoroughly beaten, Massena withdrew.

Wellington, his army having by an amazing coincidence sustained just 626 British and 626 Portuguese casualties, withdrew to the Lines of Torres Vedras, claiming that he had only stood at Busaco to give the Portuguese 'a taste for an amusement to which they were not before accustomed',[13] – victory.

The Torres Vedras Master-Stroke

Having no idea of the existence of the Lines, Massena was astonished to find them barring his path to Lisbon, and that the terrain in front of the Lines had been stripped by a 'scorched earth' policy so that he could find no provender. Loath to retreat, but powerless to penetrate the Lines, Massena's army sat outside all winter, gradually starving. As the Lines had not been intended as a continuous fortification, but a way of delaying the enemy, Wellington's strategy involved counter-attacking any French forces which might penetrate. The Lines themselves were held by Portuguese militia, the main field army being comfortably ensconced in winter quarters, warm and well-fed, whilst the French starved.

The campaign cost Massena some 25,000 men before he finally gave up and limped away in March 1811, his army wrecked by privation. The Lines of Torres Vedras were thus more effective than any battle, at no cost to Wellington, and had saved Portugal. Torres Vedras was probably Wellington's master-stroke.

Almeida and Albuera

Although the year of 1811 included several significant actions, few

William Beresford in the uniform of Marshal of the Portuguese Army. Although not the most gifted of field commanders, he was a superb organiser and was largely responsible for transforming the Portuguese forces into an invaluable part of Wellington's Peninsular Army.

involved Wellington personally. He blockaded the French garrison of Almeida, having harassed Massena's retreat for some way (including a sharp action at Sabugal on 3 April, when the excellence of the Light Division retrieved the day after Sir William Erskine, generally regarded as a madman, needlessly hazarded Beckwith's brigade to the attack of three French divisions). But on 9 March, the surrender of Badajos to Soult's army in the south upset his plans. Forced to divide his army, and with Rowland Hill on leave, Wellington was compelled to put Marshal Beresford in command of a force in the south, whilst he concentrated on Almeida, the last French toehold in Portugal.

Massena, duly reinforced, attempted to aid Almeida, and Wellington met him on yet another well-chosen ridge by the village of Fuentes de Oñoro. Massena made one attack on 3 May, which carried the village. Wellington counter-attacked and recaptured it, and two days later another French attack almost succeeded. Wellington fed in supports from his army (concealed as usual on the reverse slopes) and just held on.

Massena exhausted his army and then marched away, leaving Wellington in possession of his position, but dissatisfied with the action, never counting it as a true victory and noting that 'If Boney had been there, we should have been beat'.[14] He was even more displeased when the Almeida garrison was allowed to slip away unmolested; but the French had now been expelled from Portugal.

In the south, Beresford laid siege to Badajos, but was forced to draw out most of his forces to meet an attempted relief by Soult. The armies met at Albuera on 15 May 1811, Beresford depending upon a sizeable Spanish army (less than one-third of Beresford's 35,000 were British). He was not an especially-gifted commander, however, and collaboration with the Spanish was difficult. In the event, only the dogged spirit of the British infantry held off the French, though at the cost of probably the most concentrated carnage of any field action in the Napoleonic Wars. Although Soult was turned back, Beresford's army was shattered and Wellington admitted: 'another such battle would ruin us'.[15]

Savagery and Chivalry

The remainder of the year was passed in somewhat inconclusive operations, Massena being recalled in disgrace and replaced by Marshal Auguste Marmont. The French still retained overwhelming numerical superiority (by mid-July 1811 they had 354,461 men in Spain and 8,298 more in reserve at Bayonne), but their six armies were unable or unwilling to act in concert. The terrain was one contributory factor: being widely-separated and with communications ever being disrupted by guerrillas, rarely could the armies collaborate. Equally, the Marshals in command were unwilling to take orders even from King Joseph, and on occasion flatly refused to help each other. The guerrilla war was fought with the most horrifying brutality, massacre and atrocity being commonplace, which drained the French army not only of men but perhaps more importantly of morale. Conversely, the Anglo-French war was fought with chivalry. As George Napier of the 52nd Light Infantry noted, 'there is never any personal animosity between soldiers opposed to each other . . . I should hate to fight out of personal malice or revenge, but have no objection to fight for fun and glory'.[16] This was an attitude of which Wellington approved, even to the extent of preventing an attempt to shoot Napoleon at Waterloo. By the standards of the day, to single out an individual or kill a man in circumstances other than a pitched battle was not a truly honourable practice. In other circumstances, they 'used every exertion of mind and body to destroy one another' as George Napier noted. Yet these attitudes were not regarded as illogical, but merely civilised.

The Peninsular War – Wellington's Offensive

For the season of 1812, Wellington was at last in a position to take the offensive, rather than merely repelling the French attacks on Portugal. The first stage was the possession of Ciudad Rodrigo and Badajos, both having strong French garrisons.

Wellington's greatest weakness until at least 1812 had been in the provision of a siege-train, the heavy guns needed to batter holes in fortifications, and the engineers to conduct the siege-works. The British engineer corps was tiny, consisting exclusively of officers, with an even smaller number of enlisted men of the Royal Military Artificers to supervise the men who did the actual trench-digging, untrained infantrymen detailed for the job. The casualty-rate among the engineer officers was appalling, and the Artificers were inept and largely useless, so siege-trenches had to progress as best they could.

So short of heavy guns was the army that initially the siege-trains resembled veritable museums, using ordnance dating back to the early seventeenth century. Even so, it was possible to blast a hole in a fortress-wall, the siege-trenches being pushed ever closer to the breach, until it was deemed 'practicable', i.e. suitable to be carried by assault. At this juncture the garrison would normally surrender without impugning their honour. If they declined, however, and the breach had to be stormed – always a ghastly affair – by the unwritten 'rules of war' the besiegers were allowed to ransack the fort once it had been taken. It was a custom which was to result in the British Army's blackest day.

Rodrigo
The siege of Rodrigo began on 8 January 1812, in the most bitter weather,

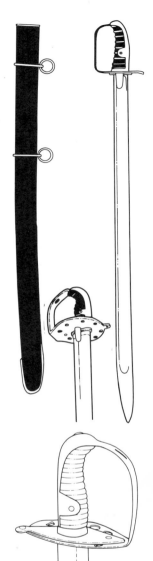

The British 1796-pattern heavy cavalry sabre was carried by dragoons and dragoon guards throughout the Napoleonic Wars. Copied from the Austrian 1775-pattern, it was a cleaver-like weapon originally with a hatchet-pointed blade. Later, it was often ground to a spear-point to enable it to be used for the thrust as well as the cut. Hilt and scabbard were plain iron.

and proceeded so well that the city fell in half the time Wellington had planned. Two breaches were open by 19 January, to be assaulted by the 3rd and Light Divisions, whilst diversionary attacks distracted the garrison. The 3rd Division's attack suffered heavily from the explosion of a mine as they entered their breach; but the Light Division stormed inside the city and, with both breaches open, the garrison surrendered.

The storm cost Wellington 59 officers and 503 other ranks – officer-casualties were always disproportionate in such operations – and included the invaluable commander of the Light Division, Robert Craufurd, killed by a shot through the spine at the edge of the breach. Following the capture of Rodrigo, the victors went on a rampage of loot and inebriation. On 28 February 1812, their commander was elevated in the peerage as a reward, to the Earldom of Wellington.

Badajos Bloodbath

Knowing that Marmont had insufficient resources to attempt to recapture Rodrigo, Wellington moved on to besiege the southern fortress, Badajos, a rather different proposition from Rodrigo in that it had a garrison of excellent quality, led by a skilful governor, Armand Phillipon. Badajoz was invested on 16 March 1812, and its outlying Fort Picurina carried by storm (for the loss of half the attackers) on 25 March. With the breaching-batteries thus able to bombard the weakest section of the defences, after in excess of 35,000 rounds had been fired at the wall, two 'practicable' breaches were opened. As Soult was known to be approaching, an immediate assault was ordered for the evening of 6 April.

The 4th and Light Divisions were detailed to storm the breaches, whilst diversionary attacks were to be made in several places, most significantly by Picton's 3rd Division against Badajoz's medieval castle, to be stormed by escalade. Though the breaches in the wall were open, the capable Phillipon had blocked them with entanglements and *chevaux-des-frises*, beams studded with sword blades.

The attack on the breaches was probably the most appalling carnage of the age; its horrors left survivors bereft of words, except to say (as did several participants) that it resembled nothing so much as the very pit of hell. From 10 p.m. until midnight more than forty attacks were made upon the breaches, until the ditches were choked with dead; but no-one got through.

Horrified by the slaughter, Wellington called off the assault. Ironically, it was two of the diversionary attacks, made when the garrison was preoccupied with the breaches, that succeeded. Leith's 5th Division and Picton's 3rd both scaled the ramparts – Picton being shot in the groin in the process – and the garrison capitulated.

What followed, however, was beyond belief. Perhaps unhinged by

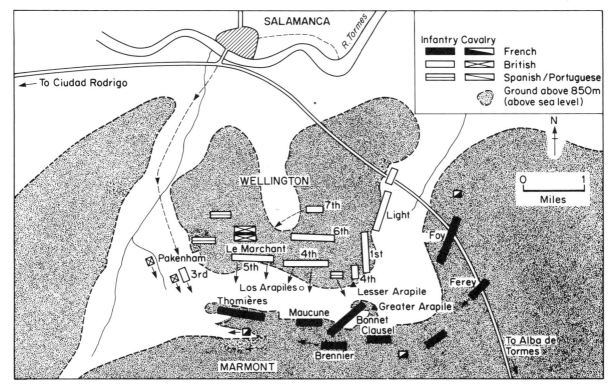

SALAMANCA

R. Tormes

← To Ciudad Rodrigo

N

0   1
Miles

WELLINGTON

7th

6th

Le Marchant   4th

Pakenham

5th

3rd

Los Arapiles ○

Thomières

Maucune

Brennier

Light

Foy

1st

4th

Lesser Arapile

Greater Arapile

Bonnet
Clausel

Ferey

To Alba de
Tormes

MARMONT

the carnage or driven mad with alcohol or the sights of horror, for two days the troops ran unchecked in the city, committing every imaginable atrocity of violence, loot and rapine upon the inhabitants who (whether it was true or not) were regarded as pro-French.

Badajoz was the most shameful episode in British military annals, and only when gallows were erected was the violence checked, by which time the troops responsible were probably sated. Conceivably the hard core of criminals in every battalion, or the rapacious Portuguese camp-followers, were largely responsible. Whatever the case, for the only period during his command, part of Wellington's army ran unchecked. As one witness remarked, the scenes in Badajoz froze the blood of even the most hardened campaigner.

Salamanca

With both border fortresses in his possession, Wellington was able to take the offensive into the heart of Spain. Though the French forces were at last officially placed under Joseph's overall command, army-commanders still refused to obey – Soult in particular being especially awkward – so the French response was ill-co-ordinated. Advancing from Rodrigo in June 1812, Wellington knew that he must strike Marmont before Joseph was able to reinforce him with his own army.

Battle of Salamanca, 22 July 1812. The British divisions are identified by their numbers (and some names) and the French commanders by name only.

Marshal Marmont, the Duke of Ragusa, was Wellington's opponent at Salamanca.

Believing Wellington to be a purely defensive general, Marmont was unperturbed even when the French and Anglo-Portuguese armies marched virtually side-by-side; but his sense of security was overturned at Salamanca on 22 July.

Interpreting the dust cloud raised by Wellington's baggage as a sign of his retreat, Marmont began a flanking-march to intercept what he believed was Wellington's rearguard. In fact, Wellington's forces were concealed on the favourite reverse slopes. As Wellington was lunching on cold chicken, he observed Marmont's army strung out on line of march. Tossing away a chicken-leg he exclaimed: 'That will do, by God!' (or, to his Spanish liaison-officer and great friend Miguel de Alava: 'Marmont is lost!').

The Allied army plunged down into the disorganised mass of French troops, who were overwhelmed and put to flight in short order. Marmont was himself severely wounded and lost about 14,000 troops; Wellington lost 4,762 and gained a further step in the peerage, to Marquess.

With Marmont's 'Army of Portugal' thus wrecked, Wellington made a triumphant entry into Madrid on 12 August, and determined to capture the fortified city of Burgos. Still appallingly equipped for siege-warfare, the Allied army had to abandon the siege when Soult finally obeyed Joseph's order and united with the armies of Joseph and Marshal Louis Suchet, preparatory to advancing against Wellington. To prevent a threat to his communications, Wellington began a withdrawal to Portugal. The retreat recalled the worst aspects of that to Corunna, with starvation and privation dogging them more closely than the French.

Whilst Wellington's withdrawal was a disappointing end to the year, it had marked the turning-point of the Peninsular War. From now it was obvious that the French were demoralized and could no longer hope to hold a country whose inhabitants were ever more hostile; and equally important, Wellington had discarded his reputation of being only a defensive general.

The Peninsular War – Final Triumphs

1813 was the year of Wellington's greatest triumphs. Contrasting to the parlous state of the French forces (denuded of their best elements to support Napoleon's campaigns against Russia and the Allies in the east), Wellington's army was never more efficient, numerous or in better spirits. By the middle of 1813 he commanded some 127,000 men, including over 52,000 British and with 46,000 Spaniards under his direct command. He was able for the first time to contemplate driving the French completely from the Iberian Peninsula.

He began to advance in late May, constantly out-manoeuvering the

French so that Joseph abandoned his capital and fell back upon the river Ebro. By capturing the northern Spanish port of Santander, Wellington was able to forsake his supply-lines with Lisbon, making Santander his supply-base instead. Thus free of the threat to his communications with Portugal, he pushed on with great speed and consummate skill, manoeuvering the French out of every position they tried to hold. Finally, Joseph and Marshal Jourdan concentrated three French armies at Vittoria, poorly-deployed and believing themselves not in immediate danger.

On 21 June 1813 Wellington mounted a multiple attack on their positions, and despite a stout resistance by elements of Joseph's army, the French were utterly routed. Joseph extricated only one piece of artillery, and though his losses were only about 8400 (to 5,158 Allied), the scale of the victory was immense. Indeed, it would have been greater had the pursuit not broken down when the Allied troops fell upon Joseph's baggage, plundering about a million pounds sterling instead of pressing on the pursuit!

Wellington was outraged at the conduct of 'our vagabond soldiers',[17] but nonetheless the French were irretrievably shattered. To demonstrate this Wellington sent Marshal Jourdan's bâton of rank to the Prince Regent; by return, the Prince sent Wellington the bâton of a field-marshal of Great Britain, the highest military rank attainable. To all practical effect, the Peninsular War was decided.

Halfpenny token of 1813. Such copper tokens were issued to remedy the shortage of small change in the Peninsular War. Depicting Wellington as field-marshal, it combines contemporary military uniform with the laurel wreath of classical antiquity.

Into France

The next step was to cross the Pyrenees into France. Napoleon had dismissed Joseph in disgrace and unified the surviving French troops into one 'Army of Spain' under Soult, and the Marshal used his limited resources to great effect in valiantly attempting to hold the line of the Pyrenees and the fortresses of San Sebastian and Pamplona.

Attempting to relieve the latter, Soult made considerable progress in the Pyrenean passes, only a running battle at Sorauren in late July finally defeating his attempt. This involved some of the heaviest fighting of the entire war; as Wellington noted, 'The battle of the 28th was fair *bludgeon* work . . . and the loss of the enemy was immense'.[18]

San Sebastian fell to a violent storming on 31 August, Pamplona on 30 October; Wellington fought his way across the Bidassoa, and carried the line of the river Nivelle on 9 November, constantly outmanoeuvering Soult. Once in French territory, Wellington sent home most of the Spaniards from his army to prevent their plundering the French civilians ('I have not had thousands of officers and soldiers killed and wounded for the remainder to plunder the French');[19] the result was that the Allied army received more cordial co-operation from the French civilians than did the French army!

223

British infantry at Toulouse, the final battle of the Peninsular War, shown in a print after A. Dupray.

The End

On 10 December Soult attacked along the Nive, but was repelled in four days of the heaviest combat. So desperate was the battle at St. Pierre on 13 December that Hill declared to his men: 'Dead or alive, my lads, we must hold our ground'.[20]

Early in 1814 Wellington began his advance on Bayonne, again outwitting Soult by crossing the river Adour by a bridge fabricated from hired boats. Soult was forced back at Orthez on 27 February (where Wellington was knocked from his horse by a grapeshot which fortunately only bruised him), and on 12 March Wellington occupied Bordeaux, whilst Soult took his army into the defences of Toulouse.

In the meantime, Napoleon's attempt to repel the invasion of France from the east had failed, and on 6 April 1814 he took the inevitable step of abdication. Four days later, before the news had reached southern France, the last battle of the Peninsular War was fought when Wellington breached the defences of Toulouse and ejected Soult from the city. Two days after this tragically unnecessary action, news of Napoleon's surrender arrived, and on 17 April Soult concluded an armistice, ending the Peninsular War.

Wellington received the news with unaccustomed levity, spinning on his heels, snapping his fingers and crying 'Hurrah!'. His five years and more of unremitting hard work had finally paid their dividend. On 11 May 1814 he was accorded the highest honour his country could bestow, the Dukedom of Wellington, following his recently-awarded Order of the Garter.

The Peninsular War cannot be over-emphasised as a contributory factor in the defeat of Napoleon; by his own admission, it was the 'Spanish ulcer' which ruined him, providing a constant drain upon men and *matériel* which became insupportable. Despite the hostility of the Spanish population, Spain alone could never have won the war; only the presence of the Anglo-Portuguese army could, and that was very much the creation of the genius who led it. Not even Marlborough could have exceeded Wellington's achievements, which is a measure of the ability of 'ar Arthur'.

Wellington himself paid tribute to the efforts of his troops in his General Order of 21 April 1814, returning his 'best thanks for their uniform discipline and gallantry in the field', and trusting that they would quit the scene of their endeavours 'with a lasting reputation, not less creditable to their gallantry in the field than to their regularity and good conduct in quarters and camp'.[21]

With the possible exception of the British Expeditionary Force of 1914, it was probably the most professional and most gallant army Britain has ever possessed.

The Hundred Days

The status of the Duke was such that once the war was ended, he was sent as one of the British representatives to the Congress of Vienna, equal faith being placed upon his diplomatic abilities as upon his military skill. Feted and lionised wherever he went, he outshone even the crowned heads and great statesmen of the Allied powers. But his military talents were required again far sooner than could ever have been envisaged.

Napoleon's Return

After chafing for some months in his exile on the Mediterranean island of Elba, Napoleon began his attempt to recapture the throne at the end of February 1815, and almost immediately resumed his position as Emperor. Just as rapidly, the Allied powers determined once again to dethrone him.

The odds against Napoleon were immense, so he decided to inflict a heavy defeat upon those Allied troops within reach, to gain a bargaining-position before he was overwhelmed by the slow-moving armies of Russia and Austria which had set out once again to invade France. Two armies lay in the newly-established Kingdom of the Netherlands. One was a polyglot force based upon a British nucleus, and the other a Prussian army under the command of the redoubtable

Wellington's chief adversary, the Emperor Napoleon, portrayed towards the end of his life in an engraving by J. François, after P. Delaroche.

The symbol of the British monarchy was the reversed GR cypher, borne here upon the brass 1812-pattern shakoplate and as worn by the line infantry in the Waterloo campaign. Many variations existed, bearing regimental identities.

old Field-Marshal Gebhard von Blücher, a stalwart septuagenarian known as *Marschall Vorwärts* ('Marshal Forward') from his aggressive style of command. The Anglo-Netherlands force was given to the only possible candidate, newly-returned from Vienna: the Duke.

His Last Army

The army was but a shadow of his Peninsular forces. The British nucleus was good, but many battalions were inexperienced as many Peninsular units had been sent to fight in North America. Even a famous regiment like the 2nd Dragoons (Royal Scots Greys) had not seen active service for twenty years; and though their quality remained as good as ever, the King's German Legion units were barely half their full strength. The remainder were Netherlanders or Germans. Of the former, many had been fighting for Napoleon only the previous year, and in general many were unenthusiastic or raw recruits. The recreated Hanoverian army was mostly inexperienced militia, and the Brunswick corps included only a few Peninsular veterans. It might not be the 'infamous army' sometimes suggested, but it was not the ideal force to face Napoleon.

Wellington had a few reliable deputies – Hill and Picton most valuably – and for the first time in his career had a really competent cavalry commander, the Earl of Uxbridge. It was Uxbridge who had led Moore's cavalry in the Corunna campaign with great skill, but had never before been employed under Wellington due to family hostility, having eloped with the Duke's sister-in-law! Conversely, the nominal second-in-command was the young Prince of Orange, son of the new King of the Netherlands. Although he had served as Wellington's aide in the Iberian Peninsula, the prince was totally inexperienced in command – a well-meaning young man who proved to be totally inept.

Nevertheless, Wellington tried to raise the overall standard of his army by blending the experienced with the raw, so that each formation contained a nucleus of battle-hardened battalions to stiffen the rest, an administrative exercise of great skill and effect.

Quatre Bras
Napoleon intended to drive a wedge between the Anglo–Netherlands and Prussian armies, and in his usual way defeat them in detail. Thus, he

'King's Colour' of the 2nd Battalion, 2nd (Coldstream) Foot Guards, the defenders of Hougoumont at the battle of Waterloo. It was crimson, with silver and gold devices.

British infantry in line, its standard formation for repelling French attacks. This engraving, after Captain George Jones, shows the 28th (North Gloucestershire) Regiment at Quatre Bras, directed by their battalion commander Sir Charles Belson (mounted left).

The actual 'Eagle' of the 45th. The flag was a subsidiary decoration to the main symbol of the regiment; the gilded, sculpted metal eagle was affixed to the head of the standard-pole.

British infantrymen from the light company of the 5th (Northumberland) Regiment, wearing the 1812 pattern shako made famous by its use at Waterloo. Published as one of Genty's prints, the drawing was made in France in 1815.

plunged across the frontier on 15 June and took the Allied commanders by surprise.

Wellington was attending the Duchess of Richmond's ball in Brussels when he received the news. Remarking that 'Napoleon has humbugged me, by God!' he put his army into motion towards a position he had already reconnoitered, the ridge of Mont St. Jean, south of the village of Waterloo on the Brussels–Charleroi road. His advance positions were further south, at the crossroads of Quatre Bras, with the Prussians to the east around Ligny.

On 16 June Napoleon detached Marshal Ney to seize Quatre Bras whilst he led the bulk of his army against Blücher at Ligny, a fierce action in which the Prussians were mauled and old Blücher incapacitated after being ridden over in a charge. His deputy, Gneisenau, took temporary command and, for some reason mistrusting Wellington, was inclined to withdraw right away to regroup – but eventually acceded to Blücher's plan of supporting Wellington come what may. Meanwhile, Ney was involved in a severe clash at Quatre Bras, the Netherlands advance-guard just holding on until Wellington arrived with elements of the British forces. Ney was beaten off in desperate fighting and Wellington withdrew in good order.

Waterloo

The defensive line at Mont St. Jean was based on a low ridge (the army assembling on its reverse slope as usual), anchored on the right flank by the château of Hougoumont and in the centre by the fortified farm of La Haye Sainte. Both were garrisoned, and Wellington determined to cling to his position until Prussian assistance arrived.

Wellington's force numbered about 63,000, only 21,000 of them British, with 156 guns. Napoleon had around 72,000 with 246 guns, a great advantage given the dubious quality of parts of Wellington's army. Ignoring the advice of Soult (mis-cast as chief-of-staff) who warned him that the British infantry was 'the devil' in action, Napoleon said he knew Wellington was a bad general and the British bad troops, and that the battle would be an *'affaire d'un déjeuner'*. He was soon to be disillusioned.

At about 11.50 a.m. on 18 June 1815 Napoleon began the attack on Wellington's position, his younger brother Jérôme (ex-King of Westphalia) leading an assault on Hougoumont at the right of Wellington's line. It was intended as a diversion to draw in Wellington's reserves, but in the event it had the opposite effect. Unable to overcome the British Guards holding the château, Jérôme fed into the fight ever more of Napoleon's reserves, but Hougoumont never fell.

Napoleon assembled a massed battery to bombard the centre of the Allied line, but was foiled largely by the shelter of the reverse slope tactic. Thus, when he threw in his first attack, the Allied troops were largely unscathed. Despite the Prince of Orange's aberrations – as at

228

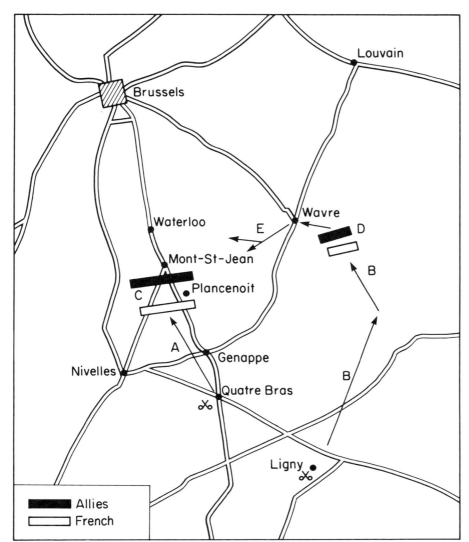

French grenadier, as shown in a watercolour most probably by J.A. Atkinson.

A Wellington's retreat from from Quatre Bras (battle, 16th June), followed by Napoleon.

B Blücher's retreat from Ligny (battle, 16th June), followed by Marshal Grouchy

C Wellington faces Napoleon at Mont–St–Jean (Wateloo), 18th June

D Prussian rearguard holds up French attack at Wavre, allowing for:

E Blücher supports Wellington at later stage of Battle of Waterloo, 18th June

Quatre Bras he sacrificed battalions by counter-attacking in line when they were easy prey to French cavalry – Picton's British infantry repelled the attack; Picton himself was killed. Uxbridge launched a cavalry counter-charge against the retreating French. In the classic manner, the

An overall view of the Waterloo campaign, 16–18 June 1815.

The Duke of Wellington in an engraving by W. Say, after Thomas Phillips. The Duke wears the uniform of the general staff of about 1814, with the many orders of chivalry which he was awarded by the Allied nations. Particularly prominent are the Order of the Garter (upper breast star), the Austrian order of Maria Theresa (large cross) and the ancient Order of the Golden Fleece (around neck).

cavalry swept aside their target, but refused to rally and were cut to pieces as they charged too far.

Throughout the action Wellington moved around the battlefield, ever at the critical point, husbanding his resources. One such re-alignment was mistaken by Ney for a withdrawal, and prompted the first of numerous French cavalry charges, all of which foundered with great slaughter upon the stolid squares of British infantry, who drove them off time and again.

By 4.30 p.m., the first elements of Blücher's Prussians had arrived on Napoleon's right wing, drawing in ever more French troops to secure the flank; but eventually Ney succeeded in cracking the centre of Wellington's position as the German Legion defenders of La Haye Sainte ran out of ammunition.

With the strongpoint in French hands, Ney made a desperate attack upon the main line. The fighting was appalling in its ferocity. Wellington told a brigade-commander that 'every Englishman on the field must die on the spot we now occupy'. And die they did, in ranks.

Then Napoleon made his last gamble by committing the Imperial Guard, his élite corps which had never been defeated. Their columns ascended the slopes towards the ravaged Allied line. At the critical point, Wellington was present – as usual – and ordered the British Guards to reveal themselves, they having been lying hidden on the reverse slope. It is doubtful whether he said the traditional 'Up Guards and at them'; more likely it was 'Stand up, Guards', or, to their commander, 'Now Maitland, now's your time!' They poured in musketry at point-blank range, and assailed in the flank by the 52nd Light Infantry which wheeled from line into an enfilade position, the Imperial Guard broke and fled.

It was the end for Napoleon. Raising his hat, Wellington signalled a general advance which, combined with the Prussian pressure on the French right, caused the total disintegration of the French army. Napoleon's final defeat was certain; but at a terrible cost, for much of the British army was still lying in formation upon the ridge, dead. Nothing more exemplified Wellington's heartfelt statement that only a battle lost could be half so terrible as a battle won.

Wellington met Blücher that evening at the aptly-named inn of *La Belle Alliance*, near to where Napoleon's headquarters had been established. The old Prussian remarked '*Quelle affaire*', which was about the only French he knew (and Wellington spoke no German). It was probably the understatement of the age.

That night Wellington wept unashamedly as he read the casualty returns. He would have been heartily glad had he realised that he had fought his last battle. The triumph was largely due to the band of redcoats who had stood impassively on the ridge throughout that terrible day – but there was another reason for victory. As Wellington

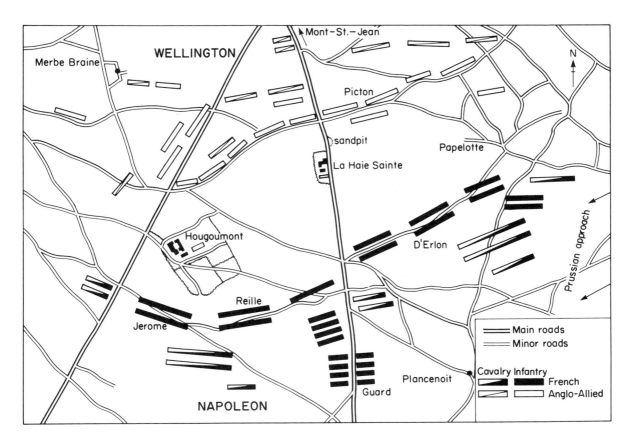

Battle of Waterloo, 18 June 1815.

himself said, 'By God, I don't think it would have done if I had not been there'.

The Great Duke

Waterloo marked the end of Wellington's military career, for as he admitted, Waterloo – 'the nearest run thing you ever saw in your life' – had finished Napoleon, or as Wellington said laconically: 'I think we've done for 'em this time'.[22]

He was by then the most famous general in Europe, eclipsing even Napoleon; and, at 46 years of age, had half a lifetime's public service still to perform. He undertook his duties – now non-military ones – with the same concern for the public weal as he had fought his campaigns. As Waterloo ended and he was riding forward in pursuit of the French, an aide begged him not to risk himself: 'Let them fire away', he said, 'The battle's won; my life is of no consequence now'.[23]

This same attitude he carried into political life, when as Prime Minister

231

Portrait of Wellington in old age, probably around 1840.

The sword carried by Wellington at Waterloo was a French weapon, with hilt and mounts of silver-gilt, made by Napoleon's own goldsmith, Biennais. How it was acquired by Wellington is not known, but probably it was a Peninsular War trophy.

he survived a brief period of unpopularity during which angry mobs stoned his London residence, Apsley House, breaking the windows. He responded by erecting iron shutters, and hence his nickname, 'the Iron Duke'. So unbending were his principles in doing what he perceived was right that he even fought a duel with the Earl of Winchilsea on 23 March 1829 over the contentious subject of Catholic Emancipation, which the Duke supported (he remarked that Winchilsea should not be positioned so near to a ditch, for 'If I hit him he will tumble in'![24]).

His political career was not of his choosing and he was a reluctant Prime Minister who found difficulty in managing a cabinet; unlike the army, the Cabinet did not obey his every word without question. As commander-in-chief of the army, his dislike of change may have had much to do with the stultification of the military system in the years before the Crimean War. Yet as Disraeli observed in *Endymion*, the Duke's government was 'a dictatorship of patriotism' which is, perhaps, not the worst system when entrusted to one of unbending moral principles.

Having become the mentor and friend of the young Queen Victoria, the Duke died at Walmer Castle (his residence as Lord Warden of the Cinque Ports) on 14 September 1852, at the age of 83, loaded with every honour which could be bestowed upon him by his own and allied sovereigns. His state funeral was such as had not been seen before, nor since. Yet pageantry and outward show were never much to the Duke's liking; 'God knows I have plenty of Orders' was his comment on the award of the Garter![25]

Queen Victoria commented that he was the greatest man his country had *ever* produced, and in the sense that none could possibly exceed his perception of duty, she was right. He was a man who had brought his country victory in the most desperate war she had yet fought and who approached civil duties with the same unswerving loyalty to crown and people.

His obituary in *The Times* in September 1852 remarked that 'The Duke of Wellington had exhausted nature and exhausted glory. His career was one unclouded longest day'. Most probably though he would have appreciated more the sentiments of his old soldiers, like Fusilier Horsefall who asked 'Whore's ar Arthur?'.

The Duke never liked fulsome praise, so that in old age, when a man helped him across the road and said: 'Never did I hope to reach the day when I might be of the slightest assistance to the greatest man that ever lived', the Duke replied: 'Don't be a damned fool'.[26] However, he could surely not have objected to the comment of Capt. Sir John Kincaid, ex-95th Rifles, whose memoirs[27] are among the most readable of all Napoleonic accounts: 'We would rather see his long nose in a fight than a reinforcement of ten thousand men any day'.

He truly was, as his nickname stated, 'the Great Duke'.

232

References

1 *Rough Notes of Seven Campaigns* J.S. Cooper, Carlisle, 1869; 1914 edn. p. 68.

2 *The Wellington Memorial* Maj. Arthur Griffiths, London, 1897 pp. 3–4.

3 *History of the British Army* Hon. J.W. Fortescue, London, 1910 Vol. V p. 17.

4 *Notes of Conversations with the Duke of Wellington* 5th Earl Stanhope, London, 1888 p. 57.

5 *Narrative of Some Passages in the Great War with France* Sir Henry Bunbury, London, 1854; 1927 edn. p. 145.

6 *Recollections of the Peninsula* 'by the Author of Sketches in India': actually Moyle Sherer, London 1825, pp. 42–43.

7 Wellington to Earl Bathurst, 21 November 1813; *Dispatches of Field-Marshal the Duke of Wellington*, (ed.) Lt. Col. J. Gurwood, London, 1834–38, XI p. 306.

8 See *British Infantry of the Napoleonic Wars* P.J. Haythornthwaite, London, 1987 pp. 7–8.

9 Cooper *op. cit.* p. 157.

10 *To All Sportsmen* George Hanger, London, 1814 p. 205.

11 *General Craufurd and his Light Division* Rev. A.H. Craufurd, London n.d. (reprinted Cambridge, 1987) p.169.

12 *Passages in the Early Life of General Sir George T. Napier, written by himself* ed. Gen. W.C.E. Napier, London, 1884 pp. 191–95.

13 *Supplementary Despatches and Memoranda of Field-Marshal the Duke of Wellington* (ed.) 2nd Duke of Wellington, London 1858–72, VI p. 607.

14 *Supplementary Despatches* VII p. 176.

15 *Supplementary Despatches* VII p. 135.

16 Napier *op. cit.* p. 177.

17 *Dispatches* X p. 473.

18 *Dispatches* X p. 602.

19 *Dispatches* X p. 287.

20 *Rough Notes of an Old Soldier* G. Bell, London, 1867; 1956 edn. p. 111.

21 *Despatches* XI, p. 668.

22 *The Creevey Papers* (ed.) Sir H. Maxwell, London, 1904 p. 142.

23 *Wellingtonia: Anecdotes, Maxims and Characteristics of the Duke of Wellington* J. Timbs, London, 1852 p. 60.

24 The story of the duel is recounted in Elizabeth Longford's *Pillar of State* London, 1972 p. 188.

25 *Dispatches* X p. 376.

26 *Words on Wellington* Sir William Fraser Bt., London, 1889 p. 108.

27 *Adventures in the Rifle Brigade* London, 1830 and *Random Shots from a Rifleman* London, 1835.

Chronology of Events

21 JUNE Defeat of Joseph Bonaparte at Vittoria.

3 JULY Appointed Field-Marshal (as from 21 June).

31 AUGUST Capture of San Sebastian.

7 OCTOBER Passage of the Bidassoa.

10 NOVEMBER Defeat of Soult on the Nivelle.

10–13 DECEMBER Defeat of Soult on the Nive.

1814 27 FEBRUARY Defeat of Soult at Orthez.

10 APRIL Defeat of Soult at Toulouse.

11 MAY Appointed Duke, and Marquess of Douro.

1815 11 APRIL Appointed 'Commander of the British Forces on the Continent of Europe'.

16 JUNE Defeat of Ney at Quatre Bras.

18 JUNE Defeat of Napoleon at Waterloo.

22 OCTOBER Appointed Commander-in-Chief of the Allied Armies of Occupation in France.

1827 22 JANUARY Appointed Commander-in-Chief, resigning on becoming Prime Minister; re-appointed August 1842.

1828 15 FEBRUARY Appointed Prime Minister (to October 1830, and November/December 1834).

1852 14 SEPTEMBER Death at Walmer Castle, Kent.

234

Bibliography

Gustavus Adolphus

The literature of the Thirty Years War is truly immense; the following representative selection is chosen because of accessibility or because of its coverage of Swedish affairs.

Cust, Sir E. *Lives of the Warriors of the Thirty Years War* London, 1865.

Fletcher, C.R.L. *Gustavus Adolphus* London, 1892.

Fuller, J.F.C. *Decisive Battles of the Western World* London, 1957.

Gardiner, S.R. *The Thirty Years War* London, 1877.

Holmquist, B.M., and Gripstad, B. *Swedish Weaponry since 1630* Stockholm, 1982 (illustrates some contemporary weaponry).

Langer, H. *The Thirty Years War* Poole, 1980.

Mackay, J. *An Old Scots Brigade* Edinburgh & London, 1885 (history of the Scottish mercenary regiments).

Parker, G. (ed.) *The Thirty Years War* London, 1985.

Roberts, M. *Gustavus Adolphus: A History of Sweden 1611–32* London, 1953–58.

Steinberg, S.H. *The Thirty Years War and the Conflict for European Hegemony 1600–1660* London, 1966.

Stevens, J.L. *History of Gustavus Adolphus* London, 1885.

Wedgwood, C.V. *The Thirty Years War* London, 1938.

Wagner, E. *European Weapons and Warfare 1618–48* London & Prague, 1979.

Marlborough

The literature on the career and age of Marlborough is vast, his biographies ranging from Lediard's initial work, through Coxe (which contains many of his letters and documents) to his descendant Sir Winston Churchill. Recommended for further reading are the invaluable modern works by Chandler. Of accounts by participants of the campaigns, that of Robert Parker is among the most interesting, and is available in a modern reprint.

Chandler, D.G. *The Art of Warfare in the Age of Marlborough* London, 1976.

Chandler, D.G. *Marlborough as Military Commander* London, 1973.

Chandler, D.G. (ed.): *The Marlborough Wars* London, 1968 (contains reprints of the memoirs of Robert Parker and the comte de Mérode-Westerloo).

Churchill, Sir W.S. *Marlborough, his Life & Times* London, 1933–38.

Coxe, W.C. *Memoirs of John, Duke of Marlborough* (originally published London 1820) footnote-references from the revised edition by John Wade, London 1847.

Donkin, R. *Military Collections and Remarks* London, 1977.

Fortescue, Hon. Sir J. *History of the British Army Vol. I* London, 1899.

Kemp, A. *Weapons and Equipment of the Marlborough Wars* Poole, 1980.

Lediard, T. *Life of John, Duke of Marlborough* London, 1736.

Parker, R. *Memoirs of the most Remarkable Military Transactions* Dublin, 1746.

Frederick the Great

Of the many biographies of Frederick, the most influential early work in English was that of Thomas Carlyle, though the English translation of Kugler should not be overlooked, being illustrated by the incomparable Adolph Menzel. Menzel's own work with C. Jany is a splendid gallery of military uniforms and unit histories. The leading modern studies in English are those of Christopher Duffy and of Nancy Mitford. In particular, Duffy's The Army of Frederick the Great is the most detailed study available in English of the Prussian army, whilst his A Military Life is essential reading, containing as it does the most comprehensive bibliography on Frederick. In German, the work of Hans Bleckwenn has rekindled much interest. In the wider aspects, Duffy's Military Experience is the best overall guide to the methods and mores of the military of the mid-eighteenth century.

Carlyle, T. *History of Friedrich II of Prussia, called Frederick the Great* London 1858–65.

Duffy, C. *The Army of Frederick the Great* Newton Abbot, 1974.

Duffy, C. *Frederick the Great: A Military Life* London, 1985.

Duffy, C. *The Military Experience in the Age of Reason* London 1987.

Frederick II (trans. Foster, T.) *Military Instruction from the late King of Prussia to his Generals* London, 1797; 5th edn. 1818.

Frederick II (trans. Foster, T.) *Particular Instruction of the King of Prussia to the Officers of his Army, and especially those of the Cavalry* issued with *Military Instruction*, as above.

Jany, C. and Menzel, A. *Die Armee Friedrichs des Grossen in ihrer Uniformerung* Berlin, 1908.

Kugler, F. *The Pictorial History of Germany during the Reign of Frederick the Great* (English edn.) London, 1845.

Mitford, N. *Frederick the Great* London, 1970.

George Washington

Biographies of George Washington are legion. Freeman's is the most extensive and comprehensive, but others are also of value. For the American War, the following lists both important standard works and others which are most useful for their content of contemporary and other illustrations.

Boatner, M.M. *Cassell's Biographical Dictionary of the American War of Independence 1763–1783* London 1973 (published in the U.S.A. as *Encyclopedia of the American Revolution*, 1966). (Extremely valuable modern study.)

Dann, J.C. (ed.) *The Revolution Remembered: Eyewitness Accounts of the War for Independence* Chicago & London, 1980. (Good collection of accounts by participants.)

Elting, J.R. (ed.) *Military Uniforms in America: The Era of the American Revolution 1755–95* (Company of Military Historians), San Rafael, California, 1974.

Fortescue, Hon. Sir J. *History of the British Army: Vol. II* London 1899; *Vol. III* London 1903.

Freeman, D.G. *George Washington* New York 1948–57. (The best biography.)

Johnson, C. *Battles of the American Revolution* Maidenhead, 1975. (A modern analysis of eight major battles.)

Little, S. *George Washington* New York, 1929.

Macksey, P. *The War for America 1775–1783* London, 1967.

Parkinson, R. *The American Revolution* London, 1971. (Good collection of illustrations.)

Peckham, H.H. *The Toll of Independence* Chicago & London, 1974. (Statistical details of actions and casualties.)

Riviore, M. *The Life and Times of Washington* London, 1967 (orig. Verona, 1965). (Useful collection of illustrations.)

Trevelyan, G.O. *The American Revolution* London, 1909–14. (Major study: single-volume edition under same title; ed. R. Morris, London 1965.)

Walker, E. (ed.) *The Addresses and Messages of the Presidents of the United States, from Washington to Harrison* New York, 1841. (Includes Washington's most important addresses as President.)

Washington, George *The Writings of George Washington* (ed. J.C. Fitzpatrick) Washington, 1931–44. (The most comprehensive collection.)

Washington, George *Writings* (ed. W.C. Ford) New York, 1889–93.

Werstein, I. *1776: The Adventure of the American Revolution told with Pictures* New York, 1962. (Useful collection of illustrations.)

Wellington

There have been very many Wellington biographies; the 'standard' is now the two-volume work by the Countess of Longford, but the others noted below are all valuable, either as purely military studies or for anecdotal material.

Fraser, Sir William B. *Words on Wellington* London, 1889.

Glover, M. *Wellington as Military Commander* London, 1968.

Glover, M. *Wellington's Army in the Peninsula* Newton Abbot, 1977.

Griffith, P. (ed.) *Wellington Commander: The Iron Duke's Generalship* Chichester, n.d.

Griffiths, Maj. A. *The Wellington Memorial* London, 1897.

Longford, Elizabeth *Wellington: Pillar of State* London, 1972.

Longford, Elizabeth *Wellington: The Years of the Sword* London, 1972.

Oman, Sir C.W.C. *History of the Peninsular War* Oxford, 1902–30.

Oman, Sir C.W.C. *Wellington's Army* London, 1912.

Rogers, Col. H.C.B. *Wellington's Army* London, 1979.

Timbs, J. *Wellingtonia: Anecdotes, Maxims and Characteristics of the Duke of Wellington* London, 1852.

Ward, S.G.P. *Wellington* London, 1963.

Wellington, Duke of (ed. Gurwood, J.) *The Dispatches of Field Marshal the Duke of Wellington* London, 1834–38.

Wellington, Duke of (ed. 2nd Duke of Wellington) *Supplementary Despatches and Memoranda of Field Marshal the Duke of Wellington* London, 1858–72.

Illustrations

Maps and battle diagrams by Chartwell Illustrators and line illustrations by Peter Komarnyckyi based upon author's references. All other illustrations from author's and publisher's collections, except for those reproduced, with thanks, courtesy of the following:

Academy of Fine Arts, Pennsylvania (page 142); Ernst-Mortiz-Arndt Universitätbibliotheck, Griefswald (page 36); Germanisches National Museum, Nurnberg (pages 8 and 48); Hertzog Anton Ulrich-Museum, Braunschweig (page 47); Historisches Museum, Frankfurt am Main (pages 8 and 41); Krigsarkivet, Stockholm (page 45); National Portrait Gallery, London (pages 50 and 188); Richard Scollins/Linda Rogerts Associates (page 25); Statens Konstmuseer, Stockholm (page 6); Verwaltung der Staatlischen Schlosser Charlottenburg, Berlin/Jorg P. Anders (page 96); Wayland (Publishers) Limited, Hove (pages 157, 184 and 185); *Wasa* Museum, Statens Sjöhistoriska Museet, Stockholm (page 16).

Index

Page numbers in *italics* refer to illustrations.

239